The Complete Book of
Business Plans

SOURCEBOOKS, INC.®
NAPERVILLE, ILLINOIS

Published by: **Sourcebooks, Inc.**
P.O. Box 4410, Naperville, Illinois, 60567-4410
(630) 961-3900
FAX: (630) 961-2168

This publication is designed to provide accurate and authoritative information in regard to the subject matter covered. It is sold with the understanding that the publisher is not engaged in rendering legal, accounting, or other professional service. If legal advice or other expert assistance is required, the services of a competent professional person should be sought.

From a Declaration of Principles Jointly Adopted by a Committee of the
American Bar Association and a Committee of Publishers and Associations

The Small Business Sourcebooks series is designed to help you teach yourself the business essentials you need to be successful. All books in the series are available for bulk sales. Feel free to call us at *630-961-3900* for information or a catalog. Other books in the series include:

- *How to Get a Loan or Line of Credit*
- *The Small Business Start-Up Guide*
- *Your First Business Plan*
- *The Small Business Legal Guide*
- *Smart Hiring*
- *Mancuso's Small Business Basics*

Library of Congress Cataloging-in-Publication Data

Covello, Joseph A.
      The complete book of business plans : simple steps to writing a powerful
business plan / Joseph A. Covello & Brian J. Hazelgren.
            p.   cm.
      ISBN 0-942061-40-3 : $29.95. — ISBN 0-942061-41-1 (pbk.) : $19.95
      1. New business enterprises—Planning.   2. New business enterprises—Finance.
3. Proposal writing in business.   I. Hazelgren, Brian J.   II. Title.
HD62.5.7.C68   1993
658.4'012 — dc20   93-41064
                                                                          CIP

Printed and bound in the United States of America.

Hardcover – 10 9 8 7 6 5 4 3
AP Paperback – 20 19 18 17 16 15

Table of Contents

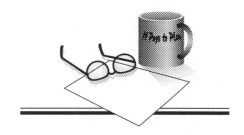

Introduction

Welcome to your future! You must be interested in knowing what the future holds for you. When you begin reading through this powerful guidebook, your future should come into a clearer focus. As you read on, you will understand what this all means.

Today's planning really *is* tomorrow's future—and now is the time to start planning or even expand your present planning for a "Tomorrow" filled with success and prosperity.

Your business planning process will become a powerful management tool that will help you realize your success easier.

A business plan is a description of your business, including its products, its markets, the people involved, and your financing needs.

A well-prepared business plan will not only assist you in plotting a course for your company—it can also serve as a vital sales tool. Suppliers of capital receive numerous re-

Remember, other things being equal, a well-prepared business plan will increase your chances of obtaining a financial commitment from outside sources.

This system is designed to assist anyone in preparing an effective business plan, one that provides the information and financial sources initially required in deciding whether or not to explore opportunities further. There are five main sections:

1. Powerful Guidelines to Writing a Winning Business Plan

2. 101-Plus Questions for Success

3. Sample Business Plan

4. The Vision: Writing Your Business Plan

5. Appendix

These five sections will walk you through topics ranging from: critical information, a question and answer section, a sample

---

"Aim at the sun. You may not reach it, but you will fly higher than if you never aimed at all."

Anonymous

---

quests for funding business ventures. Therefore, to attract their attention, your company and its products should be presented to them in a complete and professional manner.

A business plan prepared with the information needs of possible funding sources for your enterprise in mind will impress them, not only with your planning ability, but also with your general competence as a manager.

business plan, essential points with step-by-step ideas of how to write a winning business plan, and an appendix on general business information.

Good Luck and enjoy your reading!

Acknowledgments

This has been a fun and rewarding project! We would sincerely like to thank all the talented and important people who assisted and supported us throughout the entire process of researching, editing, and developing "The Complete Book of Business Plans."

Many long hours and enormous amounts of patience went into what you see here as the final package. We would especially like to say thank you to our wives Ann and Robin for believing in our dream of creating something of value. They have each been a source of strength and courage to enable us to complete this important project.

We certainly want to mention our parents who taught us that hard work and good values will take you a long way in life.

We would like to thank SCS Computers of Mesa, Arizona, for its creative help in the development of the printed copy. SCS's ideas on layout and design have been, and always will be, greatly appreciated.

Many thanks to Phyllis Ridgeway for her initial typing of the book. She really got us off to a great start.

Most importantly, we would like to thank you, the reader, for taking the initiative to consider a new venture. Your entrepreneurial spirit and determination will take you a long way in life if you channel it in the right direction. It's people like you who made this country great. We take our hats off to all entrepreneurs. They take risks so that others may enjoy employment.

Since you probably purchased this manual to help you develop a successful business plan, marketing plan, or strategic plan, we want to wish you the very best life has to offer. Congratulations on making the decision to move forward in life. Whatever your dreams and goals are, we hope that you attain all the important objectives that you have set, or will set, for yourself and your company.

Good Luck in all your endeavors.

Very Sincerely, Brian J. Hazlegren
                 Joseph A. Covello

Controlled Use and Intended Use Warranty Declaration

This product has been carefully checked for technical accuracy. We feel that the information presented in this publication is accurate, reliable, and useful. However, everything is subject to change and the authors reserve the right to make changes and improvements in the document, without prior notice. Readers should, in all cases, contact the authors regarding questions, omissions, changes, and improvements. The information contained in this product is intended to provide guidelines and a foundation for further planning and development by readers to fit their specific requirements.

As each business plan is unique and one of a kind, the authors, publisher, their employees, agents, and distributors, having no control as to how these guidelines are to be used, herein disclaim liability of any kind or nature in the use of this system, in total. No representa- tions, warranties, or guarantees are given, either expressed or implied, that this system, "Secrets to Writing Powerful Business Plans: The Entrepreneurs Guide," will raise capital for the purchaser, end user, or subsequent end user's intended use.

The use and intent of the contents of this written manual should only be for the gath- ering and accumulation of information required for a business plan in anticipation of creating a management tool, funding a new business or start-up, or for an estab- lished business seeking venture capital, banks, lenders, insurance companies, pen- sion funds, or other private sources.

The contents covered are extensive and comprehensive, covering most requirements for types or methods used in funding a business with capital.

Chapter 1

Powerful Guidelines to Writing a Winning Business Plan

I. A Few Facts

About one million new businesses are started each year in America. Of those million, only two hundred thousand will survive five years. This translates into only one in five businesses that will make it to their fifth anniversary.

That is an alarming statistic! Why in the world would only one in five businesses in the "Land of Opportunity" survive only a relatively short period of time? There are several reasons why, yet the one reason that is most common just happens to be the most controllable.

The bottom line is that there is no magic equation for success. However, one basic rule holds true: "A business owner who fails to plan, plans to fail."

A business plan helps entrepreneurs think through their strategies, balance their enthusiasm with facts, and recognize their limitations. It will help you avoid potentially disastrous errors like undercapitalizing, creating negative cash flow, hiring the wrong people, selecting the wrong location, and pursuing the wrong market.

A winning business plan requires time. Plan on fifty to one hundred hours of work to write a complete and comprehensive business plan, including research, documentation, analysis, and review.

Entrepreneurs should really start planning at least six months before they plan to open their business. This is only due to the time you need to devote to its start-up while working another job. Six months gives you time to sharpen and focus your business ideas, test your assumptions, and improve your management skills.

If you don't want to wait six months, then dig in and begin your incredible journey. Maybe you are the type of person who can accomplish the following elements in a shorter time period. Whatever category you fit in, consider these essential elements . . .

II. Your New Enterprise— Before Start-Up

Decide on the kind of business you want to start.

The answer will depend on a few important elements:

- How much money you have to invest;
- Whether you can attract other investors;
- The amount of return you want;
- Ask yourself what you do well.
- Ask yourself what you like to do most.
- Are you willing to work harder, longer hours?
- Do retail sales, manufacturing, service business, import/export (or whatever), fit your interests and/or expertise?

Consider a Start-up's Impact

- Your income will suffer.
- Your work hours will multiply.
- Your family relationships will be strained.
- You will have expended your personal cash, or be in debt.

- You will sometimes feel like you're running behind.

- You may become more irritable, or critical with people around you.

- You will see less of your friends and family.

- You may get more headaches, backaches, or stomachaches.

- You will feel guilty at times if you are not working.

- Your life, for a time, may seem like all work and no play.

Don't despair, these feelings and circumstances are a normal part of starting a business, or embarking on a new project. Just don't give up. As Robert Donovan once said, "Giving up is the ultimat̶̶̶̶̶̶

- Your state commissioner of Economic Development.

- SCORE (Service Corps of Retired Executives).

- U.S. Embassy in the country or countries you plan to do business with.

- Businesses in noncompetitive locations. (Magic phrase: "I've got a problem and I think you can help me.")

- Foreign Trade Zones Board—this entity is there to review and approve applications to import foreign goods.

- Small Business Administration (SBA).

- Newspaper Editors—send them a press release also.

Define your business. Write a mission ̶̶̶̶rds or less—that outlines ̶̶̶̶d to whom, and what

> *"Greet the da̶̶ you may expect ̶̶̶̶tion by sunset."*

Anonymous

Hot information sou̶̶

Start your research.

- Your local Chamber of Co̶̶ assist you whether you are a member or not.

- Trade shows—a one-stop shopping source for businesses, suppliers, and various consultants.

- Trade-association executives—ask them what is "hot" in the marketplace.

- Trade-magazine editors—send a press release to as many as possible.

- Local networking meetings—a tremendous source for leads. Start your own if you have to.

- Federal, state, and university programs.

̶̶ness different (Your ̶̶antage).

̶̶ useful, applicable solu-̶̶ers and managers, in the ̶̶usiness planning, finance, accounting, and promotion, and to fully utilize our management team's experience and knowledge to increase revenues of each of our client's enterprises and companies.

III. The Business Plan

Name Your Business. This is a vital decision.

Advice: Keep the name straightforward and descriptive. Make it as distinctive as possible. Avoid grandiose, overworked adjectives.

Your business name should be like a headline of an article. Describe who you are and what you do in your name whenever possible. A dangerous marketing tool is to make customers guess what you do. Your competition may already have a descriptive and straightforward name.

Select Outside Advisors. You will need a competent attorney, management consultant, accountant, insurance agent, and banker. Also helpful: A marketing consultant will save time, money, and misspent effort.

Start Writing Your Business Plan. That is why you purchased this guideline—to get you started in the right direction. (But wait until you have read all the secrets and critical elements to a winning business contained in this system.)

Convince yourself that proper business planning is an absolute necessity. *Your business plan is the heart and soul of your operation and the most important set of documents provided by you to any lending institution or potential investor.* It explains all the financing you need. Most importantly, it will give your financial sources persuasive information about your venture.

Put your business plan to multiple uses. A comprehensive and realistic business plan will help you accomplish many essential objectives, including the following:

1. Take charge of your entrepreneurial life. The business plan is evidence of your initiative. It shows that you have the discipline to focus your energies on an important project and that you understand how to achieve progress and growth, solve problems along the way, and achieve ultimate goals. The business plan is the foundation and pillars of your vision and will allow you to structure your ideas into reality.

2. Lay out a master blueprint. The business plan is to the entrepreneur what a set of detailed architectural drawings is to the builder. It determines the details of how you are going to reach your objectives. It shows you every step of the way, where you plan to go, in relation to where you

actually are. It will also help you plan, or pursue an alternate (and possibly better) route. The business plan is a powerful management tool.

3. Communicate your master plan to members of your team. The business plan constitutes a concrete statement of purpose which allows you to communicate to your colleagues a step-by-step agenda for reaching your goals. Some portions of the business plan can also be used in training and coordinating meetings, as well as teaching staff persons what their role and accountability will be in making your business function successfully.

4. Attract money to your project. Potential suppliers of capital and other needed resources (bankers, brokers, investors, future partners, etc.) will place great value on your business plan as they weigh the decision on whether to participate with you.

Your ability to create trust and respect can be greatly enhanced through interpersonal contact with these potential suppliers of capital. However, you may not even get a chance to get to know these people on a personal basis. Therefore, you must have a professional document to present in written form. Your business plan will be your initial selling tool, your business resumé, when attracting lenders to participate with you in your venture.

IV. What Potential Suppliers of Capital Look at First

There are four critical areas of the business plan that investors will weigh very heavily if they are to participate with you. These areas are:

1. Your Management Team
2. Current and Projected Financials
3. Your Products or Services
4. Your Marketing Plan

List strength/weakness (handwritten)

... of the

... ket?

... ted

... arket

... ajor

... ared

... e

... ...ues from

y... ...et analysis.

You will also want to list the strengths and weaknesses of your product or service. When covering your strengths, you need to be sure to place at least as much emphasis on marketing as you do on your product, if not more.

List several distinct advantages over the competition in the following areas:

1. Actual performance

2. Quality and reliability

3. Production efficiencies

4. Distribution

5. Pricing

6. Public image or reputation

7. Business relationships or references

If you know of any weaknesses in your product or service, list those also, and show what steps you are taking to alleviate the problem(s).

Marketing Strategies is the science of planning for and executing a promotional campaign that will generate sales for your enterprise. These strategies are to enhance, promote, and support the advantages, features, and benefits of your products and services.

This section should be designed with one word in mind: **Strategy.**

When thinking about a strategy, you will be able to specifically define your business activities, strengths, and direction. What type of strategy would you put together if your life depended on a plan to get away from an enemy who is bound and determined to see you fail?

Think of your competition as the enemy. They absolutely do not want you to succeed. Your strategy, depending upon how much you want to succeed, should be defined to capture your share of the market in as little time as possible.

How do/will your customers perceive your company and product, relative to the competition? This is critical! Let's say that one more time. How do/will your customers perceive your company and product, relative to the competition? A good way to find out is to ask them. Conduct a market survey. This is an easy and inexpensive way to find out the answer to this important question.

What can be said about your competitors' products or services that will change your customers' minds? What is your Unique Selling Advantage? (A discussion on this topic follows this section.)

What will be your strategies to promote your products and services? Will you use television or radio? Is it better to conduct seminars or participate in trade shows? Will you use telemarketing or outside sales representatives? Do you need to hire a Public Relations Agency? Will you sell your products and services locally, nationally, or internationally? Have you considered direct mail? Will you use brochures and flyers? What other creative ways will you come up with to generate leads?

Here are a few other questions you should give serious consideration:

- Are your strategies consistent with your evaluation of the marketplace and your capabilities?

- Have you defined your targeted market into a narrow window, or does your product appeal to a large market?

- Are your strategies based on facts or assumptions?

- Is your appraisal of the competition open-minded and honest?

- Is the expected return on investment sufficient to justify the risks?

- Have you thoroughly examined other strategies that your competitors are using? Could some of their strategies be adapted to your environment?

- Is your strategy legal?

Hot Marketing Tip

Another tip is to look at the gripes first, then create a marketing strategy. Look at everything about your industry that could gripe, frustrate, or irritate a potential customer.

Ask people what irritates them. Try to internalize the same problems and experience your customer's frustrations before creating your marketing strategies.

V. Your Unique Selling Advantage (USA)

It is important to understand how vital it is to adopt your own USA, and implement it from the CEO down through the sales team, and on to your clerical staff. Everybody within an organization should have a solid understanding of what sets you apart from the competition.

Your USA is that single, unique advantage, benefit, essence, appeal, or big promise that holds your product or service out to the prospect—one that no other competitor offers or advertises. You should be able to articulate in one or two crisp, clear paragraphs the Unique Selling Advantage of your business product or service.

The Backbone of your entire business concept

A. Your USA is literally the unique advantage that distinguishes your business from that of anyone else.

This is a concept that your entire enterprise should be built around.

B. Without a USA you cannot build a consistent and effective marketing campaign.

C. There is some unique advantage that you should basically build your entire marketing efforts around. You need to define it in a clear paragraph. Once you have developed your own USA, formulating a winning marketing strategy will come much easier. Therefore, tell it accurately, straightforwardly, and intelligently.

D. A USA may be that your product is made entirely of all-natural ingredients or has a guarantee for double the amount of time over your competitors. Maybe you offer three times more follow-up by calling, writing to, or actually visiting your customers after they purchase your product or service. Maybe your product is entirely handmade, the only product in your area, and the competition will take years to produce something as good as you offer. Maybe your business stays open two hours longer than all of your competitors for added convenience to your customers.

You probably get the idea. Go ahead! Create an insatiable USA that lets people feel that they cannot live a moment longer without your product or service. You will be surprised how easy this is. Have FUN!

Here is a good example of how a USA has escalated sales for a highly successful computer company:

AST Research Inc. was struggling during the personal computer wars of the late '80s. One of its founders had angrily resigned, the company had announced its first loss in eight years, and it was laying off employees for the first time in its ten-year history.

Things there are different these days. AST developed a simple, yet powerful, way to market its products. Its original break came in 1981 when IBM announced the introduction of the personal computer. AST figured people would want an inexpensive way to add options. AST has made it a point to educate the public about its **U**nique **S**elling **A**dvantages. One way was to put its advertising where the people that use such products would come across it—airports, bus shelters and taxis. Smart Idea!

There are basically six distinctive **U**nique **S**elling **A**dvantages that AST markets to its end users.

1. Probably the most important marketing plan is the company's upgradable PCs. Buyers don't have to worry that their computers will be outdated in six months. Most of them will never upgrade, but it removes the reason for postponing the purchase.

2. Add-on memory board business, which also helps to enhance virtually any IBM compatible.

3. AST sells its PCs to other computer companies such as Digital Equipment Corp. and Texas Instruments Inc., which put their own labels on them. (Imagine that!)

4. AST prices are typically 20% to 30% lower than IBM and Compaq.

5. AST was one of the first PC makers to ship PCs based on a top-of-the-line 80486 chip.

6. Low prices and high performance that provide a winning combination for recession-weary PC buyers.

This marketing plan paid off very well for AST. In 1990 its share price raised 259%. While the overall personal computer market limps along at a 5% growth rate, AST's revenues race along at 20%! While other PC makers struggle, AST's sales and profits soar. Its **U**nique **S**elling **A**dvantages are broadcast to buyers and decision makers in

the form of advertising, suppliers, and salespeople. The buyer becomes educated and is then able to make an intelligent decision. Incidentally, this powerful case of a successful USA has rocketed AST to a $650 million company. AST may soon be a billion-dollar company. *

Contents

Note—the format of your business plan or the amount of detail it contains, how fancy and image oriented it is, etc., may vary according to the intended use and readership. The following summary of the ingredients of the business plan is intended to show you the elements needed to compose a winning plan that will attract potential financial resources to your venture.

Listed below are the items that you should consider including in your business plan:

I. Cover Sheet. If you are appealing to prospective investors, money brokers, bankers, venture capitalists, etc., include a cover sheet, preferably on company stationery, displaying company emblems, logos, etc. This will help place your application in a framework of legitimacy.

Keep your cover sheet as simple as possible. Identify yourself, your business, and the institution or party to whom you are addressing your application. Include the date the plan is submitted. Here is a checklist of items to include:

A. Business information

    1. Name of business
    2. Location, address
    3. Telephone numbers
    4. Contact person(s), including titles

B. Business paragraph: promotional description of business goals, potential, and outlook.

C. Amount of capital required: current and anticipated future needs.

D. Whenever possible state the name or names of persons recommending you to the investor.

II. Table of Contents. This index will not only help your prospective lender to understand the road map you are placing before him, it will also make a statement about you (i.e., you are organized, thorough, sensitive to the needs of those you are approaching, and able to manage the "big picture"). Type up the Table of Contents last.

III. Executive Summary. This portion of the business plan must be designed to capture and hold the interest of the party to whom the plan is being presented. It is also the only portion of the business plan that everyone who sees your business plan is sure to read with care. Make sure it can be read in a few minutes. Make it good! Keep it somewhere between two and five pages of typed copy.

This critical executive summary encapsulates the entire business plan in a few paragraphs by giving the most succinct statement possible of the nature and objectives of your business:

A. Its mission.

B. Its unique "selling advantage."

C. Your projections for the future (sales and profits).

D. Your needs (capital and other resources).

E. Procedures and timetable for repaying investors.

F. The amount of capital you are requesting.

This summary is a crystallization of the entire business plan in a quick, overview format. Don't neglect this section; it will demonstrate that you can focus with clarity on your goals, and state in no-nonsense

fashion who you are, what you want, and where you are going.

IV. The Context of Your Business. This statement provides a "big picture" perspective of the industry to which your business belongs and prepares the reader to understand better how your business fits into the total picture. It should include:

A. Growth potential: in view of the trends described above, provide a statement (in dollars) of the future growth potential of the industry in which you are competing.

B. New products and developments: what new developments have arisen in the recent past that will make your product or service more attractive to the public?

C. Economic trends: evidence that spending trends are favorable to the industry.

E. Industry outlook and trends: the future of the industry according to industry leaders, experts, economists, government forecasters, and other authoritative spokespersons.

V. Profile of Your Business.

A. What is the precise nature of your business?

B. Provide a brief history of the business or how you developed your products and services.

C. What are the economic trends? Is there evidence that spending trends are favorable to the industry?

D. What is the organizational detail (legal structure, personnel resources, operational patterns, organization chart) of your business?

E. What are the factors that influence your business (i.e, local economic factors, seasonality, dependence on special vendors or suppliers)?

F. What are your patterns of research and development?

    1. The nature of your test-marketing procedures?

    2. Results achieved?

    3. Product development?

    4. Legal control of process and/or product?

G. Do you have any contracts and agreements? (Identify here and include copies in the Appendix; examples: resale agreements, service contracts, leases, etc.)

H. What are your operational procedures?

    1. For ventures involving manufacturing a product, include:

       a. Physical space requirements

       b. Machinery and equipment

       c. Raw materials

       d. Inventory and supplies

       e. Personnel requirements

       f. Capital estimates

    2. For ventures involving selling or retailing, include:

       a. Physical space requirements

       b. Purchasing procedures and plans

       c. Inventory system

       d. Staff and equipment

       e. Training

       f. Credentials

Note: This information, and similar details you may wish to include, constitutes the profile of your business. This section should provide the reader with the concept of how your business works and why it has a unique chance to shine in the marketplace.

VI. Profile of Your Specific Market.

A. Precisely state who the consumers of your products or services are.

B. The geographical scope of your market, including size and population.

C. Growth potential of your target market.

D. Your ability to satisfy the market's demands.

E. How your business plan will enable you to attract new customers while keeping the customers you have.

When developing a profile of your target market, it is important to remember that your research will determine the strength of your analysis. The time you spend on this section should be spent wisely. Your local library and your telephone will be your strongest allies. Use them to their fullest!

Take advantage of the information and statistics already available in books, directories, and

---

> *"Dost Thou love life? Then do not squander time, for that's the stuff life is made of."*
>
> *Benjamin Franklin*

---

case studies. Thorough research will impress potential investors more than you can believe. So again, spend your time wisely here.

Note: Be thorough in structuring this market profile. Show that you have done your homework with great care and due diligence.

VII. Anticipated Challenges and Planned Responses. This section of the business plan sets forth your contingency strategies for dealing with anticipated barriers and challenges. Some of the main types are these:

A. Dealing with the competition:

1. Your major competitors (similarities and differences when compared with your business);

2. Their strong points and weaknesses;

3. How your "edge" (Unique Selling Advantage) will enable you to prevail and stay on course;

4. How you guess the competition will try to block you and how you will respond.

B. Weak areas where you believe you may be vulnerable and how you intend to compensate, for example:

1. Obsolescence factors

2. Cheaper products on the horizon

3. Cyclical trends in the marketplace

4. Possible economic downturn in the future

5. Turnover of key employees

6. Seasonality of your products and services

7. Offering a benefits package to employees (whether or not to)

C. Legal factors:

1. License requirements that you must satisfy or maintain.

2. Restrictions and regulations under which you must operate, given the nature of your business.

3. Future changes in legal or governmental policies that may affect your business, and how you will respond.

4. Any governmental agencies that you need to apply to. (A franchise must comply with FTC [Federal Trade Commission] regulations; a radio station must comply with FCC [Federal Communications Commission] regulations; etc.)

D. Protection issues:

1. Patents, copyrights, trademarks, and other protection procedures you have in place.

2. How to assure that business secrets are preserved.

E. Key man contingencies:

1. The depth of your management team.

2. Management procedures in place to assure continuity of leadership.

3. Plans for responding to the loss of important personnel.

F. Staffing:

1. Personnel needs you anticipate having over time (requirements, training, benefits, expansion) and how these needs will be met.

2. Policies on minority issues.

3. Policies on temporary versus permanent staff.

4. Policies on racism, or prejudices.

Note: This section must demonstrate that you have covered the problem bases and have carefully crafted contingency plans in place. The information in this section will provide your business plan with more credibility than you think. Be practical and reasonable. Show that you have really done your homework.

VIII. Marketing Plan. We have all seen great businesses, with a super location and a unique product, go broke and close their doors. In most cases this tragic problem can be traced to poor marketing and promotion. This could be because the owner of the business did not know how to market his or her products and services.

Many business owners make the mistake of thinking they don't have to advertise or promote their "superior products or services." WRONG! Nothing could be farther from reality. Small business owners tend to ignore or (given the benefit-of-the-doubt) forget four key Marketing areas, and end up going out of business. These four critical areas are:

1. Publicity
2. Promotion
3. Merchandising
4. Market Research

Here's a secret. Read this carefully. Each of these four marketing areas does not have to cost you one dime. That's right. You don't have to spend any hard money for these free things.

Go ahead, ask the question. "HOW . . . ?"

How do you reach your customers to let them know who you are and what services you provide without spending any money?

Well first, you must define your market. Who, or what, is your targeted audience? Who will listen to your story, and who will buy from you once they have heard your case?

The first rule in the area of marketing is a very simple one: know your market. It's simple to determine who your customers are. *Entrepreneur Magazine* gives us a super idea in this area: "All you have to do is forget that you are selling your product or service, and put yourself in your customer's place." Make sense? It's almost like the Golden Rule: "Do unto others as you would have them do unto you." *Entrepreneur* goes on to say, "Ask yourself questions such as these:

• Where do I go to buy it?

• What makes me buy it?

• What media do I watch, read, listen to, that make me decide to buy?" *

*Source: *Entrepreneur Magazine*

Simply put, you must know what media your market draws to.

You must develop a rock-solid marketing plan. Your profits will literally rise or fall on the basis of how well you develop and implement your marketing plan. Here is your chance to show your entrepreneurial expertise in its best light. Carefully consider the following ideas and strategies, and implement each one of them in your plan:

A. Marketing strategies that you will be focusing on.

B. Reasons for these strategies: information, feasibility testing, competitor track record, and/or creative insight into the market.

C. Pricing Note: Pricing a product or service is sometimes as much a decision—based on customer acceptance—as cost. Therefore, consumer research and competitor track record and pricing, customer acceptance, etc., should be demonstrated as your basis. In other words, "Charge what the market will bear."

D. Your timetable.

E. Your marketing budget.

F. Guarantee policies.

G. Presentation and packaging.

H. Professional resources you will need to implement your plan.

I. How you will monitor the response of the market to your campaign.

J. How you will test one approach against another.

K. Advertising and promotional intentions.

L. Media you will use to promote your enterprise, and related costs.

IX. Financial Projections. Here is the heart of your business plan, the point in time where your vision is quantified in terms of dollars and cents, and units of time: days, weeks, months, and years. All persons reading your plan will go through your financial projections with great care. Your financials should be broken down into monthly projections for years one and two, and annually thereafter up to and including year ten. Based on this scenario you should include the following projections. These projections (sometimes called the "computation trio") should be prepared according to three scenarios: Profit & Loss Statement, Balance Sheet, and Cash Flow Statement.

A. Profit & Loss Statement: Based on the marketing plan you have developed, determine projected revenues over time. Typically, projections become outdated given the impact of all the variables at work in a given enterprise and its market environment. Adjustments will need to be made constantly as you implement mid-course corrections over time.

    Next, calculate your cost of goods and/or services sold (COGS) as well as all your anticipated fixed overhead costs. Keep in mind that your COGS will generally fluctuate with revenue volume while fixed overhead costs will exist on a continued monthly basis.

    The net difference of total revenues less total costs will determine the profit or loss of your enterprise.

B. Balance Sheet: The balance sheet gives a profile of the worth of your company at a given moment in time. This statement lists all of the company's assets (cash, accounts receivable, inventory, machinery and equipment, real estate, etc.) and all of the company's liabilities (accounts payable, notes payable, taxes and interest payable, salaries and wages currently owed, etc.).

    The difference between the assets and the liabilities constitutes the net worth of the company (also called the owner's equity) at any particular moment in time. If you have a track record when the business plan is developed (as in an expansion of an existing operation) then the balance sheet may show considerable equity. If you are starting out with a new venture, the balance sheet may be very simple and show little equity. Work with your local accounting team to develop the details of the balance sheet (in quarters or years).

C. Cash Flow Statement: When you plot expected revenues against anticipated expenses, and tally the running net balances by unit to time, you are projecting your cash flow. Cash flow totals are a critical index of how successful your business will be. Be sure to identify all changes in detail. Leave nothing to the imagination. Be conservative and realistic.

Note: As in all numbers exercises, work with your accountant on the details.

X. Implementation Schedule. This portion of the business plan accomplishes the following:

A. Identifies when you expect needed financing to kick in.

B. Lists the main steps of the marketing campaign charted by date.

C. Gives the scheduled dates of the production and delivery programs that will fulfill the obligations of sales.

The implementation schedule will enable you to coordinate and manage your enterprise in a systematic and controlled way. This section of your business plan is of critical importance both internally (as a management tool) and externally (as a means of persuading others that you have the "smarts" to put your project into effect).

XI. Statement of Resource Needs. If you are using your business plan for the purpose of generating needed resources from lenders or investors, this item will summarize your precise needs (amount, terms, date needed) and identify how the resources will be used. In the case of financing, your cash-flow projections will, of course, reflect how these funds will be repaid.

In the case of capitalization involving equity partners, your projections will give an indication of the growth of equity and the anticipated timetable for the sharing of profits.

XII. Appendix. This section of the business plan might include some or all of the following:

A. Footnotes from the text (i.e., assumptions used in projections, further sources of information).

B. Supporting documents.

C. Articles, clippings, special reports.

D. Biographies.

E. Bibliographies.

F. Graphs and charts.

G. Copies of contracts and agreements.

H. Glossary of terms.

I. References: lenders, investors, or other bankers, suppliers, trade creditors, etc., who can give positive feedback on your past performance.

Practical Tips

I. Be Realistic. Build your business plan with a sense of realism and practicality. Do your homework carefully and think through every detail that could have a bearing on the success of your project. Your business plan should be a carefully crafted action document, not a speculative piece of fortune-telling.

II. Document Your Claims. Where you are basing projections on specific assumptions (i.e., projections about market response to your goods or services), give evidence that these assumptions are based as closely as possible on fact. Assemble and apply expert opinion to substantiate your projections. Use newspaper and magazine articles, university studies, interviews of prominent people who are familiar with your market, etc.

III. Create a Unique Selling Advantage. If you have an "edge" that will raise your chances and persuasively identify you as separate from your competitors, emphasize this advantage boldly.

IV. Be Flexible. Your business plan is a road map that allows you to check your position, velocity, and direction on a constant basis. As you monitor your progress, you will need to implement midcourse corrections periodically. You will certainly need to adjust your business plan from time to time as your assumptions are updated according to real-life feedback from the "trenches" and as market conditions shift.

V. Use Technology to Good Advantage. Modern computers and computer software can be a tremendous help to you in developing portions of your business plan, especially the financial portions. With the help of computers, you can play "what if" and gain valuable insight into future outcomes, based on the strategic adjustment of variables (i.e., pricing services in relation to variable costs). Have your local accounting experts explain the details.

You might wish to invest in the equipment and software to service your own needs in these regards. Computer hardware is very much within the reach of most budgets these days, and recent software developments place effective software programs within easy reach as well.

VI. Attend to Packaging. The business plan should be clean, conservative, simple, well-prepared, clearly written, error-free, and appropriately bound. Your plan should look impressive though not slick. You don't want to make a statement about being a big spender on superficials. If you are presenting the business plan to prospective financial sources, you should bind the materials in such a way that they will open flat on a desk top. For internal use, the business plan should be organized in a three-ring binder, where updates can be easily incorporated.

VII. Present the Plan Skillfully and Graphically. Consider using projection technology and similar support equipment when presenting your plan to prospective funders. Presenting economic and chart-oriented information in attractive, visual ways will help to solidify your position.

Patents, Copyrights, Trademarks, and Secret Formulas

There are countless stories about companies in the multimillion-dollar range whose origination was based on an idea from Ralph Waldo Emerson which basically said: "Build a better mousetrap and the world will come knocking at your door."

That quotation was never more true than in today's world of high technology and expanding markets. Companies from far and wide are being developed on a world-wide basis to produce and distribute products that were never even dreamed of just ten years ago.

If you are a start-up business, or even an established business that has new products, ideas, or technology that will improve someone's standard of living, and want to place your product on the market, your products should be patented, or trademarked, and all your written material should be copyrighted.

The two basic kinds of patents are either Mechanical or Design. The distinction between the two is that a Mechanical Patent is for a new product that operates mechanically, something no one has ever developed before. A Design Patent is an improvement to a previously patented product. That is, its design makes the older product better. However, there is a great possibility of infringement on the older patent if all you did was change the design, leaving the mechanics to operate as they used to.

A case in point, one which everyone would understand, is automobiles. Here, the design changes are radical, changing every month if you follow closely the trends in the marketplace. Each change in design is Design Patented. Design Patents last for three years. Mechanical Patents last for 17 years and can be renewed thereafter.

Note: We strongly suggest that you seek council of an attorney who specializes in patents, copyrights, trademarks, and secret formulas.

Government Contracts

Many new businesses have been established just to handle government contracts. If you are establishing a new business to handle government contracts, or if you are already established and handling government contracts, this should be totally revealed in your Business Plan.

There are many advantages and disadvantages to this. You must use your own knowledge and expertise to determine these factors. Obtaining a contract is not easy. Yet the government spends hundreds of billions of dollars annually on just about everything you can think of. Government contracts are a very lucrative source of business.

What your business is and what your expertise is will determine whether you are capable of handling a government contract.

You must bid for a government contract, and if you are successful, this business could mean your ultimate success.

On the other hand, all government contracts are subject to cancellation or withdrawal, in which case you may have spent many thousands of dollars that cannot be recovered. All contracts carry a "save or hold harmless" clause.

For small businesses that wish to pursue the government contracts and don't know where to start, again, go to some of the sources already mentioned in this guideline. The U.S. Small Business Administration (SBA), Office of Procurement and Technical Assistance, and Service Corps of Retired Executives (SCORE) are excellent sources. They can assist you in getting on the mailing list for contracts in your industry.

You may also look into those companies that already hold contracts with the government. You may be in a position to sub-contract from them.

Your Business Plan should indicate whether your company is in a position to handle government contracts, and to what degree you can handle them.

Finding financing to fulfill a government contract is easy—

But you still need a Business Plan

Business Resource Directory

I. General

National Federation of Independent Business, 53 Century Boulevard, Suite 250, Nashville, TN 37214; (800) NFIB-NOW (634-2669). Packing the free enterprise muscle of its 570,000 members, NFIB lobbies Congress on small-business issues and provides information to members on regulations, legislation, and federal agencies. Counselors troubleshoot business problems, and case

workers will intervene with federal agencies on members' behalf.

American Marketing Association, 311 S. Wacker Dr., Suite 5800, Chicago, IL 60606-5819; (312) 542-9000. Valuable source of marketing information. Publishes periodicals such as the bi-weekly *Marketing News* and *The Journal of Marketing.* $130 National Membership. www. ama.org

American Management Association, 1601 Broadway, New York, NY 10019; (212) 586-8100, (800) 262-9699. Founded in 1923; 700,000 members worldwide. Corporate memberships available. Individual membership fee of $45 or $225 per year includes access to My World website, telephone support, and library services. Members get preferred rates on publications, purchasing, finance, human resources, insurance, manufacturing, marketing, and many others.

Small Business Administration, 409 3rd St. SW, Washington, DC 20416; (800) U-ASK-SBA. Whatever the business question, chances are the SBA answer desk will have a solution, or at least be able to refer you to one. The line is staffed from 9 a.m. to 5 p.m. EST. www.sba.gov

SBA Small Business Development Centers. These provide education and seminars, conferences, networking reference books, and lots of other resources for entrepreneurs and managers. Each of the state hub-SBDCs administers the activities of field offices at state colleges and universities, Chambers of Commerce, and corporations, at more than 600 locations across the U.S. Call (800) U-ASK-SBA for the nearest location and its calender of events.

II. International Trade

Central and Eastern Europe Business Information Center, 1401 Constitution Ave., NW, U.S. Department of Commerce, Ronald Reagan Building, R-CEEBIC, Washington, DC 20230; (202) 482-2645; fax (202) 482-3898. The center can assist small and medium-sized companies with questions about exporting, setting up joint ventures, financing of trade promotion opportunities, and foundations or individuals interested in promoting the economic development of their city or state. www.mac.doc.gov/eebic/email.htm

International Council for Small Business, St. Louis University, 3674 Lindell Blvd., St. Louis, MO 63108; (314) 977-3628; fax (314) 977-3627; EMAIL icsb@slu.edu. Dr. Robert Brockhaus, Executive Director. ICSB is a non-profit association with members in fifty countries open to anyone wishing to exchange ideas and information on economic development and business management. Membership comprises small-business owners, consultants, corporate officers, government officials, educators, and professionals. www.icsb.org

Office of the U.S. Trade Representative, Executive Office of the President, 600 17th St. NW, Washington, DC 20508; (888) 473-8787. This office is the president's primary agent for negotiating and administering trade agreements with foreign countries. www.ustr.gov

Customs Service Public Information Division, 1300 Pennsylvania Ave. NW, Washington, DC 20229; (202) 972-1770. For questions on trade tariffs, quotas, or other specific customs requirements, this division answers over the phone, provides advisory services, or will send you information.

referrals, or copy and send you materials.

III. Copyright, Trademarks, and Patents.

U.S. Patent and Trademarks Office, General Information Services Division, U.S. Patent and Trademark Office, Crystal Plaza 3, Room 2C02, Washington, DC 20231; (800) 786-9199 or (703) 308-4357. The nation's repository of bright ideas offers information through its public service center. A free booklet, "Basic Facts About Patents," is available. www.uspto.gov

The International Trademark Association, 1133 Avenue of the Americas, New York, NY 10036; (212) 768-9887. Nonprofit association devoted to the trademark concept. Answers inquiries, produces publications, and sponsors seminars. www.inta.org

IV. Other Government Programs

The U.S. Government Purchasing and Sales Directory, Superintendent of Documents, U.S. Government Printing Office, Washington, DC 20402-9371 (Stock No. 045-000-00272-1). This directory provides addresses of government purchasing offices. The publication is $28.00. www.gpo.gov

Procurement Automated Source System (PASS) is a computerized listing of small businesses. Being on this list can increase your exposure, but it does not guarantee solicitations or contracts. To get listed, write to U.S. Small Business Administration, PASS, 409 3rd St. SW, Washington, DC 20416.

"Feel the pride in how far you have come, and confidence in where you are going."

Anonymous

U.S. International Trade Commission Library, 500 East St. SW, Washington, DC 20436; (202) 205-2000. This library holds a wealth of data on commercial policy, foreign trade, and trade statistics. Staff members will answer telephone inquiries and make

WHEW! We have taken quite a long journey up to this point. Do you have a solid understanding of the importance of a comprehensive business plan? You should at least understand why you need a plan, and what areas, topics, strategies, etc., are needed.

Now, the rest is up to you. Keep in mind that there are professional consulting firms that can give you advice and suggestions about your enterprise. We hope that you have enjoyed reading this material so far. It was created to help anyone in business who must create a business plan to raise capital, expand their current market, or develop an internal document for their company to follow.

In the next section, you will be introduced to some additional questions that will help you formulate a better game plan. So, sharpen your pencil and get ready to create the vision of where you want to take your enterprise. ENJOY!

"It is the greatest of all mistakes to do nothing, because you can only do a little. Do what you can."

Sidney Smith

Chapter 2

101-Plus Questions to Success

The following *checklist* will help you create a better overall picture of how to structure your business plan. It is intended to assist you in thinking through the key elements of your enterprise. This *checklist* will give you most of the answers that are needed to write a comprehensive plan.

1. What is the nature of your business (retailing products to consumers; real estate sales; manufacturing; mail order; etc.)?

    ....

    ....

    ....

2. What phase is your business in?

    A. Start-up ....

    B. Expansion ....

    C. Cash flow shortage ....

    D. Other ....

3. What is your corporate structure?

    A. Sole proprietor ....

    B. Partnership ....

    C. Limited partnership ....

    D. Minority-owned ....

    E. Woman-owned ....

    F. Corporation   C Corp. ☐   S Corp. ☐ ....

    G. Not for profit ....

    H. Other ....

4. Who is your management team?

    A. President ....

    B. Vice President ....

    C. Secretary ....

    D. Treasurer ....

    E. Controller ....

    F. Marketing Manager ....

    G. Sales Manager ....

    H. Operation Manager ....

    I. Human Resource Manager ....

5. Who is on your outside consultant team?

    A. Legal...

    B. Management consultant ....

    C. Marketing ....

    D. Accounting ....

    E. Computer software ....

    F. Computer hardware ....

6. What is your unique selling advantage? (Give details on why your product/service is unique.)

    ....

    ....

    ....

    ....

7. What are your goals and objectives? ....

    ....

    ....

    ....

    ....

8. What would you like to achieve in annual sales volume?

    A. Year one $ ....

    B. Year two $ ....

    C. Year five $ ....

    D. Year ten $ ....

9. How do you plan to achieve your annual sales volume goals? ....
....
....

10. What do you want for yourself, both personally and financially? ....
....
....
....

11. What will you develop? ....
....
....
....

12. What will you achieve? ....
....
....
....

13. How will your company fit into the industry? ....
....
....
....

14. How will your investors receive their return on investment (go public in five years, be acquired in four years, etc.)?
....
....
....

15. What is your customer profile? (Give details on your typical customers.)

    A. Business Customer ....

    Type of business ....

    Size of business (Approximate annual revenues) ....

    Geographical area ....

    Number of employees ....

    Years in business ....

    B. Individual Consumer ....

    Age ....

    Income ....

Sex ....

Occupation ....

Family size ....

Culture ....

Education ....

16. Who is your competition?

    A. ....

    B. ....

    C. ....

    D. ....

    E. ....

    F. ....

    G. ....

    H. ....

17. How is your competition promoting its product or service?

....

....

....

18. What are your company plans?

    A. Sales and marketing plans ....

....

....

    B. Technical and engineering ....

....

....

    C. Franchise or distributor plans ....

....

....

    D. Personnel ....

....

....

19. How much capital do you need for two years of operation? ....

20. What will the capital be used for? ....

....

21. What type of borrowing structure are you looking for?

    A. Debt only ....

    B. Debt/Equity ....

    C. Limited partnership ....

    D. Stock purchase ....

    E. Venture capital ....

22. What type of payback to the lender/investor are you looking for? ....

23. What equipment do you need? (Please list type of equipment and retail costs, i.e., machinery and equipment, furniture and fixtures, vehicles, office machines and equipment, telephone systems.)

    ....

    ....

    ....

24. What inventory do you need? (List type of inventory you need.)

    ....

    ....

    ....

25. Will you be leasing office/warehouse space, or purchasing? Give details.

    ....

    ....

    ....

26. What existing loans do you have? ....

    ....

    ....

27. What will you do with these loans? ....

    ....

    ....

28. Will you/do you have salespeople? If yes, please indicate their territories, commissions, and salary structures.

    ....

    ....

    ....

29. How many salespeople do you/will you have on staff during the next 24 months?

    A. Outside ....

    B. Inside ....

30. What are all your business assets? ....

....

....

31. What are all your business liabilities? ....

....

....

32. When does your fiscal year end? ....

33. What were the past three years' prior results? ....

Sales	**Yr. 1**	**Yr. 2**	**Yr. 3**
Cost of sales (Variable costs)	....	....	....
Gross profit	....	....	....
Operating expenses (Fixed costs)	....	....	....
Profit or loss	....	....	....

34. What type of inventory do you have?

    A. FIFO (First in, first out) ....

    B. LIFO (Last in, first out) ....

35. How much inventory do you/will you carry in an average month? ....

....

36. How much in receivables do you carry on average?

    A. 30 days ....

    B. 60 days ....

    C. 90 days ....

    D. 120 days ....

    E. Over 120 days ....

    F. TOTAL ....

37. How will you be promoting your product or service? ....

....

....

....

....

....

38. How much will you spend on advertising in a typical year? (List in dollars and as a percentage of gross revenues.)

   ....

   ....

   ....

39. Have you defined your market into a narrow window?

   ....

   ....

   ....

40. What is your market? (E.g., do you market only to the medical profession?)

   ....

   ....

   ....

41. What is your current and/or anticipated market share over the next five years? (E.g., 25%, 30%?)

   ....

42. How much working capital will you need?

   A. One year ....

   B. Two years ....

43. Who are your suppliers?

   1. ....

   2. ....

   3. ....

   4. ....

   5. ....

   6. ....

   7. ....

   8. ....

   9. ....

44. Do you have:

   A. Letters of recommendation? ....

   B. Endorsements? ....

   C. References? ....

45. Do you have one or two (or more) faithful customers who buy from you on a regular basis?

   ....

46. What percentage do they represent of your overall business? ....

47. Give some background information on the management team. (Graduated from college, worked for a Fortune 500 Company, increased sales 50%, developed new personnel handbook, etc.)

   ....

   ....

   ....

   ....

   ....

   ....

   ....

   ....

   ....

48. What is your primary means of distribution (dealers, salespeople, mail order, etc.)?

   ....

   ....

   ....

49. What are your coverage areas for distribution? ....

   ....

   ....

50. Does your marketing strategy incorporate any of the following:

   A. Executive Selling (i.e., owners or managers of your company out in the field selling)?

   ....

   B. Direct Sales Force? ....

   C. Manufacturer's Reps? ....

   D. Distributors? ....

51. If so, please give some details. ....

   ....

   ....

52. How do you set your prices? ....

53. What are your profit margins? ....

54. What is your present situation? ....

   ....

55. Financial Resources:

    Current cash available is: ....

    Your current ratio is:

$$\frac{\text{Current Assets}}{\text{Current Liabilities}} = \quad \text{..}$$

    What is your Quick Ratio?

$$\frac{\text{Cash and Equivalents} + \text{Accounts Receivable} + \text{Notes Receivable}}{\text{Total Current Liabilities}}$$

    ....

56. Are you aware of the Small Business Administration (SBA) procedures for obtaining a loan?

    ....

57. What is the precise nature of your business? ....

    ....

    ....

    ....

58. Provide a brief history of the business and tell how you develop your products or services.

    ....

    ....

    ....

59. What are the economic forecasts that indicate spending trends are favorable to your specific industry?

    ....

    ....

    ....

60. Is your business seasonal? ....

61. If yes, how will you maintain cash flow for the slower times of the year? ....

    ....

    ....

    ....

62. Do you, or will you, depend on special vendors or suppliers to successfully operate your business?

   ....

63. Do you have any licenses or agreements that are required to operate your business?

   ....

   ....

   ....

64. How will your product or service differ from similar products or services? ....

   ....

   ....

   ....

65. How will you satisfy your customers' needs and wants?...

   ....

   ....

   ....

66. Will your products or services save your customers time, money, or both? ....

   How? ....

   ....

   ....

67. Are there any case studies that have been performed that will help you back up your claims?

   ....

   ....

   ....

68. What is the life cycle of your product or service?...

   ....

   ....

69. How many competitors share your market? ....

70. Who are they and where are they located? ....

   ....

   ....

   ....

   ....

   ....

71. How is the share of the market distributed among the major participants? ....

....

....

....

72. What are the *strengths* of your management team? ....

....

....

....

73. What are the *strengths* of your products or services? ....

....

....

....

74. What are the *strengths* of your marketing plan? ....

....

....

....

75. What are some of the *weaknesses* for the same areas listed under "Strengths"?

   A. Management team ....

   ....

   ....

   B. Products or services ....

   ....

   ....

   C. Marketing plan ....

   ....

   ....

76. What advantages do you have over your competition in the following areas:

   A. Performance? ....

   ....

   ....

   B. Quality and reliability? ....

   ....

   ....

   C. Production efficiencies? ....

....

....

   D. Distribution? ....

....

....

   E. Pricing? ....

....

....

   F. Public image? ....

....

....

   G. Business relationships or references? ....

....

....

77. Who or what is your target market? ....

....

78. What strategies may be adopted to your environment that your competition is using?

....

....

....

79. How will you promote your products and services (television, radio, seminars, brochures, salespeople, direct mail, etc.)?

....

....

....

80. What are the associated costs for each area of promotion? ....

....

....

....

81. What are the associated frequencies of media coverage? ....

....

82. Who is your management consultant? ....

83. Who is your attorney? ....

84. Who is your banker? ....

85. What type of computers do you need to operate your business? ....

....

....

86. How many computers do you need? ....

87. What kind(s) of software do you need (business management, accounting, word processing, mailing lists, etc.)?

....

....

....

88. What other equipment do you need to operate your business? ....

....

....

....

....

89. Does your product need to be patented? ....

90. If so, have you applied for a patent? ....

91. What is the sales tax rate for each state, city, or county in which you plan to transact business?

....

....

....

92. Do you have a current personal financial statement? ....

93. When is your business financial statement updated (monthly, quarterly, annually)?

....

....

....

94. What is your break-even point, according to your financial projections? ....

....

....

95. Does your business have a current profit and loss statement, balance sheet, cash flow statement, and at least two years' financial projections?

....

....

....

96. What do you have to pledge as collateral (inventory, accounts receivable, fixed assets, stocks, other marketable securities, contracts, etc.)?

....

....

....

97. Do you have any other financing that will be paid off with your new proceeds?

....

....

....

98. If so, what and how much? ....

....

99. Do you have any co-signers or other guarantors for your new proceeds?   Who?

....

....

....

100. Do you have controlling interests in other businesses? ....

....

....

....

101. Are there any supporting documents you can use that will help you solidify your claims to the investor/lender (newspaper articles, quotes by industry experts, magazine articles, brochures, graphs, charts, copies of contracts, etc.)?

....

....

....

102. How do you produce your product or service (internally/in-house, externally/subcontract, etc.)?

....

....

....

....

103. Will your current production philosophy change in future years? If so how? ....

....

....

....

104. What is your current production capacity in units of output and in dollars on a monthly basis?

....

....

....

105. Can your current facility handle future growth demands?.................................

....

....

....

106. Have you established lead times for the ordering of inventory?...........................

....

107. Does your current facility allow for flexibility with regard to growth? ....

....

....

....

108. If a new building is being considered, have you planned for:

   A. Adequate warehouse/office space for future expansion? ....

   B. Efficient loading docks and ground-level door entrances? ....

   C. Ease of transportation to roadways, railroads, and airports? ....

   D. Convenient to customers and suppliers? ....

109. Have you properly negotiated your lease (lease rates, free rent, term of lease, responsibility for roof repairs and maintenance, etc.)?

....

110. What are your lease rates? ....

111. Has your facility been properly designed to allow for efficient use of space and productivity in:

   A. Office? ....

   B. Warehouse?...

112. Is your facility accessible to the handicapped? ....

....

Chapter 3

Disclaimer

The information in this Sample Business Plan was compiled for intended use as an example only. All information in the Sample Business Plan is fictitious. Resemblance to any actual company is purely coincidental and is not intended to compete with or to divulge proprietary ideas, company structure, or financial status of any company.

Sourcebooks, Inc., and the authors of this guidebook disclaim any responsibility for this Sample Business Plan. The information is intended to be used as a guide only. We strongly recommend that the reader consult with an attorney, accountant, or other business advisor to verify that the format and structure is appropriate for his or her circumstances.

Home Improvements, Inc.

December 1993

Michael X. Swann

President

1234 East Main Street

Suite 1012

Anywhere, Arizona 85999

(602) 555-1919

Table of Contents

Executive Summary

In 1991, Home Improvements, Inc. (HII), was formed. During the past year, the company has positioned itself as a leader in the sales and distribution of durable and energy efficient aluminum siding and double pane windows.

The purpose of operation of the company is to provide customers with exterior aluminum siding that is attractive, yet provides a high degree of durability and energy efficiency to home owners and business owners.

Now, HII is at a point where it is entering two separate phases that are projected to cut operating costs by 15 percent and increase sales by 30 percent. By buying direct from the manufacturer, HII will realize better purchasing power, and gain hands-on control of the manufacturing and assembly process. This will also cut down on delivery time to the customer, resulting in a faster cash flow to the company.

Our mission statement is as follows:

To provide customers with high-quality exterior aluminum siding and double pane windows where we can be proud of the integrity and craftsmanship of each product sold to the end-user, and offer superior customer service throughout the warranty phases of the product, always remembering that each customer may be a tremendous source of referral business to our company.

Background

For many years people have had one of two choices when considering purchasing exterior siding for their home or office:

1. Purchase high-quality aluminum siding at a premium price, or

2. Settle for a low-quality exterior siding made of wood composite, steel, or low-grade aluminum offered at a lower price.

Potential customers need to be educated on the important fact that all exterior siding is NOT made the same. When they settle for a lesser quality product, the end results are frustrating and costly.

At HII, we only sell the most highly rated siding on the market today. The company will NOT sell cheaply manufactured products. However, to accomplish this, HII is currently forced to purchase materials from a single manufacturer. This presents a problem because HII does not have an alternate source for the product; as well it is costly to the customer and to HII in potential lost revenue due to higher prices.

As stated, HII is procuring its material as a complete product. Senior management has decided to buy raw material direct from other manufacturers. The product that HII purchases is manufactured in Asia and the United States. These companies have mastered the art of designing and manufacturing aluminum siding through advanced technology. Consequently, the product they provide is superior to any other on the market. Buying direct from the manufacturer will enable HII to save tens of thousands of dollars in the upcoming years, whereby the company can pass these savings on to the customer.

Our operation was producing $200,000 in sales by the end of 1991. This figure is represented by only eight months of operation. These results far exceed industry standards for a start-up enterprise of our size.

Revenue projected for fiscal year 1994, without external funding, is expected to be $480,000. Annual growth thereafter is projected to be an average of 15 percent per year through 1996.

Concept

The condition of the industry today is such that people are rapidly becoming aware of the need to protect their assets more than ever before. It has been shown that aluminum siding not only protects your home, but the beauty and attractiveness adds to its value.

Compared to competitive products, our product is made of the highest quality materials available. There are some companies that sell cheaply manufactured siding made of low-grade aluminum, steel, or wood composites.

The ability to educate customers on the superior quality of our product is a capability unique to our trained salespeople. Each of the company's sales personnel is required to complete a four-week training course before selling to the general public. This is absolutely essential to the success of our business, because of the "value-added" sale that salespeople will encounter. Since our product is made of higher quality materials, the cost of purchasing the material is higher. Plus, the company is presently buying a finished product direct from a single manufacturer. Once the "middleman" is eliminated, that will no longer be a problem.

Our strategy for meeting the competition is to buy raw material direct from various manufacturers, and produce the finished product at HII. This will lower our prices to the customer. Presently, HII has a 30 percent market share in the Arizona market. Implementation of this strategy will result in a 20 percent increase in market share by the end of the first year.

Target Market

The typical customer profile for the company falls into two separate categories:

1. Households with an annual income of $30,000 to $50,000 and

2. Retired persons in medium- to upper-income housing.

HII is rapidly moving into its third marketing phase, namely expansion of its market base into rural geographical areas, and has relocated to a larger facility in Anywhere, Arizona.

One additional product that HII will provide its customers with is a state-of-the-art rain gutter system that is especially useful in draining water from the perimeter of a customer's house or property.

Another area that will eventually be developed includes:

An agreement with an Anywhere-based aluminum manufacturing company to supplement parts, thereby lowering shipping costs for some components of the aluminum siding. This will enable HII to purchase components from a local manufacturer.

All products from HII are protected by the trademark and copyright laws, and patents, from the original manufacturer.

Responses from customers indicate that our current product is enjoying an excellent reputation. Inquiries from prospective customers suggest that there is considerable demand for exterior aluminum siding and double pane windows. Relationships with leading OEMs (Original Equipment Manufacturers), retailers, major accounts, manufacturers, and distributors substantiate the fitness of the future outlook and potential of the industry.

Objectives

Our objective, at this time, is to propel the company into a prominent market position. We feel that within five years HII will be in a suitable condition for an initial public offering or profitable acquisition. To accomplish this goal we have developed a comprehensive plan to intensify and accelerate our marketing activities, product development, services expansion, engineering, distribution, and customer service. To implement our plans we require a line of credit of $150,000 for the following purposes:

1. Purchase one container of aluminum materials for inventory—$50,000.

2. Expand current operations into the rural areas of the United States—$30,000.

3. Procurement of production and computer equipment—$60,000.

4. For general working capital—$10,000.

These items will enable HII to maximize sales with an extensive campaign to promote our products and services. It will also reinforce Customer Support services to handle the increased demands created by the influx of new orders and deepened penetration into new markets.

Management

Our management team consists of individuals whose backgrounds consist of 30 years of corporate development with major organizations, as well as over 25 years of sales and design within the home improvement industry.

Marketing

Conservative estimates suggest HII's market share, with our intensified and accelerated marketing plan, product development, manufacturing, and customer service, would be about thirty percent (30%) in the Arizona market.

The fundamental thrust of our marketing strategy consists of television, radio, printed advertising, and one-on-one selling in the home. Television and radio advertising have been the most successful marketing methods for HII, compared with flyers, direct mail, and display ads in magazines and newspapers.

We intend to reach prospective clients by continued advertising via television and radio. The marketing promotion tactics will consist of a New Leads Flow System. The customer calls the 1-800 number. The leads are forwarded to HII, whereby HII sends out product information. A subcontracted telemarketing firm calls the original leads and sets appointments for the sales personnel to go on.

None of the competitors of HII are advertising as intensely by television and radio. Our company can be characterized through our marketing efforts as the business that creates a positive and stable image for customers to see.

HII enjoys an established track-record of excellent support to our customers. Their expressions of satisfaction and encouragement are numerous, and we intend to continue our advances in the marketplace with more unique and instrumental offers.

Finance

In 24 months, we will have reached our stated goals and objectives and our lending institution will be able to collect its return on investment. The original loan will be paid down to a balance of zero (as projected in the Balance Sheet for year three).

Present Situation

The current situation of the organization is very exciting. We have recently completed a move to a larger and more efficient facility. This move will enable the company to streamline its method of operation and increase its bottom line.

Market Environment

The marketplace is undergoing tremendous technological change. New technology of exterior aluminum siding is making our product increasingly attractive, stronger, and less costly. We are poised now to take advantage of these changes, and expect to become an important supplier of aluminum siding and double pane windows.

Products and Services

The present stage of exterior siding and double pane windows is the mature stage. This is primarily due to the strong influence of committed manufacturers and the demand for exterior siding.

Product Life Cycle

Our current product line is primarily manufactured in the United States and Asia. Then it is assembled in Anywhere, Arizona. By buying direct from the manufacturer, HII will cut out 15 percent of our current costs. HII will then be able to pass these savings on to our customers.

Pricing and Profitability

Current prices are increasing by 10 percent due to rising labor and material costs in the U.S. and Asian marketplace.

Customers

Current customers are using our exterior siding and double pane windows for added home value, energy savings, storm protection, and noise reduction. They are requesting that we continue promoting our products in their area, so that the value of their neighborhoods will increase, especially during a tough real estate valuation period.

Distribution

We currently have one service center in Anywhere, Arizona. Our plans are to open additional offices and distribution centers in Indianapolis, Ind., and Knoxville, Tenn., once the results of operations warrant such centers. Once in place, these centers will reduce freight costs as well as damage occurring during shipment.

Management

Most of our management is in place, and HII enjoys a solid managerial staff with many years of experience directly related to the industry.

Financial Resources

Current cash available is $22,500 (as of 12/31/93)

Our Current Ratio is:

$$\frac{\text{Current Assets}}{\text{Current Liabilities}}$$

$$\frac{51}{51} = 1{:}1 \ (100\%)$$

Our Quick Ratio is:

$$\frac{\text{Cash} + \text{Accounts Receivable}}{\text{Current Liabilities}}$$

$$\frac{26}{51} = 0.51{:}1 \ (51\%)$$

Objectives

The long term goal of Home Improvements, Inc., is to go public. With the additional capital provided, management intends to expand into rural America, and purchase raw material, inventory, and equipment for the manufacturing and assembly of our products. With such an expansive network, we feel we can better serve our target market of middle to upper income households and retired persons.

Management also feels that with such a network, they will have stronger buying power and will be able to get more favorable pricing from manufacturers and vendors. This favorable pricing of material and equipment should allow the company to be more price competitive.

The final goal is to become a manufacturer of aluminum siding and maintain the company's distribution and sales operations.

Intermediate goals are to solidify our existing location and bring the company to a more profitable position. Long-term goals call for a 10 percent profit margin by the end of year five.

In order to achieve these goals, management has set two simple objectives for fiscal 1992. The primary objectives of our organization are to:

1. Open up the rural sales offices upon funding.

2. Increase advertising spectrum through television and radio.

3. Purchase direct from OEMs.

4. Begin attending national and international trade shows.

5. Hire new personnel and purchase newer equipment.

6. Increase training for current and new salespeople.

For the company to achieve these immediate goals, the line of credit needs to be structured to long-term debt. This restructuring will better match the terms of the loan with the use of the proceeds. Long-term expansion and restructuring will also significantly improve the cash flow of the company over the next fiscal year.

The industry is expanding, and more locations will be needed. Senior management expects to spend the majority of its time and marketing efforts on expanding current and new territories. The required funding is necessary to maintain expected growth. Net profits after tax from sales should approximate a total of $1.5 million over a ten-year period. Total sales for the same period of time are projected to be over $21 million.

Position for Growth Goals and Objectives

1. Understand customers, competition, and industry.

2. Product/service/channel/customer congruency.

3. Product/service life cycles.

4. Growth by fields of interest.

5. Balance people/management/business goals.

6. Transition from single-point to distributed management.

7. Operate at 50 employees.

8. Develop values and culture.

9. Hire the best people.

We plan to maintain one distribution and service center in Anywhere, add two sales and distribution offices, and 20 sales-only offices by 1996.

Management

Home Improvements, Inc., was founded in 1991 by Michael X. Swann, who, after a careful study of the exterior siding industry, found a tremendous void of service and quality products.

This became the principal reason that Mr. Swann wanted to start his own distribution company in the industry. The opportunity to create an entity that offered superior service and products was reflected in his enthusiasm to begin Home Improvements, Inc.

The legal form of *Home Improvements, Inc.*, is an Arizona Corporation.

Of the people who make up the development staff, there are several executives, who hold the following positions:

> Michael X. Swann, President
>
> Mary V. Jonstone, Vice President—Finance
>
> Roger Armstrong, Director of Marketing
>
> John Herbert, Manager of Production

The founders and key managers of HII have combined experiences exceeding 25 years in the siding and distribution industry.

The strength of the HII management team stems from the combined expertise in both management and sales areas. This has produced outstanding results over the past year.

The leadership and alignment characteristics of HII's management team have resulted in broad and flexible goal setting to meet the ever-changing demands of the quickly moving marketplace requiring our products. This is evident when the team responds to situations requiring new and innovative capabilities.

Responsibilities

Michael X. Swann, President and General Manager

Manage market planning, advertising, public relations, sales promotion, merchandising and facilitating staff services. Identifying new markets, maintaining corporate scope and market research. Researching and identifying foreign markets.

Mary V. Jonstone, Vice President—Finance

Management of working capital including: receivables, inventory, cash, and marketable securities. Financial forecasting including: capital budget, cash budget, pro forma financial statements, external financing requirements, and financial condition requirements.

Roger Armstrong, Director of Marketing

Manage field sales organization, territories, and quotas. Manage sales office activities, including customer/product support/service.

John Herbert, Manager of Production

Service, manufacturing, raw materials management, and installation.

Outside Support

An outside Board of Directors, including highly qualified business and industry experts, will assist our management team to make appropriate decisions and take the most effective action; however, they will not be responsible for management decisions.

Management Team

Michael X. Swann, President

Mr. Swann's professional experience includes many different areas in the sales and distribution arena. He has been involved in sales, marketing, and distribution of several services and products for large corporations such as: Big Shoe Stores, Fresh Pine Inc., and Home Siding 4 You. His experience covers many diverse areas, and he has received several awards as the top sales representative for his efforts.

After learning the basic techniques of the siding industry, Mr. Swann worked with the development of sales and distribution for Home Siding 4 You (HSY).

While working for HSY, Mr. Swann was involved with the implementation of a sales and marketing program that increased the company's revenue by 45 percent.

There he enjoyed considerable success as National Sales Manager and Director of Sales and Marketing. However, he became interested in developing a more efficient way to operate a company within the same industry.

With ideas in mind, Mr. Swann conducted a feasibility study to determine the viability of a product capable of competing in the siding industry. When he found that such a market was worthwhile and could be developed, Mr. Swann formed Home Improvements, Inc., in 1990.

Mary V. Jonstone, Vice President—Finance

Ms. Jonstone comes from a diverse background in finance and management. She served as a Department Manager for 12 years at VALUE Department Stores and House and Yard, Inc.

Ms. Jonstone has been overseeing the Finance Department for Home Improvements, Inc., since the company's inception.

Roger Armstrong, Director of Marketing

Mr. Armstrong's background in sales and marketing has been a big asset to the company. After earning a degree in marketing, Mr. Armstrong went to work as a sales representative for Steel Boxes, Inc. He enjoyed a successful career there.

Mr. Armstrong then moved on to a management position with the multinational corporation Better Products, Inc. As a manager, he was involved with day-to-day operations of inventory control, hiring and training personnel, and developing departmental policies and procedures.

Mr. Armstrong also worked for Top Aluminum for three years, where he earned the Top Sales Representative Award for the entire United States.

Mr. Armstrong has enjoyed a high degree of success at HII. He has helped develop the present sales and marketing structure of the company. As a sales professional, he trains and assists new sales representatives. As a Marketing Manager, he is involved with development of marketing strategies and market research.

John Herbert, Manager of Production

Mr. Herbert has a solid ten years of qualified experience specifically in the siding industry. His knowledge of the requirements for proper installation is an important asset to the company.

Mr. Herbert is responsible for several areas related to each project. He oversees everything from the bidding process to the completion of the job, which also includes the timely satisfaction of the customer.

People/Talent We Require

The HII development team recognizes that additional staff is required to properly support marketing, sales, research, and support functions.

Currently, HII is composed of eight personnel. Over the next five years, 50 personnel will be required to meet the demands of the projected market. These staff requirements will include personnel in the following areas:

Management

Marketing

Sales

Engineering

Customer Relations

Administration

Manufacturing

Skilled Assembly Labor

Field Service Technicians

Product Description

HII products are manufactured in Japan, Korea, Florida, and South Carolina, then assembled in Anywhere, Arizona. State-of-the-art tooling and strict quality control procedures produce dependable, custom-hardened aluminum alloy siding.

To fight against weather conditions, each panel is technologically slotted and overlaid on fiberglass insulation of high density. This provides extra insulation value inside the HII siding panel during the entire year.

Trim pieces and eave underpanels are made from extruded aluminum that give the final touches to an attractive product along with securing additional energy efficiency.

The colors available are

> White
>
> Cream
>
> Dark Brown
>
> Dark Wood Grain
>
> Beige
>
> Sky Blue
>
> Aqua Green
>
> Sunflower Yellow

Custom colors can be chosen from HII's Custom chart, which includes an additional forty colors to choose from. Delivery times for custom colors are usually three weeks longer than for our standard colors.

Pay Back

For most customers, HII siding and double-pane windows will pay for themselves in terms of energy savings within 12 years. Research has proved that between 10 percent and 15 percent savings of annual energy costs may be realized by each homeowner. During the hotter months, HII siding and windows intercept solar radiation, thus providing insulation value that allows air conditioners to work about 30 percent less.

In the winter, HII aluminum siding and double-pane windows provide a pleasant insulating blanket. This insulated exterior shield keeps the cold air from entering, and keeps the heat inside the home.

Here are a few of the other outstanding features of HII aluminum siding:

- Premium quality and efficiency
- Lower warranty costs
- Improved energy-efficiency
- Improved home value

Even a moment's reflection will prove that personal satisfaction in one's home is worth a fortune. There really isn't a price one could place on the peace of mind that our products give to the home owners. These are some of the nonmonetary benefits of owning HII aluminum siding.

Useful Purpose and Key Benefits

These combined capabilities provide added value, energy savings, noise abatement, and protection from storms.

This, in turn, can be used to create a sense of greater need in the minds of customers. These are benefits that are worth the extra money and, during our history, have convinced customers to buy from HII.

Tests

Completed tests have shown that HII aluminum siding has been subjected to many tests of impact by hard and soft objects. These tests are in accordance with the common rules of the Product Durability Testing Requirements set forth by U.S. regulations. The test resulted in a performance that is highly superior to that which the regulations require.

Product/Service Life Cycle

The life cycle of HII aluminum siding is estimated to be 60 years. The manufacturer's warranty covers all exterior parts for 5 years.

Market Analysis

Market Definition

Currently, the Arizona market distribution is shared by nine participants. Home Improvement, Inc., enjoys approximately 30 percent of this market share. There are four other major competitors that share an approximate 60 percent, and the remaining competitors share a combined total of 10 percent.

The stability of this market segment is expected to increase. However, some volatility has been introduced to the market with the announcement of a national recession.

The exterior aluminum siding market is growing at a rapid rate. The market for siding in the United States is virtually untapped. The United States is a very immature market with tremendous growth potential.*

Over the past 3 years, companies have developed and shown the additional features that can be provided for this type of industry. These companies have focused on the use of technological advances to steadily improve the quality of aluminum in exterior siding.

The report, *New Consumer Product Reports*, also states that firms selling home value added products will prosper greatly in the coming decade.

Strengths

In marketing, our most powerful assets are the uses of television and radio for advertising and promotion. The public awareness of the HII products and services has been greatly enhanced due to our intense advertising policies.

With a 30 percent market share, HII has the largest share of the market spread among six other competitors. This is not only due to our marketing strategies but includes our superior customer service.

Weaknesses

There are some handicaps inherent in our market. The only notable marketplace disadvantages are the prices that customers believe they will have to pay for their home beauty and energy efficiency. Typically, an average job will cost around $13,000, if the entire home is covered with siding and double-pane windows.

Corporate weaknesses, at this time, consist only of not enough sales personnel. However, we are taking steps to interview competent sales professionals, which we feel should alleviate this problem.

There are no environmental threats with our product.

Customers

The person who influences the decision to buy is the housewife. She will also permit the purchase to be made. Generally speaking, the housewife is the person who will also choose the color and the areas where the siding will be added to the home.

*Source: Westeck, Improved Contracting Unit

The most typical customers for our product/service are households earning between $30,000 and $50,000 per year, and retired persons living in middle- to upper-class housing developments.

It is likely that potential customers are going to be familiar with aluminum siding and double-pane windows, and that they will readily accept our advertising approach, provided that we educate them in the proper manner. It is also important to point out that our marketing and advertising efforts have been targeted to people concerned about home added value and energy efficiency, and to retired individuals.

It is easy to understand why the principal buying motives are geared toward our products, because retired persons and housewives are looking for added comfort in and around their homes.

Research indicates that these groups of customers are not as sensitive to pricing differences among competitors. In fact, research also indicates that these people are willing to spend their money on ways that will improve their way of life. It is our task to educate the customer on the superior quality of our products and service.

Housewife

Age: 35-65

Income: ....Fixed

Sex: ....Female

Family: ....Full nest

Geographic: ....Suburban

Occupation: ....Housewife

Attitude: ....Security-minded

Married Couples

Age: 35-55

Income: ....Medium to high

Sex: ....Male or female

Family: ....Married or no children

Geographic: ....Suburban

Occupation: ....Varies

Attitude: ....Security-minded, energy-conscious

Older Couple

Age: 55-75

Income: ....High or fixed

Sex: ....Male or female

Family: ....Empty nest

Geographic: ....Suburban

Occupation: ....White-collar or retired

Attitude: ....Security-minded

Elderly

Age: ....70+

Income: ....Fixed

Sex: ....Male or Female

Family: ....Empty nest

Geographic: ....Suburban

Occupation: ....Retired

Attitude: ....Security-minded

Competition

Competitive threats today come primarily from three major competitors, and three other dealers in Arizona.

HII's products perform in virtually all situations where there is a home or office where the siding and windows can be added.

The ability to offer superior beauty, with full capability to provide an insulating blanket for the home or office, is unique to such an attractive addition to any building or structure.

Our research indicates that its performance is superior to anything else on the market today. In all comparisons, the products that HII provides have more features and have superior performance than competitive products. In most cases, the number of differences is substantial. A complete technical comparison is available.

Competitive Products and Services

Companies that compete in the U.S. market are Home Siding 4 You (HSY), U.S. Aluminum (USA), North East Siding (NES), and Quality Home Products (QHP). All companies mentioned charge competitive prices.

Most of these products do not provide the same capabilities when the construction of the siding is compared to HII's product.

For example, our aluminum siding has been subjected to many trials of impact with hard and soft objects, in accordance with the common rules of the Product Durability Testing Requirements set forth by U.S. regulations. It turned out to be highly superior to what the regulations require.

Competitive Roundup

The following chart illustrates how HII compares with the competition in several different key areas.

	Competition	HII
Estimated Share of Market (HSY, USA, NES, QHP)	60%	30%
Rank:1=Weak to 5=Strong		
Product line	4	5
Quality	4	5
Technology	4	5
Advertising effectiveness	2	5
Sales force excellence	3	5
Distribution	3	4
Seriousness of competition	3	5
Price	4	4
Installation	4	5
Ease of use	4	5
Appearance	3	5
Quality	3	5
Design	4	5
Useful life	4	4
Responsiveness	3	5
24-Hour availability/support	1	5
Technical expertise	4	5
Repair service	3	5
Efficiency	3	5
Guarantee/warranty	5	5
On-time capability	4	5
Upgrades	4	4
Standing in industry	3	5

Observations and Conclusions

It appears from the above information that some of our competition is faring well in this tough market. However, it is clearly apparent that HII is offering a superior product and service at a competitive price.

Marketing Strategy

HII's marketing strategy is to enhance, promote, and support the fact that our products/services are superior to others in the market.

Comprehensive Plan

The overall marketing plan for our product is based on the following fundamentals:

1. The segment of the market(s) planned to reach.

2. Distribution channels planned to be used to reach market segment: television, radio, sales representatives, and mail order.

3. Share of the market expected to capture over a fixed period of time.

To prove the value of exterior aluminum siding and double-pane windows, we will demonstrate two areas that sell our products: Added Value and Energy Efficiency. These two areas are a great concern to the customers who purchase our products.

The lack of exterior aluminum siding and double-pane windows in everyday situations is demonstrated by the numerous studies on neighborhood values and energy efficiency.

Because our product is constructed with a high-grade aluminum and installed over superior insulation, an extra value is added to the home year round. Based on an actual comparison, our product saves an average of 10 percent to 15 percent in energy costs.*

Product Strategy

Exterior aluminum siding and double-pane windows should be treated as a long-term product. The consumer can recoup his investment within the term of a 30-year mortgage, if one only considers energy savings. However, if one considers the added value of property, there is no price to place on return on investment.

Positioning

Our products are seen by consumers as a product that protects their homes, as well as protecting their pocketbooks through energy savings.

Its unique advantages can be exploited to arrive at a winning position in the consumer's mind.

In terms of market segmentation advantages, we can use these factors already mentioned to arrive at a winning position here.

By repositioning our product from a cost to an investment in the home, and as an overall attractively appealing package, exterior aluminum siding and double-pane windows become a smart investment for any consumer.

Outside Suppliers

HII is presently using the firm Superior Media Marketing for the overall television and radio marketing strategy. This has been a good relationship that has lasted since the inception of the company. Superior Media Marketing has the buying power, technical, and marketing expertise

*Source: County Gas & Electric

that is necessary for a successful campaign. HII is also working closely with TRICO Business Solutions for additional marketing consulting.

Marketing Responsibilities

The President of HII, Mr. Swann, will be responsible for these marketing decisions:

New business development

Dealer and OEM support

Sales generation tools

Corporate graphics standard

Brandmark recognition

Direct response promotion

Telemarketing—scripts/training

Product position and identification

Selling tactics (Refer to section on Selling Tactics for details.)

Advertising and promotion (Refer to section on Advertising and Promotion for details.)

Includes:

Company positioning (identity) within market

The identity is consistent throughout all areas of communication

Promotional tools

Brochures and catalogs

Other collateral materials

Advertising

Targeted advertisements

Media selection and strategy

Sales support

Distributor and retailer support packages

Representative support (sales tools)

Communication within channels of distribution

Feedback loops

Lead generation

Lead referral and follow-up systems

Information gathering and dissemination

Strategy Review

Based on the marketing strategies, advertising and promotion, and selling tactics sections, the following questions have been reviewed and answered:

Do the strategies define means for achieving the objectives management sets?

Are the strategies consistent with our evaluation of the marketplace and our capabilities?

Is the return on investment sufficient to justify the risks?

What are the chances of a competitor executing a similar strategy? In that case, what would happen?

Have we made sure our strategies are based on facts, and not assumptions?

Does the overall strategy leave you critically vulnerable to a shift in market behavior?

Is our appraisal of the competition open-minded and honest?

Is our strategy legal?

Is the success of our strategy based on our ability window? What are the chances of failure?

Have we thoroughly examined alternative strategies? Do we have a sound, deductive rationale for our recommendations?

Advertising and Promotion

Home Improvements, Inc. (HII), recognizes that the key to success at this time requires extensive promotion. This must be done aggressively and on a wide scale. To accomplish sales goals, HII will require an extremely capable advertising agency and public relations firm.

The company plans to do most of its advertising on television and radio, in major metropolitan cities.

Once an agency selection is made, its assistance in developing a comprehensive advertising and promotion plan will be needed. Advertising will be done independently and cooperatively with Distributors, OEMs, retailers, and companies with whom HII has joint marketing/sales relationships.

Advertising and Promotion Objectives

The primary reason for such a heavy advertising campaign is to position HII as the leading supplier of exterior aluminum siding and double-pane windows in the U.S. market.

By so doing, HII plans to generate qualified sales leads for field sales representatives, who will be able to take faster action in closing sales. This will be accomplished by cutting out 80 percent of their time directly involved with prospecting. HII's experience has been that sales representatives can optimize the impact of their time by using a promotional campaign like the one that will be used to generate leads.

Media Objectives

The objectives that HII will obtain with a television and radio advertising campaign will give the company greater public awareness. Television and radio advertising will establish an image of HII as a solid organization that is very professional, completely reliable, and highly visible in the market. This is in addition to the fact that HII has maximized efficiency in selection and scheduling of sales representatives' time.

Media Strategy

It is the aim of senior management to position HII in select primary publications, radio stations, and television stations with high specific market penetration. Therefore, it is important to schedule adequate frequency to impact the market with a positive corporate image and superior products and services.

Plans are to work closely with a reputable advertising agency to maximize ad life with monthly and weekly exposure of the advertisements.

To get the most out of our promotional budget, the media coverage will focus on two targeted audiences:

1. Households who are concerned about home value and energy-efficiency, and

2. Retired individuals in high income areas.

An advertising campaign will be built around the added-value and energy-efficiency of our product, beginning with a "who we are" position and supporting it with ads that reinforce the added value and energy efficiency message. It is important that a consistent message and frequency be maintained throughout the year.

Advertising Campaign

The best way to reach our potential customers is to develop an intense advertising campaign promoting the company's basic premise—"Value you can count on!"

To maintain our stable image, the delivery and tone of promotional statements will be based on hard-driving reality that creates a sense of urgency to protect one's assets and energy savings.

Ads will convey the look and feel of a home that is attractive, comfortable, and energy-efficient.

Research indicates that television and radio advertising is not heavily used by any of our competitors. The consumer mindset is that they are eager to purchase a product that will offer a solution to possibly diminishing property values that may face their neighborhoods.

Ideally, after becoming familiar with our product and service(s), consumers will be able to take action by calling a toll-free number to place their order, or request that additional information be sent to them, or set up an appointment with a sales representative.

To eliminate the biggest objections to immediate action, the advertisements must address known and anticipated objections, such as how much is their property worth?

Because HII's product is so unique, it is important to develop a promotional campaign that is consistent and easy to understand.

Accordingly, HII has created a system of research and response to ensure the maximum benefit of its advertising dollars. One way to measure the effectiveness of its advertising is to count the number of responses and purchases per 100 customers—given a particular ad.

Research shows that television commercials will bring in an average of 48 leads per day. Further research indicates that for every 100 phone-in leads, the following results are typical:

29% Are not really interested at this time.

18% Do not own their home, or are not interested in buying aluminum siding for their future home.

3% Give incorrect information (i.e., wrong phone number).

10% Request that we call at a later date.

40% Turn into an actual appointment.

From the 40 percent, research indicates that approximately 20 percent, or one in every five appointments, turns into a sale.*

Preliminary Media Schedule

	Customers	Budget
Projected sales (per month)	15	$105,000
Monthly cost of advertising		25,000
Anticipated Profits (per month)		8,000

We expect to reach a total monthly audience of 10 million potential customers.

Promotion

In addition to standard advertising practices, HII will gain considerable recognition through these additional promotional mediums:

• Trade programs that are offered throughout the Southwest and Northwest Regions.

• Press releases sent to major radio stations, newspapers, and magazines.

• Radio advertising on secondary stations.

The number of trade shows attended will be increased from two to five each year. These shows will be attended both independently and with companies with which HII has joint marketing/ sales or OEM agreements.

Reports and papers will be published for trade journals and technical conferences. These reports will be written by an outside consulting agency and edited by senior management.

Incentives

As an extra incentive for customers to remember HII's name and the service that HII provides, plans are to distribute coffee mugs, hats, and tee shirts with the company logo and slogan. This will be a gratis service that will be provided to keep the name in front of customers.

*Source: Marketing Survey Source, Inc.

Direct Mail

In the past, the company has used direct mail as a marketing avenue to generate leads. The type of direct response piece was a house-to-house coupon mailer. This did not generate the responses that it had hoped for.

Senior management was presented with ideas of new plans to refocus direct mail efforts in the form of personal letters, with a detachable return voucher. Research has proved that this is a more effective way of reaching our targeted markets, with a greater success ratio.

Corporate Capabilities Brochure

Objective: To portray HII as the leading supplier of state-of-the-art exterior aluminum siding.

Recommended contents: Use the current corporate brochure with minor revisions to the first page, displaying new management, sales personnel, and new facilities.

Management: With the new brochure, a portrayal of dedicated, experienced, and professional managers is important to depict a team that will ensure complete satisfaction.

Sales: Portray HII's full selling team, including representatives and distributors, as a savvy, dedicated support group with one overriding mission: customer satisfaction.

Marketing: Present the marketing department in its role of market research, product development, new product management, etc., providing improved product ideas to the user.

Sales Support Collateral Materials

An additional form of advertising in the home will be used by each sales representative. Each will carry a Video Introduction Tape and give a home presentation. The video tape will be designed to give an accurate description of all the benefits of having exterior aluminum siding. It will enable sales representatives to close more sales, as well as attract new Distributors.

In addition, each sales representative will carry a Presentation Binder that is in a "flip chart" format to keep their thoughts in a unified and easy to understand style.

The following is a list of items that will assist the communications process during their sales presentations.

• Ads	• Newsletters
• Brochures	• Post Cards
• Business Cards	• Price Lists
• Catalogs	• Promotions
• Charts	• Proposals
• Data Sheets	• Questionnaires
• Direct Mail	• Reports
• Resumes	• Stationery
• Handouts	• Telephone Scripts
• Videos	• Letters

Investment in Advertising and Promotion

For the first 12 months of the project, advertising and promotion will require $48,000. On an ongoing basis HII feels that it can budget its advertising investment at 15 percent of total sales.

This figure is necessary because of the specific goals HII plans to meet. Industry averages for dollars spent on advertising and promotion are considerably less because competitors are not using television and radio as a marketing tool.

Selling Tactics

Current Selling Methods

HII's marketing strategy incorporates plans to sell its line of products/services through several channels:

Executive selling

Direct sales force

Distributors

Mail-order/direct response

Telemarketing

Joint marketing relationships

Executive Sales

Because our customers tend to be overly conscientious about spending large amounts of money, it is important that our company president and senior managers present our product and service to our customers on occasion.

Direct Sales

The majority of sales will be through direct sales by the HII sales staff. HII anticipates hiring ten additional sales representatives to cover additional territories and markets to sell specific products.

We have chosen to use a direct sales force because our products require considerable customer education and postsales support — directly from the company. Our price point, pricing structure, and profits are such that our cost of sales warrants that sales be handled on an individual basis in this manner.

Distributors

One of the key elements designed into the HII marketing plan is the targeting of its distributors. It is important to select distribution channels already in existence and staffed with professionals possessing appropriate backgrounds and clientele.

HII products are pertinent to the nature of the distributor's business and to the well-being of its customer base. Also, it is significantly less difficult for us to reach distributors and educate them as to the benefits available in using exterior aluminum siding.

This strategic marketing approach takes full advantage of the tremendous momentum inherent in the fact that these professionals are already involved with parallel products and services. They already have expertise and have been practicing in their field for a long time.

By operating within these distribution channels in this manner we feel that we can maintain control of our market. In addition, we can generate growth at a reasonable pace and obtain excellent sales results.

• See Distribution Section for detailed plan of action.

• See also Advertising and Promotion section on "Direct Mail," regarding appropriate distributors.

Distribution

HII will use several different distribution channels. The determining factors in choosing these channels are

• Customer profile

• Geography

• Seasonal concerns

• Efficient use of funds

• Feasibility of using channels of similar products already on the market

Method

The primary means of distribution will be through company sales representatives. Secondary means of distribution will be through third-party distributors.

An important advantage of these alternate channels is flexibility. By using more than one method, HII will have more control and also more options with which to respond to special needs and circumstances.

Other features of our secondary channels are low cost, quick start-up, increased capacity to reach more customers that are not necessarily influenced by advertising and promotional methods.

Coverage

Metropolitan target areas indicate the highest level of consumer interest.

Because our distribution network is easy and cost-efficient to implement, we can enjoy delivery almost immediately. This, in turn, will reduce shipping time and increase customer satisfaction. To date, none of our competitors is able to achieve this.

Roll-Out Program

We have selected from ten key market areas based on proximity — easy to sell into, contact, deliver to, have customers come to, etc.

Trade Incentives

It is the intention of senior management to offer incentives to regional distributors, such as allowances, co-op accruals, warehouse flushing promotions, etc.

Customer Service

Our customers emphasize that support is one of their major concerns. They are constantly impressed with the support provided by HII. Hot-line service is currently available to all customers enrolled in a maintenance/support program.

We intend to provide free postsale consultation for customers. The purpose for this service is to ensure customer satisfaction and loyalty and, in addition, allow us to increase sales as well as maintain a high profile within our service area.

Another service to add value is to provide warehousing of customer inventory. This allows us to book larger orders and provide faster order response.

Support to distributors is provided as required. This allows them to perform efficiently as a sales force. We intend to treat the distributors as an extension of the HII direct sales force, and they will be given the same support as the HII internal sales staff.

Technical support to marketing and sales functions will be strengthened. Pre- and postsales situations involving the application, presentation, and demonstration of HII products will be supported by our customer service and marketing staff.

Returns and Cancellation Policy

At this time, general trade customs for handling cancellations are to provide a full refund of any down payment, if a cancellation occurs within 3 business days from the signing of the contract.

Refunds are made only on the price of the package, plus applicable taxes, and do *not* include shipping costs.

Credit card refunds are credited to the customer's account and cash or check payments are refunded within 30 days of receipt of returned merchandise in good condition.

Business Relationships

HII has formed some very important relationships with major companies in the industry. The following is a list of existing relationships:

OEM Relationships

OEMs (Original Equipment Manufacturers)—The major advantage of selling through OEMs is to provide a means of more rapidly penetrating the market. Also, these relationships provide HII with national coverage through established sales forces.

We are presently buying from, or developing relationships with, the following OEMs:

1. Craft Aluminum, Inc.

2. All Seal Windows

3. Custom Improvements, Inc.

4. Quality Built Materials

5. Protection Plus, Ltd.

Joint Marketing Agreements

Joint marketing with established companies will produce revenues, credibility, and market presence.

HII is pursuing joint marketing agreements with other organizations to further the name of our products and services in the U.S. markets. Our plans include having them market our exterior aluminum siding and double-pane windows within their product line.

Third-Party Supplier Agreements

We feel that we require additional components to enhance the attractiveness of our products and services to customers. Because we do not currently have the resources to procure the exterior aluminum siding from OEMs, we rely on a single manufacturer for the availability of our product line.

Financial Projections

Current Assets

1. *Cash*—reflects limited amount of cash on hand at any balance sheet date. Positive generation of cash is to be applied against outstanding loan.

   Cash on hand can be eliminated upon implementation of a "direct disbursement" program for both checking and payroll accounts. This will allow Home Improvements, Inc., to maximize the management of cash by borrowing only when required and to apply monies received directly against the bank loan payable.

2. *Accounts Receivable*—are minimal to Home Improvements, Inc. Company policy dictates cash before installation or approved financing from reputable finance companies on the majority of projects.

3. *Inventory*—is to be purchased on a container-load basis at a precalculated reorder point determined by lead times provided by the manufacturers. Product on hand will be items already categorized as "work-in-process." Stock available for sale is scheduled to turn over in a 6- to 8-week period.

Fixed Assets

1. Production and assembly of the aluminum siding requires light machinery. The major piece of equipment required is a 20-inch radial-arm saw for aluminum cutting. This equipment will be purchased on an as-needed basis with available cash funds.

2. Thirty thousand dollars has been scheduled for 1st quarter 1994 for the purchase of new commercials, new equipment, and office furniture.

3. *Depreciation*—Equipment and furniture have been considered to be either 7-year or 5-year property per Modified Accelerated Cost Recovery System (MACRS). Whole year depreciation has been estimated for all equipment.

Liabilities

1. *Accounts Payable*—Includes amounts due on inventory purchases as well as noninventory items such as supplies, tools, telephone, travel, and entertainment.

2. *Taxes Payable*—for unpaid Federal, State, FICA, FUTA, SUI, and medical withholding based on current and expected headcount.

Selling, General, and Administration

1. *Officer Wages*—for all years have been reflected at market value.

2. *Employee Wages*—includes all Home Improvements, Inc., employees including sales, general administration, and warehouse. Wage increases for nonofficer employees are calculated at 5 percent per annum.

3. *General Administration Expenses*—have been increased annually by approximately 6 percent to reflect inflationary increases.

Break-Even Analysis:

Projected for the first quarter of 1994   ($ 000)

Sales			34
COGS	Materials	7	
	Labor	4	
Total COGS			11
Gross profit margin			23
Selling expenses	Commissions	3	
	Advertising	4	
Total selling expenses			7
Profit before G&A expenses			16
Total G&A expenses			16
Break-even			0

Appendix

Letters of Recommendation

Market Survey Data

Television and Radio Advertising Statement

Property Value and Statistics

Mechanical Designs of the Product

Company Brochures

Note:

The appendix should include all documentation that will support and add value to your organization. The above outline only covers several examples of items that could be included in the appendix of your business plan. Some examples of what to include appear on the following pages.

HOME IMPROVEMENTS, INC.
PROFIT & LOSS STATEMENT
YEAR ONE - 1991
Rounded to Hundreds ($00)

	1	2	3	4	5	6	7	8	9	10	11	12	YEAR ONE
SALES	30,0	30,0	30,0	40,0	40,0	40,0	40,0	40,0	40,0	50,0	50,0	50,0	480,0
COGS—MATERIALS	6,0	6,0	6,0	8,0	8,0	8,0	8,0	8,0	8,0	10,0	10,0	10,0	96,0
LABOR	3,6	3,6	3,6	4,8	4,8	4,8	4,8	4,8	4,8	6,0	6,0	6,0	57,6
TOTAL COGS	9,6	9,6	9,6	12,8	12,8	12,8	12,8	12,8	12,8	16,0	16,0	16,0	153,6
GROSS PROFIT/MARGIN	20,4	20,4	20,4	27,2	27,2	27,2	27,2	27,2	27,2	34,0	34,0	34,0	326,4
SELLING—COMMISSIONS	3,0	3,0	3,0	4,0	4,0	4,0	4,0	4,0	4,0	5,0	5,0	5,0	48,0
ADVERTISING	3,6	3,6	3,6	4,8	4,8	4,8	4,8	4,8	4,8	6,0	6,0	6,0	57,6
TOTAL SELLING	6,6	6,6	6,6	8,8	8,8	8,8	8,8	8,8	8,8	11,0	11,0	11,0	105,6
PROFIT BEFORE G&A	13,8	13,8	13,8	18,4	18,4	18,4	18,4	18,4	18,4	23,0	23,0	23,0	220,8
TOTAL G&A (SCHEDULE)	15,7	15,7	15,7	15,8	15,8	15,8	16,1	16,1	16,1	16,2	16,2	16,2	191,4
PROFIT(LOSS)BEFORE TAX-	-1,9	-1,9	-1,9	2,6	2,6	2,6	2,3	2,3	2,3	6,8	6,8	6,8	29,4
ESTIMATED INCOME TAX													7,4
PROFIT AFTER TAX													22,0

HOME IMPROVEMENTS, INC.
GENERAL & ADMINISTRATIVE EXPENSE
YEAR ONE - 1991
Rounded to Hundreds ($00)

	1	2	3	4	5	6	7	8	9	10	11	12	YEAR ONE
SALARIES—EMPLOYEES	8,8	8,8	8,8	8,8	8,8	8,8	8,8	8,8	8,8	8,8	8,8	8,8	105,6
SALARIES—OFFICERS	2,0	2,0	2,0	2,0	2,0	2,0	2,0	2,0	2,0	2,0	2,0	2,0	24,0
PAYROLL TAXES/BENEFITS 1,0	1,0	1,0	1,0	1,0	1,0	1,0	1,0	1,0	1,0	1,0	1,0	12,0	
VEHICLE EXPENSE	,3	,3	,3	,3	,3	,3	,3	,3	,3	,3	,3	,3	3,6
INSURANCE	,2	,2	,2	,2	,2	,2	,2	,2	,2	,2	,2	,2	2,4
LEGAL & ACCOUNTING	,2	,2	,2	,2	,2	,2	,2	,2	,2	,2	,2	,2	2,4
GENERAL OFFICE EXP	,1	,1	,1	,1	,1	,1	,2	,2	,2	,2	,2	,2	1,8
POSTAGE	,1	,1	,1	,1	,1	,1	,2	,2	,2	,2	,2	,2	1,8
OFFICE SUPPLIES	,2	,2	,2	,2	,2	,2	,3	,3	,3	,3	,3	,3	3,0
TELEPHONE	,5	,5	,5	,6	,6	,6	,6	,6	,6	,7	,7	,7	7,2
RENT	,8	,8	,8	,8	,8	,8	,8	,8	,8	,8	,8	,8	9,6
UTILITIES	,2	,2	,2	,2	,2	,2	,2	,2	,2	,2	,2	,2	2,4
DEPRECIATION	,9	,9	,9	,9	,9	,9	,9	,9	,9	,9	,9	,9	10,8
TRAVEL	,2	,2	,2	,2	,2	,2	,2	,2	,2	,2	,2	,2	2,4
ENTERTAINMENT	,1	,1	,1	,1	,1	,1	,1	,1	,1	,1	,1	,1	1,2
MISCELLANEOUS	,1	,1	,1	,1	,1	,1	,1	,1	,1	,1	,1	,1	1,2
TOTAL G&A EXPENSE	15,7	15,7	15,7	15,8	15,8	15,8	16,1	16,1	16,1	16,2	16,2	16,2	191,4

HOME IMPROVEMENTS, INC.
QUARTERLY BALANCE SHEET
YEAR ONE - 1991
Rounded to Hundreds ($00)

	MARCH	JUNE	SEPT	DEC
ASSETS				
CURRENT ASSETS:				
CASH	52,5	45,0	38,6	36,3
ACCOUNTS RECEIVABLE	6,0	8,0	8,0	10,0
INVENTORY	120,0	120,0	120,0	120,0
TOTAL CURRENT ASSETS	178,5	173,0	166,6	166,3
FIXED ASSETS:				
MACHINERY & EQUIPMENT	30,0	30,0	30,0	30,0
FURNITURE & FIXTURES	10,0	10,0	10,0	10,0
TOTAL FIXED ASSETS	40,0	40,0	40,0	40,0
ACCUMULATED DEPRECIATION	8,2	10,9	13,6	16,3
NET FIXED ASSETS	31,8	29,1	26,4	23,7
TOTAL ASSETS	210,3	202,1	193,0	190,0
LIABILITIES & STKHLDRS EQUITY				
CURRENT LIABILITIES:				
ACCOUNTS PAYABLE	30,0	30,0	30,0	30,0
PAYROLL TAXES PAYABLE	1,0	1,0	1,0	1,0
TOTAL CURRENT LIABILITIES	31,0	31,0	31,0	31,0
LONG-TERM LIABILITIES:				
LEASES PAYABLE	20,0	19,0	18,0	17,0
BANK LOAN PAYABLE	150,0	135,0	120,0	105,0
STOCKHOLDERS EQUITY:				
COMMON STOCK	10,0	10,0	10,0	10,0
PRIOR YEAR PROFIT (LOSS)	5,0	5,0	5,0	5,0
CURRENT YEAR PROFIT (LOSS)	-5,7	2,1	9,0	22,0
TOTAL EQUITY	9,3	17,1	24,0	37,0
TOTAL LIABILITIES & S/E	210,3	202,1	193,0	190,0

HOME IMPROVEMENTS, INC.
CASH FLOW STATEMENT
YEAR ONE - 1991
Rounded to Hundreds ($00)

	MARCH	JUNE	SEPT	DEC	YEAR ONE
NET INCOME (LOSS)	-5,7	7,8	6,9	13,0	22,0
SOURCE:					
DEPRECIATION	2,7	2,7	2,7	2,7	10,8
USE:					
PURCHASE—PROP & EQUIP	,0	,0	,0	,0	,0
SOURCE (USE) FROM OPERATIONS	-3,0	10,5	9,6	15,7	32,8
(INCREASE) DECREASE:					
ACCOUNTS RECEIVABLE	-2,0	-2,0	,0	-2,0	-6,0
INVENTORY	-95,0	,0	,0	,0	-95,0
INCREASE (DECREASE):					
ACCOUNTS PAYABLE	-20,0	,0	,0	,0	-20,0
PAYROLL TAXES PAYABLE	,0	,0	,0	,0	,0
LEASES PAYABLE	,0	-1,0	-1,0	-1,0	-3,0
(INCREASE) DECREASE:					
CASH	-30,0	7,5	6,4	2,3	-13,8
DISTRIBUTION TO STOCKHOLDERS	,0	,0	,0	,0	,0
CHANGE IN LOAN BALANCE	-150,0	15,0	15,0	15,0	-105,0
BALANCE BEGINNING OF QTR	,0	150,0	135,0	120,0	,0
LOAN BALANCE END OF QTR	150,0	135,0	120,0	105,0	105,0

HOME IMPROVEMENTS, INC.
PROFIT & LOSS STATEMENT
YEAR ONE - 1991
Rounded to Hundreds ($00)

	1	2	3	4	5	6	7	8	9	10	11	12	YEAR ONE
SALES	70,0	70,0	70,0	80,0	80,0	80,0	100,0	100,0	100,0	110,0	110,0	110,0	1080,0
COGS—MATERIALS	14,0	14,0	14,0	16,0	16,0	16,0	20,0	20,0	20,0	22,0	22,0	22,0	216,0
LABOR	9,1	9,1	9,1	10,4	10,4	10,4	13,0	13,0	13,0	14,3	14,3	14,3	140,4
TOTAL COGS	23,1	23,1	23,1	26,4	26,4	26,4	33,0	33,0	33,0	36,3	36,3	36,3	356,4
GROSS PROFIT/MARGIN	46,9	46,9	46,9	53,6	53,6	53,6	67,0	67,0	67,0	73,7	73,7	73,7	723,6
SELLING—COMMISSIONS	7,0	7,0	7,0	8,0	8,0	8,0	10,0	10,0	10,0	11,0	11,0	11,0	108,0
ADVERTISING	10,5	10,5	10,5	12,0	12,0	12,0	15,0	15,0	15,0	16,5	16,5	16,5	162,0
TOTAL SELLING	17,5	17,5	17,5	20,0	20,0	20,0	25,0	25,0	25,0	27,5	27,5	27,5	270,0
PROFIT BEFORE G&A	29,4	29,4	29,4	33,6	33,6	33,6	42,0	42,0	42,0	46,2	46,2	46,2	453,6
TOTAL G&A (SCHEDULE)	26,5	26,5	26,5	26,5	26,5	26,5	28,7	28,7	28,7	28,7	28,7	28,7	331,2
PROFIT (LOSS) BEFORE TAX	2,9	2,9	2,9	7,1	7,1	13,3	13,3	13,3	13,3	17,5	17,5	17,5	122,4
ESTIMATED INCOME TAX													43,4
PROFIT AFTER TAX													79,0

HOME IMPROVEMENTS, INC.
GENERAL & ADMINISTRATIVE EXPENSE
YEAR TWO - 1992
Rounded to Hundreds ($00)

	1	2	3	4	5	6	7	8	9	10	11	12	YEAR TWO
SALARIES—EMPLOYEES	14,4	14,4	14,4	14,4	14,4	14,4	16,0	16,0	16,0	16,0	16,0	16,0	182,4
SALARIES—OFFICERS	5,0	5,0	5,0	5,0	5,0	5,0	5,0	5,0	5,0	5,0	5,0	5,0	60,0
PAYROLL TAXES/BENEFITS	1,6	1,6	1,6	1,6	1,6	1,6	1,7	1,7	1,7	1,7	1,7	1,7	19,8
VEHICLE EXPENSE	,4	,4	,4	,4	,4	,4	,4	,4	,4	,4	,4	,4	4,8
INSURANCE	,3	,3	,3	,3	,3	,3	,3	,3	,3	,3	,3	,3	3,6
LEGAL & ACCOUNTING	,3	,3	,3	,3	,3	,3	,3	,3	,3	,3	,3	,3	3,6
GENERAL OFFICE EXP	,2	,2	,2	,2	,2	,2	,3	,3	,3	,3	,3	,3	3,0
POSTAGE	,2	,2	,2	,2	,2	,2	,3	,3	,3	,3	,3	,3	3,0
OFFICE SUPPLIES	,3	,3	,3	,3	,3	,3	,4	,4	,4	,4	,4	,4	4,2
TELEPHONE	,8	,8	,8	,8	,8	,8	1,0	1,0	1,0	1,0	1,0	1,0	10,8
RENT	,8	,8	,8	,8	,8	,8	,8	,8	,8	,8	,8	,8	9,6
UTILITIES	,3	,3	,3	,3	,3	,3	,3	,3	,3	,3	,3	,3	3,6
DEPRECIATION	1,2	1,2	1,2	1,2	1,2	1,2	1,2	1,2	1,2	1,2	1,2	1,2	14,4
TRAVEL	,3	,3	,3	,3	,3	,3	,3	,3	,3	,3	,3	,3	3,6
ENTERTAINMENT	,2	,2	,2	,2	,2	,2	,2	,2	,2	,2	,2	,2	2,4
MISCELLANEOUS	,2	,2	,2	,2	,2	,2	,2	,2	,2	,2	,2	,2	2,4
TOTAL G&A EXPENSE	26,5	26,5	26,5	26,5	26,5	26,5	28,7	28,7	28,7	28,7	28,7	28,7	331,2

HOME IMPROVEMENTS, INC.
QUARTERLY BALANCE SHEET
YEAR TWO - 1992
Rounded to Hundreds ($00)

	MARCH	JUNE	SEPT	DEC
ASSETS				
CURRENT ASSETS:				
CASH	6,2	13,1	16,7	11,4
ACCOUNTS RECEIVABLE	14,0	16,0	20,0	22,0
INVENTORY	130,0	130,0	150,0	150,0
TOTAL CURRENT ASSETS	150,2	159,1	186,7	183,4
FIXED ASSETS:				
MACHINERY & EQUIPMENT	50,0	50,0	50,0	50,0
FURNITURE & FIXTURES	20,0	20,0	20,0	20,0
TOTAL FIXED ASSETS	70,0	70,0	70,0	70,0
ACCUMULATED DEPRECIATION	19,9	23,5	27,1	30,7
NET FIXED ASSETS	50,1	46,5	42,9	39,3
TOTAL ASSETS	200,3	205,6	229,6	222,7
LIABILITIES & STKHLDRS EQUITY				
CURRENT LIABILITIES:				
ACCOUNTS PAYABLE	37,0	37,0	37,0	37,0
PAYROLL TAXES PAYABLE	1,6	1,6	1,7	1,7
TOTAL CURRENT LIABILITIES	38,6	38,6	38,7	38,7
LONG-TERM LIABILITIES:				
LEASES PAYABLE	26,0	25,0	24,0	23,0
BANK LOAN PAYABLE	90,0	75,0	60,0	45,0
STOCKHOLDERS EQUITY:				
COMMON STOCK	10,0	10,0	10,0	10,0
PRIOR YEAR PROFIT (LOSS)	27,0	27,0	27,0	27,0
CURRENT YEAR PROFIT (LOSS)	8,7	30,0	69,9	79,0
TOTAL EQUITY	45,7	67,0	106,9	116,0
TOTAL LIABILITIES & S/E	200,3	205,6	229,6	222,7

HOME IMPROVEMENTS, INC.
CASH FLOW STATEMENT
YEAR TWO - 1992
Rounded to Hundreds ($00)

	MARCH	JUNE	SEPT	DEC	YEAR TWO
NET INCOME (LOSS)	8,7	21,3	39,9	9,1	79,0
SOURCE:					
DEPRECIATION	3,6	3,6	3,6	3,6	14,4
USE:					
PURCHASE—PROP & EQUIP	30,0	,0	,0	,0	30,0
SOURCE (USE) FROM OPERATIONS	-17,7	24,9	43,5	12,7	63,4
(INCREASE) DECREASE:					
ACCOUNTS RECEIVABLE	-4,0	-2,0	-4,0	-2,0	-12,0
INVENTORY	-10,0	,0	-20,0	,0	-30,0
INCREASE (DECREASE):					
ACCOUNTS PAYABLE	7,0	,0	,0	,0	7,0
PAYROLL TAXES PAYABLE	,6	,0	,1	,0	,7
LEASES PAYABLE	9,0	-1,0	-1,0	-1,0	6,0
(INCREASE) DECREASE:					
CASH	30,1	6,9	3,6	5,3	24,9
DISTRIBUTION TO STOCKHOLDERS	,0	,0	,0	,0	,0
CHANGE IN LOAN BALANCE	15,0	15,0	15,0	15,0	60,0
BALANCE BEGINNING OF QTR	105,0	90,0	75,0	60,0	105,0
LOAN BALANCE END OF QTR	90,0	75,0	60,0	45,0	45,0

HOME IMPROVEMENTS, INC.
PROFIT & LOSS STATEMENT
YEARS THREE TO TEN
Rounded to Thousands ($000)

	YEAR THREE	YEAR FOUR	YEAR FIVE	YEAR SIX	YEAR SEVEN	YEAR EIGHT	YEAR NINE	YEAR TEN
SALES	1,240	1,430	1,640	1,890	2,170	2,500	2,870	3,300
COGS—MATERIALS	260	300	350	410	470	550	640	740
LABOR	160	190	220	260	300	350	400	460
TOTAL COGS	420	490	570	670	770	900	1,040	1,200
GROSS PROFIT/MARGIN	820	940	1,070	1,220	1,400	1,600	1,830	2,100
SELLING—COMMISSIONS	124	143	164	189	217	250	287	330
ADVERTISING	186	215	246	283	325	375	430	495
TOTAL SELLING	310	358	410	472	542	625	717	825
PROFIT BEFORE G&A	510	582	660	748	858	975	1,113	1,275
TOTAL G&A (SCHEDULE)	477	505	521	550	565	593	611	640
PROFIT BEFORE TAX	33	77	139	198	293	382	502	635
ESTIMATED INCOME TAX	8	20	47	74	120	150	212	269
PROFIT AFTER TAX	25	57	92	124	173	232	290	366

HOME IMPROVEMENTS, INC.
GENERAL AND ADMINISTRATION EXPENSE
YEARS THREE TO TEN
Rounded to Thousands ($000)

	YEAR THREE	YEAR FOUR	YEAR FIVE	YEAR SIX	YEAR SEVEN	YEAR EIGHT	YEAR NINE	YEAR TEN
SALARIES—EMPLOYEES	288	294	300	308	316	324	334	344
SALARIES—OFFICERS	72	78	84	88	92	96	100	104
PAYROLL TAXES/BENEFITS	28	30	31	32	32	33	34	35
VEHICLE EXPENSE	6	7	7	8	8	9	9	10
INSURANCE	4	5	5	6	6	7	7	8
LEGAL & ACCOUNTING	6	7	7	8	8	9	9	10
GENERAL OFFICE EXP	4	5	5	6	6	7	7	8
POSTAGE	4	5	5	6	6	7	7	8
OFFICE SUPPLIES	5	6	6	7	7	8	8	9
TELEPHONE	12	13	13	14	14	15	15	16
RENT	14	14	14	16	16	17	17	17
UTILITIES	6	7	7	8	8	9	9	10
DEPRECIATION	17	20	23	26	29	32	35	38
TRAVEL	5	6	6	7	7	8	8	9
ENTERTAINMENT	3	4	4	5	5	6	6	7
MISCELLANEOUS	3	4	4	5	5	6	6	7
TOTAL G&A EXPENSE	477	505	521	550	565	593	611	640

HOME IMPROVEMENTS, INC.
BALANCE SHEET
YEARS THREE TO SIX
Rounded to Thousands ($000)

	YEAR THREE	YEAR FOUR	YEAR FIVE	YEAR SIX
ASSETS				
CURRENT ASSETS:				
CASH	24	71	126	121
ACCOUNTS RECEIVABLE	25	25	30	35
INVENTORY	150	170	200	220
TOTAL CURRENT ASSETS	199	266	356	376
FIXED ASSETS:				
MACHINERY & EQUIPMENT	70	90	110	130
FURNITURE & FIXTURES	30	40	50	60
TOTAL FIXED ASSETS	100	130	160	190
ACCUMULATED DEPRECIATION	48	68	91	117
NET FIXED ASSETS	52	62	69	73
TOTAL ASSETS:	251	328	425	449
LIABILITIES & STKHLDRS EQUITY				
CURRENT LIABILITIES:				
ACCOUNTS PAYABLE	65	65	75	80
PAYROLL TAXES PAYABLE	5	5	5	5
TOTAL CURRENT LIABILITIES	70	70	80	85
LONG-TERM LIABILITIES:				
LEASES PAYABLE	40	60	55	50
BANK LOAN PAYABLE	0	0	0	0
STOCKHOLDERS EQUITY:				
COMMON STOCK	10	10	10	10
PRIOR YEAR PROFIT	106	131	188	280
CURRENT YEAR PROFIT	25	57	92	124
DISTRIBUTION TO STOCKHOLDERS	0	0	0	-100
TOTAL EQUITY	141	198	290	314
TOTAL LIABILITIES & S/E	251	328	425	449

HOME IMPROVEMENTS, INC.
BALANCE SHEET
YEARS SEVEN TO TEN
Rounded to Thousands ($000)

	YEAR SEVEN	YEAR EIGHT	YEAR NINE	YEAR TEN
ASSETS				
CURRENT ASSETS:				
CASH	163	182	197	186
ACCOUNTS RECEIVABLE	40	45	50	60
INVENTORY	240	250	280	300
TOTAL CURRENT ASSETS	443	477	527	546
FIXED ASSETS:				
MACHINERY & EQUIPMENT	150	170	190	210
FURNITURE & FIXTURES	70	80	90	100
TOTAL FIXED ASSETS	220	250	280	310
ACCUMULATED DEPRECIATION	146	178	213	251
NET FIXED ASSETS	74	72	67	59
TOTAL ASSETS:	517	549	594	605
LIABILITIES & STKHLDRS EQUITY				
CURRENT LIABILITIES:				
ACCOUNTS PAYABLE	80	85	95	95
PAYROLL TAXES PAYABLE	5	5	5	5
TOTAL CURRENT LIABILITIES	85	90	100	100
LONG-TERM LIABILITIES:				
LEASES PAYABLE	45	40	35	30
BANK LOAN PAYABLE	0	0	0	0
STOCKHOLDERS EQUITY:				
COMMON STOCK	10	10	10	10
PRIOR YEAR PROFIT	304	377	409	449
CURRENT YEAR PROFIT	173	232	290	366
DISTRIBUTION TO STOCKHOLDERS	-100	-200	-250	-350
TOTAL EQUITY	387	419	459	475
TOTAL LIABILITIES & S/E	517	549	594	605

HOME IMPROVEMENTS, INC.
CASH FLOW STATEMENT
YEARS THREE TO SIX
Rounded to Thousands ($000)

	YEAR THREE	YEAR FOUR	YEAR FIVE	YEAR SIX
NET INCOME	25	57	92	124
SOURCE:				
DEPRECIATION	17	20	23	26
USE:				
PURCHASE—PROP & EQUIP	30	30	30	30
SOURCE (USE) FROM OPERATIONS	12	47	85	120
(INCREASE) DECREASE:				
ACCOUNTS RECEIVABLE	-3	0	-5	-5
INVENTORY	0	-20	-30	-20
INCREASE (DECREASE):				
ACCOUNTS PAYABLE	28	0	10	5
PAYROLL TAXES PAYABLE	4	0	0	0
LEASES PAYABLE	17	20	-5	-5
(INCREASE) DECREASE:				
CASH	-13	-47	-55	5
DISTRIBUTION TO STOCKHOLDERS	0	0	0	-100
CHANGE IN LOAN BALANCE	45	0	0	0
BALANCE BEGINNING OF QTR	45	0	0	0
LOAN BALANCE END OF QTR	0	0	0	0

HOME IMPROVEMENTS, INC.
CASH FLOW STATEMENT
YEARS SEVEN TO TEN
Rounded to Thousands ($000)

	YEAR SEVEN	YEAR EIGHT	YEAR NINE	YEAR TEN
NET INCOME	173	232	290	366
SOURCE:				
DEPRECIATION	29	32	35	38
USE:				
PURCHASE—PROP & EQUIP	30	30	30	30
SOURCE (USE) FROM OPERATIONS	172	234	295	374
(INCREASE) DECREASE:				
ACCOUNTS RECEIVABLE	-5	-5	-5	-10
INVENTORY	-20	-10	-30	-20
INCREASE (DECREASE):				
ACCOUNTS PAYABLE	0	5	10	0
PAYROLL TAXES PAYABLE	0	0	0	0
LEASES PAYABLE	-5	-5	-5	-5
(INCREASE) DECREASE:				
CASH	-42	-19	-15	11
DISTRIBUTION TO STOCKHOLDERS	-100	-200	-250	-350
CHANGE IN LOAN BALANCE	0	0	0	0
BALANCE BEGINNING OF QTR	0	0	0	0
LOAN BALANCE END OF QTR	0	0	0	0

Chapter 4

The Vision: Writing Your Business Plan

Introduction

When preparing your business plan, it is important that you remember to use what you have seen and learned in the first three sections.

Visualize where you are now and where you want to be. Visualize what you have read and what you have written. It is now time to take this vision and transfer it to paper.

It is with this step that your vision will be truly communicated to others. It is with this step that your business will increase its chance of becoming a successful enterprise.

The following pages in this section have been created for you as a guideline in the development of your business plan. As all business plans differ from one another, it is highly suggested that you add, subtract, or change the format to create the optimum business plan for your enterprise.

When in presentation form, your business plan will be similar to the Table of Contents in the business plan in Section Three. However, during the development period, you may choose to complete any area in any order you like.

This section has been prepared in the following topic order:

I. Your Management Team

Leading the Way

How important is your business management team? It is extremely important! Whether your company is a start-up or an established company, potential lenders and investment groups will only finance a company with a management team that has balance and the ability to provide four essential elements of management:

1. Planning

2. Organization

3. Control

4. Leadership

What is meant by balance? The management team as a whole must have the human, technical, and conceptual skills applicable to both the production and delivery of your product and/or service. Therefore, it is a must that your team have skills in marketing, finance, and operations at a minimum.

The strength of your management team must be strongly stated and related in your business plan. An organization with a formal structure (figure MT.1) will be able to enhance its ability to raise capital as well as provide it with a road-map for achieving its goals. This will be done in less time and with less expense.

After reviewing table MT.1, take some time to mentally review your proposed or existing management team. Remember to use honesty in the judgment of yourself and each member of the team. Do not let the "he is a nice guy," or "he never misses a day's work" syndrome influence reality.

Refer to data chart MT.1 and complete for each key management team member.

Your Formal Organization

After fully completing data chart MT.1, begin to develop a formal organizational flow chart. One important item to remember is the structure and size of your organization. It is reasonable for small to medium-sized businesses to have a management team consisting of only one, or possibly two, key management personnel.

If this is the case, it is highly suggested that outside consultants and professionals be hired to fill in the gaps to provide expertise that is necessary to strengthen your management team. Example MT.1 provides a useful example of an overall organizational structure, while example MT.2 shows a further breakdown by department.

Incorporate Your Management Team into Your Formal Organization

To this point, you have identified the abilities of your key management team and the formal organizational structure of your company. Now, in the final step we must blend the two together to see if each key function within your organization can be met by at least one team member. Examples of functions include:

- Marketing
- Advertising
- Sales
- Finance—Controller/Treasurer
- Inventory control
- Purchasing

- Operations
- Production
- Distribution
- Receiving
- Human resources
- Legal

Use data chart MT.2 to incorporate key management personnel with key functions. For any responsibilities which cannot be covered by current management, check the column for outside services required. You may want to consider contacting outside consultants and professionals who specialize in these areas to assist you.

Now that you have determined your management structure and who should be a part of your management team, let's begin telling the story (use additional paper if needed or preferred).

Management

Tell why and by whom the corporation was started.

Management Team

Of the people who make up the development staff, there are several executives who hold the following company positions:

....

....

....

Explain combined experiences, strengths, leadership abilities, and all positive characteristics.

....

....

....

Responsibilities

List each manager separately and explain his or her various responsibilities.

....

....

....

Outside Support

Include all outside professional consultants and industry experts who give support to your management team.

....

....

....

Management Resume

Give a brief, yet comprehensive, resume of the qualifications of each manager.

....

....

....

People/Talent Required

List current and future needs of required company staff. Estimate number of employees as well as positions needed to effectively operate the business.

....

....

....

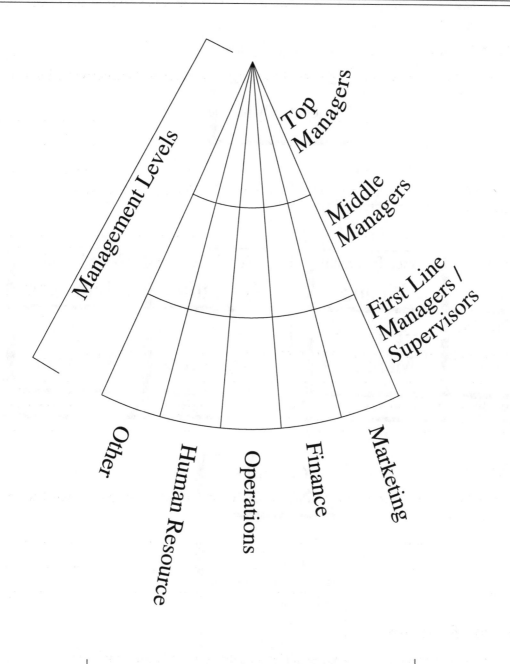

Labels on figure: Top Managers, Middle Managers, First Line Managers / Supervisors, Management Levels, Other, Human Resource, Operations, Finance, Marketing

Departments of Management

Figure MT.1

Depending on the structure and size of your organization, the number of management levels and departments will vary.

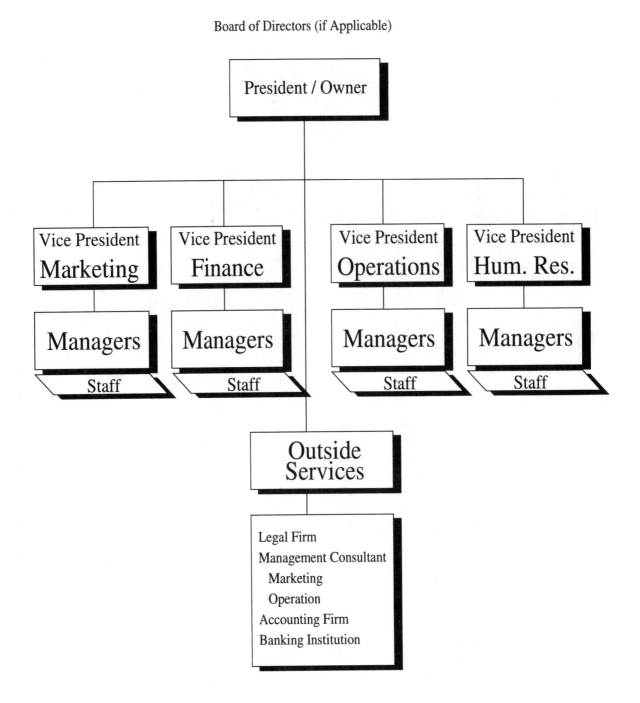

Board of Directors (if Applicable)

President / Owner

Vice President Marketing | Vice President Finance | Vice President Operations | Vice President Hum. Res.

Managers | Managers | Managers | Managers

Staff | Staff | Staff | Staff

Outside Services

Legal Firm
Management Consultant
   Marketing
   Operation
Accounting Firm
Banking Institution

Example MT.1

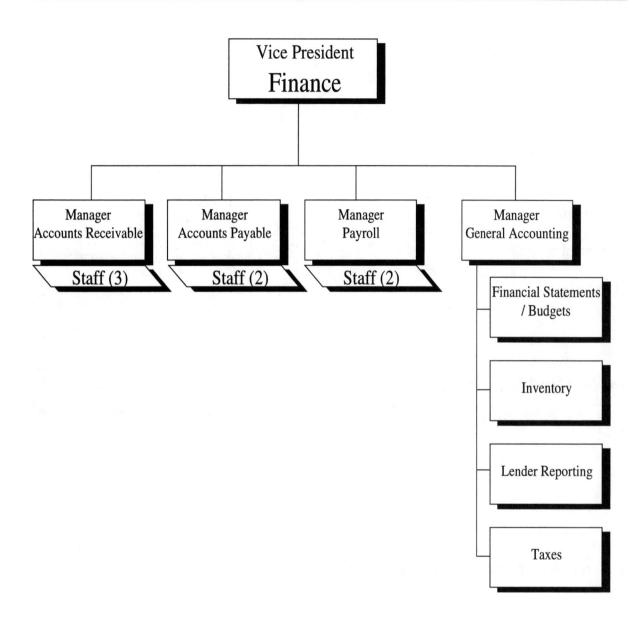

Example MT.2

Department of Manager _____

Name of Manager _____

Skills	**Grade**	**Grading Key**
Conceptual	☐	1 = Exceptional
		2 = Good
Technical	☐	3 = Average
		4 = Shoud not be manager
Human	☐	

Describe Strengths of Manager:

Describe Weaknesses of Manager:

Overall Grade (see key above) ☐

Data Chart MT.1

Managers / Key Functions					Outside Services Needed

Data Chart MT.2

II. Product/Service Description

Outside Appeal

Will your product/service be easily recogniz-able and understood by lending organiza-tions? It is very important to identify your product/service clearly, as well as all aspects of the purchasing, manufacturing, packaging, distribution, etc., of the product/service.

Potential lenders and investment groups will only lend capital if they have confidence that the process has been clearly researched, identified, calculated, and thoroughly thought out.

Product/Service Description

In brief and concise paragraphs, explain all important information regarding your product/service.

....
....
....
....
....
....
....
....

Added Value

List and explain all value-added features your product/service has. It is important to clearly state why your product/service is such a great item (i.e., what makes it unique).

....
....
....
....
....
....

Tests/Approvals

List and explain all test ratings, approvals by government regulations, etc., that add substance to your product/service.

....

....

....

....

....

Product/Service Life Cycle

Identify product life, warranty, guaranty, etc., that cover each product/service provided.

....

....

....

....

III. Market Analysis

Do Your Homework

Have you clearly identified your market? It is also very important that you show all relevant data which supports what you have carefully researched, the market.

Potential lenders and investment groups must be clearly convinced that the market you have identified is feasible for the distribution of your products and services.

Market Definition

Clearly identify your market, including competitors, market share, potential market share, market stability, market share and growth, success of product/service in other markets, etc. Include supporting documentation from third-party independent sources (i.e., magazine and newspaper articles, books, trade reports, government statistics, surveys).

....
....
....
....
....

Strengths and Weaknesses

Identify marketing strengths (i.e., sources of advertising and promotion, public awareness).

....
....
....
....

Identify market weaknesses (i.e., public acceptance, per capita income).

....
....
....
....

Customer Profile

Identify your customers including the decision maker, per capita income, age, sex, family, geographic location, occupation, attitude, etc.

....

....

....

....

Competition

Identify all competitors and how your company will effectively compete and continue to gain market share.

....

....

....

....

Provide charts, graphs, data which support your claims.

....

....

....

....

IV. Marketing Strategies

Selling Tactics

Now let's identify your sales force. You should clearly think through the advantages and disadvantages of commissioned versus salaried salespeople. You may even want to offer a combination of a base of $500 per month, plus a $250 car allowance, plus commissions, bonuses, and health insurance. Identify all these parameters in this section.

In the initial stages of your business, will you need to personally go out into the market and promote your product/service?

....

....

....

Identify how soon you believe it will be before you will need to hire other salespeople.

....

....

Will you only hire salespeople who have a college degree?

....

Do your sales personnel need to be licensed by a state regulatory agency?

....

Will you be selling your products/services through a network of dealers or distributors?

....

Will they have protected territories?

....

Where are the protected territories?

....

....

....

Are your pricing policies set to market or industry standards?

....

Will your salespeople be able to compete with the prices that you have established?

....

Your Unique Selling Advantage

Explain your USA briefly.

....

....

....

Why would anyone want to buy your product or service?

....

....

....

Will it make their life more comfortable? How?

....

....

....

Will it save them time or money? How?

....

....

....

Will you offer more customer service than your competition?

....

....

....

If so, how will you offer superior customer service?

....

....

....

Will your customer's life-style be any different if they purchase your product/service? How?

....

....

....

Which professional organizations do you belong to that will mean something of value to your customers?

....

....

....

What are some of the weaknesses that your competition has?

....

....

....

How can you take their weaknesses and turn them into strengths for your enterprise?

....

....

....

Establish Marketing Objectives

Establish marketing objectives for your next campaign. To help meet these objectives four critical goals should be considered:

1. To increase brand awareness by a specific percentage.

2. To generate high-quality leads for your sales force.

3. To improve the morale of your direct sales force.

4. To increase sales by a specific percentage within a certain time frame.

Once the campaign is underway, begin tracking results. Conduct a few preliminary studies a few weeks into the campaign to measure the results, but don't expect these results to be final. In most cases, you should give your campaign at least 12 months to realize final results. Your target expectations may be realized sooner, which would be the result of a well-planned and well-executed marketing strategy.

Advertising and Promotion

Develop a realistic budget for advertising by allocating about 5 percent of expected annual revenues. Include in your advertising campaign a good mixture of promotional items. If your budget is relatively small ($100 to $200 per month) definitely include business cards, letterhead, envelopes, a brochure, and stamps at a minimum. These items will give your business plenty of exposure if you carefully follow up on literature sent out.

There are so many different ways to promote your business without spending a lot of money. Do a little research on the associated costs in your area of the following items:

- Radio advertising on one station during morning drive time hours (6:00–9:00 a.m.).

- The cost of a convention hall, hotel, auditorium, gymnasium, classroom, library, etc., that holds 30–50 people at one time. This will be for a seminar you could give.

- How much would a live-remote radio campaign cost? Usually for the cost, this type of promotion is a tremendous investment.

- Have you researched how effective a press release can be for your business? If an editor of a newspaper or a producer of a radio or television show likes your idea, they will conduct an interview about you and your product or service. This is free exposure that only costs you the price of a few letters and stamps.

- Look in the Yellow Pages under Television Stations, Radio Stations, Newspapers, and Magazines for the telephone numbers. Ask for the name of the business editor or producer. Send them a personalized, double-spaced press-release that is one or two pages in length. Follow up in two weeks to find out if they received your material. Don't ask them if they are going to do a story on you. Simply remind them about your unique product, service, or idea.

- A newsletter is another inexpensive way to keep your name in front of your customers. You could charge for a subscription, or send it out free each month, or every quarter, to existing, new, and prospective customers.

- Tee-shirts, pens, coffee mugs, paper weights, hats, etc., are a relatively inexpensive way to advertise your business. Check the costs by interviewing several advertising specialties companies and include this in your business plan. These promotional items are a subtle reminder to your clients every time they see your name.

- Offer to give public speeches to several different organizations. The speaking and seminar business will enable you to promote your products and services at a relatively low out-of-pocket cost. Some organizations to choose from are:

1. Business and trade organizations

2. Civic groups

3. Convention planners

4. Service organizers

5. Business firms and organizations

6. Political affiliations

7. Fraternal organizations

8. Athletic clubs

9. Professional associations

You will be pleasantly surprised at the enormous number of organizations you probably never knew existed, as you scan the Yellow Pages or various reference sources available in the library.

Clearly define the costs of promoting and holding seminars. Include costs for the room, beverages, overhead projectors, writing boards, tables, chairs, microphones, pens and paper, and your printed material.

Next, decide how much to charge, or if you should give free seminars. Other factors to be considered when deciding the price for your presentation are: operating costs, cost of materials, audiovisuals, promotional costs, clerical support, transportation, lodging, etc.

How should you determine your price? The only way to find out is by testing. It won't take you long to find out what price is appropriate for your program.

V. The Financials

More Than Just Dollars and Cents

For most entrepreneurs the development of an idea or concept is the easy part. Turning it into a profitable reality takes thorough research, especially as it relates to determining (1) potential markets, (2) a realistic selling price for your products and services, (3) assets needed to produce and deliver, (4) costs associated to produce, (5) advertising and promotion dollars needed to obtain market share, (6) fixed general and administration costs necessary to support the above, including what employee head count is needed to support and operate your enterprise.

In this section you will develop a set of financials that will include profit and loss statements, balance sheets, and cash flow statements. A thorough understanding of how they are conceived and developed must be a top priority. Presenting potential lenders or investors with a set of financials is meaningless if they are a foreign language to you. Therefore, before you dive in and begin crunching numbers, become familiar with the financial statements in "Sample Business Plan," in Chapter Three.

If uncertainty exists about your overall knowledge and understanding of financial statements, it is suggested you do one or more of the following:

1. Purchase accounting, learning, and reference workbooks from a local bookstore.

2. Reference accounting workbooks at your local library.

3. Take an accounting class at an accredited college or university.

4. Obtain help from an outside accounting firm familiar with your line of business.

Your Financial Management Tool

It is important for every business to prepare financial statements on a monthly basis, regardless of its size or structure (i.e., sole proprietor, partnership, corporation).

Experience shows that many business owners/ managers feel that monthly financial statements are senseless, useless, or are just not needed in their business. This is a big mistake! Financial statements are Key Management Tools. Take the time to learn and interpret what the financial statements are telling you. It could mean the difference between success and failure for your business.

Determining Your Numbers

By this stage of the game, whether you are a start-up or an existing business, you should fully understand how to project, forecast, estimate, calculate, etc., all items included in your financial statements.

If assistance is needed, we suggest you contact a competent accounting firm. It will be able to assist you in the completion of this portion of the business plan.

The following pro-forma schedules will aid you in your preparation. Please note that only one copy is provided for the profit and loss statement, balance sheet, and cash flow statement. We suggest you use these as a master set. Copies can be easily made, hole-punched, and inserted into the guidebook.

For years one and two, we recommend presenting your profit and loss statements on a monthly basis, and your balance sheets and cash flow statements on a quarterly basis. Present years three through ten on an annual basis.

Profit & Loss Statement

Balance Sheet

Cash Flow Statement

VI. Present Situation

In this section you should clearly define how
you have come to your current position.
Build the story of how your idea was conceived up to your present position.

Explain the current market environment. Is it undergoing changes in technology, demographics, competition, customers, financial conditions, etc.?

....

....

....

....

What is the present stage of your industry (i.e., infancy, intermediate, or mature stage)?

....

....

....

Are there any factors that could contribute to the growth or decline of your product? Indicate both the weak and strong points here. It will look like you really have done your
homework.

....

....

....

....

Where are your products assembled or manufactured?

....

....

....

What is your product's average life cycle?

....

....

....

With regards to pricing and profitability, are current prices from suppliers increasing, decreasing, or remaining constant?

....

....

....

Indicate how you plan to make whatever adjustments are necessary to manage these possible changes in prices.

....

....

....

How are your current customers using your products/services? If your business is a start-up enterprise, how will potential customers use your products/services?

....

....

....

Where will your main distribution center be? Do you have any plans to open other offices and distribution centers? If so, indicate when and where.

....

....

....

Give some additional information about your management team. Are they all in place? Will you need to hire additional managers or consult with outside consultants?

....

....

....

Finally, provide some information about your current financial resources.

Current cash available is $XXXX (as of X/X/X)

....

Current Ratio is: $\dfrac{\text{Assets}}{\text{Liabilities}}$ =XX/XX (XX%)

....

....

Current Quick Ratio is: $\dfrac{\text{Cash + Accounts Receivable}}{\text{Current Liabilities}}$

....

....

VII. Objectives

In this section you will develop short- and long-term goals. Here is where you really need to begin formulating a vision of where you want to be in a few years. Important: make sure that you balance your enthusiasm with realism. It is a good idea to use "checks and balances" when you visualize your company's progress. In order to achieve your goals, set a few simple objectives for each year (1–5).

With these ideas in mind, let's begin writing down what it is you want to achieve.

Are your long-term objectives to stay a one-person shop, or become a large company with several hundred employees?

....

....

Do you want your company to go public by selling its stock?

....

....

Do you want to pass the leadership down to your children, great-grandchildren, etc.?

....

What will you accomplish with the additional capital (i.e., open new offices, purchase equipment, hire key personnel, expand your marketing and advertising)?

....

....

Will you develop a stronger network of suppliers and/or buyers as time goes on? How?

....

....

....

Will you become a manufacturer at any time? When?

....

....

....

Write down what your intermediate goals are.

....

....

....

What profits are expected to be generated in years 1–5?

....

....

In order for you to achieve your immediate goals, do you have any debt that must be restructured or paid down? Explain why in detail here.

....

....

....

What will be your expected net profits after tax from sales?

....

....

Take these net after tax profits for a period of ten years, and show the total for that period of time.

....

....

....

Next, indicate total sales revenue for the same period of time.

....

....

....

Finally, write down ten objectives or goals you plan to achieve with your business.

....

....

....

....

....

....

....

....

....

....

VIII. Executive Summary

As you have already read, the Executive Summary is a critical piece of this puzzle. This is the section that everyone who sees your business plan will read first; however, you should prepare it last.

By preparing the Executive Summary last, you will be able to write it more easily, and with far greater impact. You will have already compiled all of your data in the other sections of your business plan. Now simply transfer the "sizzle" of the plan into smaller paragraphs.

Begin by explaining when your company was formed and what you sell, distribute, manufacture, etc.

....

....

....

Next, explain what the purpose of your operation is by stating what you will provide your customers in the way of products and services.

....

....

....

Indicate what phase of operation your business is. Show that projections demonstrate you will cut operating costs by a certain percentage and increase sales by a certain percentage.

....

....

....

These two important items will result in a faster cash flow to the company.

Next, refer back to how to develop a "Mission Statement" and create your own mission statement.

....

....

....

....

Now give some background information on:

- The market ....
  ....
  ....

- Your customers' buying habits ....
  ....
  ....

- How you will educate your customers about your product/service? ....
  ....
  ....

- What type of quality products/services do you sell? ....
  ....
  ....
  ....

- Whether you will be able to buy at a lower cost with different suppliers. ....
  ....
  ....
  ....

- Who you are buying your supplies from? ....
  ....
  ....
  ....

- How much has your operation produced in annual sales over the past 3–5 years?
  ....
  ....
  ....

- If you have operated at a loss, indicate why, and how you will correct this problem.
  ....
  ....
  ....

- Revenue projections for your next fiscal year, and projected annual growth rate (by percentage) for the next 5 years.
  ....
  ....
  ....

Now, begin explaining the concept of your product/service. Use comparisons of similar products/services.

....

....

....

Indicate any special training required for you or your staff, managers, salespeople, etc., to properly manufacture, sell, and distribute your product/service.

....

....

....

Follow this up with what strategies you will use to meet the competition. While you are on this subject explain the market share you presently enjoy, or will enjoy.

....

....

....

The next step is to clarify your target market. Define your typical customer profile using the information you wrote down earlier in Chapter Three. Also indicate any additional products you believe your targeted market will respond to favorably.

....

....

....

Next, explain if your products are protected by copyright, trademark, and U.S. patent laws.

....

....

....

Are responses from customers or potential customers favorable, or positive? Indicate this also.

....

....

The next steps that you will take are relatively easy. You have already compiled the data in other sections. Just give the most important details in a succinct fashion. The next "mini-sections" within your Executive Summary should be in the following order:

- Objectives

- Management

- Marketing

- Finance

These sections along with the previous sections will compile a solid Executive Summary, and give powerful, persuasive information to the reader.

IX. Appendix

Your Appendix should include all of the back-up documents to the data you have already shared.

In this section you will want to provide as many supporting documents as you can. Two good places to find most of your important information will be the library and your customers.

Your public library carries previously written articles, publications, newsletters, reports, statistics, etc., that will help you verify your claims. Also look for Market Survey Data that has been performed by an independent surveying company.

Your customers may be your strongest ally, not only from a credibility position. If you can persuade loyal, satisfied customers, and/or respected people in the community to write you a letter of recommendation, you will be miles ahead of your competition. Get them to write the letter on their letterheads.

In the Appendix Section, also include your brochures, mechanical designs of your product, contracts, media information, surveys, etc.

Congratulations! You have compiled a good, solid business plan, if you followed the steps in this guidebook. We hope you have enjoyed the entire process, because if we had to bet wages on the outcome, you understand your business much better now.

Good luck in all your endeavors!

Chapter 5

Financial Ratios, Glossary and Chart of Accounts

Financial Ratios

Financial ratios are used to show what condition the business is in. They assist in determining the actual meaning of financial statements, and are especially accurate for comparing similar businesses. Financial ratios are a combination of dividing, adding, and multiplying one entry of the financial statement by another.

There are four major categories of financial ratios:

1. Solvency Ratios, which describe your ability to pay debts.

2. Profitability Ratios, which measure relative profitability.

3. Efficiency Ratios, which measure how efficiently funds are used.

4. Leverage Ratios, which measure the indebtedness of the business (i.e., how much debt the business is carrying).

Whenever you are looking to raise capital, borrow money, lease equipment, or establish a line of credit, potential financial sources will use a variety of financial ratios to judge the condition of your business. Here are a few of the possible ratios they may use in their judgment:

Solvency Ratios

Quick Ratio. Cash plus accounts receivable divided by current liabilities. The larger the number, the better the protection to short-term creditors. A ratio of 1.0 or better is taken as a statement that the business is in a "liquid" condition.

Current Ratio. Current assets divided by current liabilities. The larger the number, the better the margin of safety for covering current liabilities. A ratio of 2 or better is considered good.

Current Liabilities to Net Worth (%). Current liabilities divided by net worth times 100. The lower the %, the better the protection to investors and creditors. As a rough guide, anything less than 66% is considered reasonable.

Total Liabilities to Net Worth (%). Total liabilities divided by net worth times 100. The lower the %, the better the protection to creditors. As a rough guide, anything over 100% is a red flag to creditors and investors.

Fixed Assets to Net Worth (%). Fixed assets divided by net worth times 100. This ratio varies significantly from industry to industry. The lower the %, the better the use of capital.

Profitability

Return on Sales (profit margin) (%). Net profit (after taxes) divided by net sales times 100. The higher the better.

Return on Total Assets (%). Net profit (after taxes) divided by total assets times 100. The higher the better. Indicates the efficiency of the use of assets employed.

Return on Equity (net worth) (%). Net profit (after taxes) divided by net worth times 100. This is one of the most quoted ratios. It measures the management's ability to make a good return for the net worth of the business.

Return on Investment (%). Net profit (after taxes) divided by the invested capital times

100. This is another popular ratio, indicating management's ability to make satisfactory profit on invested capital.

Efficiency Ratios

Collection Period (days). Accounts receivable divided by annual sales and multiplied by 365. Extremely low or high numbers are problematic. In theory the lower the number of days the better, but too low a number may lead to lost sales due to credit problems.

Net Sales to Inventory (inventory turns). Annual sales divided by inventory. In theory the higher the better. A low number may indicate too much inventory on hand. An excessively high number may indicate sales are being lost due to too little inventory on hand.

Net Sales to Working Capital. Annual net sales divided by working capital. This measures the efficiency of management's use of working capital. The higher the number the better.

Cost of Sales to Inventory. Annual cost of sales divided by inventory. This is very similar in concept to inventory turns. The only difference is that it uses the more accurate cost-of-sales figure.

Accounts Payable to Sales (%). Accounts payable divided by annual sales times 100. A low % may mean the business is not getting good terms from its suppliers. An excessively high % may indicate a problem in paying suppliers.

Cost of Sales to Accounts Payable. Annual cost of sales divided by accounts payable. An excessively low ratio may indicate a problem in paying suppliers. An excessively high ratio may mean that management is not getting good terms from its suppliers.

Leverage Ratios

Fixed Assets to Net Worth. Fixed assets divided by net worth. The lower the number, the better for creditors; however, a low

number may also indicate an inefficient or obsolete facility.

Debt to Net Worth. Total liabilities divided by net worth. The higher the number, the greater the risk to creditors.

Glossary

Accounts Payable. The monies owed to suppliers of goods and services to the business.

Accounts Receivable. The monies that are owed the business from the sales of goods and services.

Accrual Basis Accounting. The accounting method that is used by most larger businesses. It records the sale, expense, or other event when it actually occurs, rather than when the cash changes hands. It is not the actual receipt of payment that is important but the "right" to receive it. The sales or costs are said to be "accrued."

Administrative Expense. Such expenses as salaries, stationery, printing, office supplies, telephone, depreciation of office equipment, and rent.

Amortization. The gradual payment of a debt through a schedule of payments or the process of writing off an intangible asset against expenses over the period of its economic useful life.

Back-End Selling. Selling additional products and services to existing customers that have previously purchased from you at an earlier date.

Backward Integration. Where a company owns or controls the suppliers of goods or services to its primary operation.

Bad Debt. Debts to the business that are either uncollectible or likely to be uncollectible.

Balance Sheet. Describes the assets, liabilities, and net worth of the company on some fixed day.

Board of Directors. A group of individuals elected by stockholders, who, as a body, manage the corporation.

Bookkeeping. See Single Entry Bookkeeping, Double Entry Bookkeeping.

Break-Even Analysis. The method of determining the exact point at which the business makes neither a loss nor a profit. It is usually calculated as a point where sales have grown at a greater rate than costs and the two lines cross.

Budgeting. The planning and coordination of the various operations and functions of a business to attain, over a specific period of time, and the control of variations from the approved plan to achieve the desired results.

Business Plan. A written document that describes the business, its objectives, strategies, operating plans, business environment, and marketing strategies, together with a financial forecast. It is the road map for managing the business.

Business Receipts. Sales and/or receipts from the operations of the business.

Capital. The general term for monies invested in the business.

Capital Plan or Capital Budget. A plan that describes the purchase of capital items such as equipment, buildings, and plant.

Cash Basis Accounting. An accounting system where the sale or expense is recorded only when the transfer of cash occurs. It is primarily used by small businesses that operate with cash.

Cash Flow, Cash Projection. The systematic charting of the sources and uses of cash in a business.

Collateral. Personal or business assets that a borrower assigns to the lender to help ensure debt payment. If the loan is in default, then the lender may assume possession of the asset.

Company Thrust. Describes the overall direction of the company.

Convertible Loan. A loan to the business whereby the lender has the option of either repayment of the loan or taking part ownership of the business at some future date.

Corporation. An organization formed under a state statute for the purpose of carrying on an enterprise in such a way as to make the enterprise distinct and separate from the persons who are interested in it.

Cost of Goods and Services. Also known as variable cost. Cost directly associated with making or providing the goods or services. These usually include raw material costs, certain utility costs, labor, and variable overhead.

Critical Issues. Issues that are currently unresolved or unpredictable or outside your control that could affect the performance of business.

Current Assets. Cash and property in your possession that can be liquidated quickly.

Current Liabilities. Debts that must be met within a relatively short time, such as short-term loans, accounts payable, and accrued taxes.

Customer Profile. Description of the customer, including type, characteristics, and habits (see also Demographics).

Cyclicality. Rise and fall of the business in some relationship to the economic ups and downs.

Debt Financing. The use of borrowed money to finance a business. The loan is repaid and the lender does not receive part ownership of the business.

Demographics. Profiling the customers by age, sex, family size, income, occupation, education, religion, culture, social class.

Depreciation. The process of expensing the decrease in value of a fixed asset over its useful life.

Direct Labor. Labor costs directly associated with production or contract work.

Double Entry Bookkeeping. A bookkeeping method where transactions are first entered in a journal or log, then posted to ledger accounts to show income, expenses, assets, liabilities, and net worth. In the double entry system, each account has a left side for debits and a right side for credits.

Equity. The value of the assets minus the liabilities for the business. Also known as net worth.

Equity Financing. A method of securing monies from an investor in which the investor becomes part owner of the business for the investment.

Exit. The ability of an investor to exit a venture by turning his investment and profit into cash or other easily traded instrument.

Expenses. See operating expenses.

Exporting. Selling products and services outside a company's general geographical area. Usually associated with the conduct of overseas trade through several types of well-established channels for foreign distribution.

Fiscal Year. The definition of the year for a company for financial, accounting, planning, and tax purposes. Usually 12 calendar months.

Financial Reports. Reports that show the financial status of a company at a given time.

Financial Statement. A written presentation of financial data prepared from the accounting records. The usual financial statements include a balance sheet, income statement (or profit and loss statement), and cash flow statement.

First In, First Out (FIFO). A method of valuing an inventory of merchandise. This method assumes that the goods first acquired are the goods first sold, in typical grocery store style. It is the method in most common use, largely because it conforms most nearly to the physical flow of the inventory.

Fixed Asset. Equipment, plant, buildings, machinery that are not sold in the normal course of business.

Fixed Expenses, Fixed Costs. Those business costs that essentially do not vary when sales volume changes.

Forecasting. The calculation of all reasonable probabilities about the business future.

Forward Integration. Where a company owns or controls the marketing or distribution of its products or services.

Franchise. A business that is contractually bound to operate on another company's concept and operating principles.

General and Administrative Expenses. Expenses that are directly associated with the management of the business and not with either making or selling the product or service.

Geographic Market Factors. Geographic service area of the business and the different natural clusters of population.

Goals. See Objectives.

Goodwill. An intangible asset related to the customers' positive attitude or perception of the business. It often includes a complete listing of customers.

Horizontal Integration. Where a company owns or controls many like businesses in the same industry.

Importing. Buying products and services from individuals or companies outside the general geographical area of a business. Usually associated with buying from overseas.

Income Statement. A standard accounting method for determining the profit and loss of a business over some time period. Usually yearly, quarterly, or monthly.

Incorporation. The act of forming a corporation.

Industry Life Cycle. The almost universal cycle of events that virtually every industry undergoes from embryonic, through growth, maturity, and finally slow retrenchment.

Inside Sales Force. Those personnel who are in direct contact with customers but who do not leave their place of work in the performance of their duties.

Intangible Asset. Assets that are associated with goodwill, trademarks, patents, copyrights, formulas, franchises, brands, customer lists, and mailing lists.

Interest. The amount paid on borrowed money.

Interim Financing. Acquisition of funds for a short term when it is planned that by the end of that period, necessary financing for a longer term will be provided.

Inventory. Items that have been produced or purchased and will ultimately be sold. May include raw material inventory, work in progress inventory, and finished goods inventory.

Inventory Financing. (1) The process of obtaining needed capital for a business by borrowing money with inventory used as collateral or (2) as in the case of a trade acceptance, a method used for financing the purchase of inventories.

Joint Venture. Partnership (often short term) between two or more businesses to accomplish some task or business.

Last In, First Out (LIFO). A method of valuing an inventory of merchandise. This method is the inverse of the first-in-first-out method and assumes that the units sold are those most recently acquired and that the units on hand are those first acquired.

Leverage. The use of credit/borrowing to increase the ability to buy a business or conduct business. Highly leveraged means a business that has a high debt level.

Line of Credit. An advance commitment by a bank to lend up to the amount indicated. Business people who anticipate the financing of current operations by bank loans usually ask their banks for a line of credit in order that they may know in advance how much they can borrow at a particular bank, without collateral, should the need arise.

Liquidity. The degree of cash that can be generated in a short time from the sale of assets.

Management Consultant. A specialist outside a business who advises the business on management matters. Professional consultants have three basic advantages over company officers and employees:

1. They bring in a point of view attained by experience with many enterprises; they can see things in proper perspective.

2. Their approach to problems is generally impartial, but it is advisable for management, when retaining a consultant, to emphasize that a predetermined result is not being sought.

3. Since such investigations are the consultants' operations, efforts are more concentrated on your investigation.

Market. A clearly defined group of people, area, or group of things that can be classified together as having some common need or other common trait.

Market Analysis. Process of determining the characteristics of the market and the measurement of its capacity to buy a commodity. It investigates the potential market for an industry.

Marketing. The act of identifying, satisfying the needs of, selling to, and servicing customers.

Marketing Mix. The array of marketing methods used to sell customers.

Marketing Plan. The combination of market analysis and marketing strategies that defines who your competitors and customers are and how you will promote your business to successfully get customers to buy from you.

Market Research. The act of discovering information about a particular market. The information typically relates to the type of customers in that market, their buying habits, unfilled needs, product or service information, plus many other factors.

Market Segments. The logical breakdown and grouping of customers or customer needs or products.

Market Share. The sales of your business divided by the total sales of your industry for either your local market or the national or international market. Usually expressed as a percentage.

Net Income. See Net Profit.

Net Profit After Taxes. Net profit before taxes less federal, state, or local income, or franchise taxes.

Net Profit Before Taxes. Net sales or total receipts less all cost and expense items and before federal, state, or local income, or franchise taxes.

Net Sales. Total sales less discounts, returned goods, and freight costs.

Net Worth. The value of the assets minus the liabilities for the business.

Net Worth of a Customer. A calculated formula used to indicate the dollar value of a customer's patronage every time he or she buys from you. (Total number of purchases divided by 12.) This formula is used to calculate monthly advertising and marketing expenditures.

Notes Payable. An account in the general ledger showing the liability for promissory notes incurred by the business.

Notes Receivable. An account in the ledger showing the amount of negotiable promissory notes received (1) from customers in payment for goods sold and delivered, and (2) from other debtors.

Operating Expenses. Those expenses of the business that are not directly associated with the making or providing of the goods or services. They usually include administrative, technical, and selling expenses.

Operating Statement. See Income Statement.

Operational Plan. The detailed action plan you will take to implement the strategies and to reach desired goals. It usually covers the near-term action items, up to one, two, or three years in the future.

Outside Sales Force. Personnel who perform their selling function and meet with customers either at the customer's location or outside the salesperson's business office.

Partnership. The Uniform Partnership Act defines the arrangement as an "association of two or more persons to carry on as co-owners of a business for profit."

Patent. An exclusive right granted by the federal government to make, use, and sell an invention for a fixed period of time.

Preferred Stock. Stock that is given a preference over other forms of stock within the same corporation primarily with respect to dividend payments.

Product Mix. The grouping of products into categories so that the change in their relative amounts can be compared.

Profit. See Net Profit.

Profit and Loss Statement. See Income Statement.

Pro Forma. A projection of future (often financial) activity.

Projected Financials. An estimation of future financial earnings and expenses.

Proprietorship, Sole. An individual owner of a business who has not incorporated or does not have a recognized partner. The owner is liable for all the debts of the business to the full extent of his or her property.

Public Offering. When a business goes into the financial market to secure capital financing by offering shares or stock in the company to the public.

Quick Ratio. Cash plus Accounts Receivable divided by Current Liabilities.

Receivable. See Accounts Receivable.

Reorganization. A process involving a recasting of corporate capital structure, which the corporation may be compelled to undergo because of either imminent or immediate insolvency.

123

Retained Earnings. Net profit after taxes that is retained in the business as working capital and not paid out as dividends to stockholders.

Return on Equity. Profit on the total equity in the company.

Return on Gross Operating Assets (RGOA). Profit on the total assets used in the business.

Return on Investment (ROI). Profit on the invested capital.

Return on Sales. Profit on net sales.

Revenues. Used interchangeably with sales. Often used for businesses that do not physically sell something, such as rental companies, contracting businesses.

Seasonality. Annual rise and fall of the business according to seasonal demand variances.

Securities and Exchange Commission (SEC). Government body that is chartered to maintain order and rules of the stock and securities exchanges.

Selling Expenses. Expenses incurred in selling or distributing a product or service.

Single Entry Bookkeeping. A simple system of recording business transactions where single entries are made into a daily, weekly, or monthly journal.

Small Business Administration (SBA). An independent agency of the Federal Government, under the general direction and supervision of the President. The SBA is authorized to furnish credit either as a maker of a direct loan or as a guarantor in part of a loan made by a bank to a business.

Strategic Role. A term used by larger, more mature businesses that identifies the type of business, its charter, and operating boundaries.

Strategic Opportunity. An opportunity or goal that will change the basic thrust or strategies of the business.

Strategy. The basic method used to reach the goal.

Tactical Plan. See Operational Plan.

Taxes. A "four-letter" word that most people hate, others become nauseated when it is spoken, and still others downright detest.

Trade Receivables. See Accounts Receivable.

Trade Payables. See Accounts Payable.

Unemployment Insurance. A Federal-State system that provides temporary income for workers when they are unemployed due to circumstances beyond their control.

Unique Selling Advantage (USA). The essential appeal a business owner develops to share with staff members and customers. It is all the unique reasons why customers should buy from your company, all stated in one crisp, easy-to-understand paragraph.

Unsecured Loan. A loan made with no actual collateral or security posted to guarantee payment of the loan.

Variable Cost. Costs that vary directly with sales. These include raw material costs, certain utility costs, labor, sales commissions.

Variances. An accounting term for the difference between what was forecast and what actually happened.

Venture Capital. A pool of investment dollars made by private investors who provide counsel designed to enhance the investment, and who usually will require controlling or a major interest in the company.

Vertical Disintegration. The breaking up of manufacturing and supply operations into discrete smaller units that are completely separate entities, often independently owned.

Working Capital. Current Assets less Current Liabilities.

Sample Chart of Accounts

Title

Current Assets

    Cash—Checking

    Cash—Savings

    Cash—Payroll

    Petty Cash

    Accounts Receivable

    Allowance for Bad Debts

    Inventory

    Prepaid Expenses

    Prepaid Insurance

    Prepaid Taxes

    Loans and Exchanges

Property and Equipment

    Land

    Building

    Accumulated Depreciation—Building

    Building Improvements

    Accumulated Depreciation—Building Improvements

    Leasehold

    Leasehold Improvements

    Accumulated Depreciation—Leasehold Improvements

    Equipment

    Accumulated Depreciation—Equipment

    Furniture and Fixtures

    Accumulated Depreciation—Furniture and Fixtures

    Vehicles

    Accumulated Depreciation—Vehicles

    Other Fixed Assets

    Accumulated Depreciation—Other Fixed Assets

Other Assets

    Officers' Loan Receivable

    Utility Deposits

    Goodwill

    Accumulated Amortization—Goodwill

    Organization Costs

    Accumulated Amortization—Organization Costs

Current Liabilities

    Accounts Payable

    Employee Health Insurance Payable

    Sales Taxes Payable

    Federal W/H Tax Payable

    FICA W/H Taxes Payable

    State W/H Taxes Payable

    Local W/H Taxes Payable

    Accrued Interest

    Accrued Salaries/Bonuses

    Other Accrued Expenses

    Notes Payable—current portion

    Current Portion of Long-Term Debt

Long-Term Liabilities

    Long-Term Debt

Note Payable Officer

    Note Payable—Long Term

Equity

    For a Corporation

        Common Stock

        Additional Paid-in Capital

        Retained Earnings

For a Partnership

  Partner's Capital #1

  Partner's Capital #2

  Partner's Drawing #1

  Partner's Drawing #2

For a Sole Proprietor

  Capital

  Drawing

Sales

  Sales

  Sales for Resale

  Sales Discounts

  Sales Retained and Allowance

Cost of Sales

  Purchase—Materials

  Labor

  Purchase Discounts

  Purchase Retained and Allowance

Selling Expenses

  Salaries

  Bonuses

  Taxes Payroll—Sales

  Auto Expense

  Commissions

  Advertising + Promotion

  Travel

  Entertainment

  Miscellaneous Expenses—Sales

General and Administrative

  Salaries—Office

  Salaries—Officers

  Bonuses

Taxes—Payroll

Outside Services

Auto Expense

Bank Service Charges

Contributions

Dues and Subscriptions

Insurance—Medical

Insurance—Other

Interest Expense

Legal and Accounting

Miscellaneous Expense

Office Expense

Postage Expense

Equipment Rental

Rent Expense

Utilities

Repairs and Maintenance

Depreciation Expense

Amortization Expense

Supplies Expense

Taxes—Other

Telephone

Travel

Entertainment

Income Taxes

  Federal Income Tax

  State Income Tax

Sample
Business Plans

Disclaimer

The information in these Sample Business Plans was compiled for intended use as examples only. All information in these Sample Business Plans is fictitious. Resemblance to any actual company is purely coincidental and is not intended to compete with or to divulge proprietary ideas, company structure, or financial status of any company.

Sourcebooks, Inc., and the authors of this guidebook disclaim any responsibility for these Sample Business Plans. The information is intended to be used as a guide only. We strongly recommend that the reader consult with an attorney, accountant, or other business advisor to verify that the format and structure is appropriate for his or her circumstances.

A Business Plan For:

The Alamo Park Hotel

San Antonio, Texas

May 1, 1994

Table of Contents

Summary Statement

The Alamo Park Hotel is expected to begin operations in 1995 upon approval and contractual agreement from the West Hotel Franchising committee. The founders will be Jerry Knife, president, and his daughter, Carrie Snow. The company will be incorporated in the state of Texas. It will offer $3 million in public stock and obtain $2 million in loans and investments and $700,000 in personal capital. The hotel will be located in San Antonio, Texas. It will have 100 rooms, a lounge, meeting facilities, room service, and a kitchen. The Alamo Park Hotel will offer superb service and hospitality to its patrons. The hotel anticipates several competitive advantages:

1. The location of the hotel is close to the highway that runs through western Texas, is accessible to the airport, and is in a nice area of San Antonio.

2. The market for hotel lodging is increasing yearly by 8 percent to 10 percent.

3. Major surrounding area competitors do not have the quality of service the Alamo Park Hotel does for the money.

4. The total time expected to pay off debt is expected to be 20 years in lieu of having excess cash to pay dividends and profit to the owners.

As a result of these conditions, The Alamo Park Hotel believes it can capture a good share of the hotel market. The total investment costs are projected to be $4.5 million, and forecasted sales for the first year of operations (1995) are $1,212,292. The common stock outstanding will be 40 percent; Jerry Knife will own 41 percent and Carrie Snow will own 19 percent.

I. Company Analysis

Background of Company: West Hotel International was founded in 1954 by M. K. Certain, a California-based hotelier with 23 years' experience in the lodging industry. By 1963, West Hotel (BH) was the largest motel chain, consisting of 699 members and 35,201 rooms.

West Hotel members receive many benefits in marketing and operational support services. The member dues help provide an international reservation system, the STAR property-to-property reservation network, quality assurance programs, marketing programs, corporate advertising, public relations, educational and professional development, group purchasing, and design consulting services.

STAR uses computers to book and confirm reservations for guests in 30 seconds around the world. BH is an industry leader in airline data links. It offers a telecommunications device for the deaf. BH has a marketing department that provides market research, sales promotion, and special use directories for specific market segments. (See Exhibit I-A for more information on member services.)

West Hotel's headquarters are located in Dayton, Ohio. It is considered the world's largest hotel chain, with 3,300 independently-owned hotels and 264,000 guestrooms located in 2,400 cities and 36 countries. It plans to have more than 5,000 properties in 60 countries by the year 2000. BH plans to add 150 new properties in 1991 to its North American network (Exhibit I-B).

The international reservations and data processing centers are located in Dayton, Ohio and Wichita, Kansas. They project that more than 620 reservations sales agents will take more than 9 million reservations calls in 1995 through their toll-free 1-800 number (Exhibit I-B).

West Hotel publishes a yearly road atlas and travel guide, an atlas and hotel guide, and offers frequent guest programs that allow participants to earn points to receive free room nights and travel amenities (Exhibit I-B).

West Hotel is rated second in the industry in number of rooms (Exhibit I-C). It claims to have the lowest affiliation rates over a ten-year period compared to the competitive industry (Exhibit I-D).

Purpose of the Company: To construct a hotel under the West Hotel franchise name in the year 1993. The hotel will be independently owned by partners Carrie Snow and her father Jerry Knife.

The purpose of the hotel will be to serve the tourism and travel needs of the growing San Antonio area. It will be a lodging facility with 100 guestrooms, lobby, lounge, meeting facilities, adequate parking, swimming pool and Jacuzzi, and limited room service. The hotel will have a comfortable, but modern and appealing atmosphere to serve both business and vacation travelers.

Profits will provide a comfortable living and a future investment opportunity for the owners of the hotel. Another purpose will be to establish a business under their own management control and objectives.

Principal Roles

Carrie Snow

Education: A college graduate of the University of Texas in 1991 with a degree in Small Business Management.

Work History: San Antonio Plaza Resort, after graduation from UT. She was a Conference Sales Manager, selling conventions and banquet facilities to patrons. Aug 91–May 94.

Sensations Niteclub—Waitress—May 90–Aug. 91.

Sherman Inn—Exec. Secretary—May/Sept 89.

Bell Captain—Christmas Break

Activities: Certified P.A.D.I. Scuba Diver, Weight Training, Aerobics, Running, Skiing.

Jerry Knife

Education: High school diploma and some college from Texas University.

Work History: Omaha Public Power—operator 1967–1977.

City of San Antonio—Street Foreman—1988–1985.

Self-Employed—Evaporative Coolers—1981–1985.

Self-Employed—Pacific Fish Imports—1985–1990.

Merchant Marine—Seaman—1990–1991.

Self-Employed—Venture Capitalist—1991 to present.

Activities: Travel, work, family.

Reasons for Entering Business: Jerry Knife was looking for an investment opportunity to plan for his future retirement. He has been watching the hotel industry for some time now and he saw the healthy profits that could be made in the business. His wife June Knife has worked for First Federal Bank for 14 years and she wanted to work for a family business with more flexibility and to see some of her hard work pay off for a family business. Jerry also wanted his daughter Carrie to be successful in a career that she knew she wanted to be in. The two decided to open a business together, since they are both entrepreneurial-minded and have the same interests in business: investment and management control opportunities. Jerry would be the major backing for the financial investment by raising capital and applying for a bank loan to help construction. Carrie will be owner of 19 percent until Jerry retires or decides to give her more shares in the company. The business will be a corporation with 40% of public common stock outstanding.

Current Organizational Structure: The hotel will have 18 to 22 employees, depending on the season. The job duties are as follows:

Owner, Chief Financial Officer and Purchasing Agent: Jerry Knife. Duties include making the final decisions for management and operations; in charge of paying debts and collecting accounts receivable; dealing with investors; purchasing hotel supplies, lounge supplies, and vending.

Sales and Marketing Manager, Human Resource Director: Carrie Snow. Duties include selling guest rooms to business travelers, conventions, vacationers, and setting promotions; placing ads and promotions for the hotel rooms, lounge, meeting rooms, and special functions in the hotel; hiring employees, managing employees and overseeing the general day to day operations of the hotel.

Guest and Conference Service Manager: June Knife. Duties include attending to guests' needs, complaints, and requests; setting up conference meetings and arranging for beverages and food for the meetings. June will also train newly hired employees.

Legal and Accounting: Will be contracted out to a Certified Public Accountant and a Corporate lawyer (when needed). Duties for CPA include preparing monthly financial statements, cash flow analysis, preparing profit and loss statements, and tax preparation.

Department Managers: Each department will have a manager appointed from within the department to oversee the daily operations of the department, scheduling, hiring, purchase orders, etc.

Front-Desk Personnel: There will be four full-time desk clerks. One will be the night auditor, working 11 p.m.–7 a.m. Monday through Friday. He or she will check in guests and answer the PBX (phone system) throughout the night as well as keep daily auditing records. The other three will check in guests, answer the PBX and direct calls, take reservations, file guest bills, do light typing, and perform any other reasonable duties that the management or guest requests.

Housekeeping Department: There will be three to six full-time maids, depending on the season. Duties include: Clean rooms—full clean, average 30 minutes: change linens, clean bathroom, vacuum, dust, empty trash, stock toiletries, and make sure room is clean and ready for new guests. Partial clean for stayovers, average 20 minutes: make beds, change linens if necessary, restock towels and toiletries, clean bathroom, and empty trash. Each day one housekeeper will be assigned to thoroughly clean the hotel lobby, lobby bathrooms, lounge, meeting room (if necessary), straighten chairs, and clean up trash around the pool area. There will be an in-house laundry room for the housekeepers to wash linens daily.

Lounge Personnel: There will be three full-time bartenders. Bar will be open from 12 p.m. to 1 a.m. daily. One head bartender, whose duties include: Set bar schedules for bartenders and waitresses, order liquor supplies, manage bar operations, and tend bar. The other two bartenders' duties include: Tend bar, clean behind bar, and count drawer at end of shift. There will be two waitresses who will each work three or four nights a week from 5 p.m. until the bar has slowed down later in the evening. A third waitress will be hired during the pool season to waitress the pool and lounge area during the day. Duties include: Serve customers cocktails, refill happy hour hors d'oeuvres bar, pick up trash, straighten up chairs and wipe tables.

Meeting Room Personnel: There will be one full-time person to set up meeting facilities and serve beverages and food to the attendees. On days when there are no conventions, he or she will help out in other areas of the hotel, bag pulls when large groups come in on a bus, etc., help in kitchen, and any other needed duties that arise.

Room Service: There will be two part-time room service and kitchen attendants at the hotel. There is no restaurant in the hotel, but the lounge will serve a small menu of sandwiches and daily specials. The kitchen will be open for delivery to rooms or bar from 5 p.m. to 10 p.m. The food will be cooked to order by these employees and delivered to the guestroom or waitress in the bar to serve to the lounge customer. Each morning from 7 a.m. to 10 a.m. there will be free continental breakfast, including rolls and coffee, served either in the lounge or by the pool, depending on the weather. This will be prepared the night before by the kitchen help and put out by the desk clerks in the morning.

Maintenance and Landscape: There will be one full-time person to attend to maintenance and the hotel grounds. Duties include: Repair any damaged equipment or fixtures on the property grounds, etc. Maintain the property grounds equipment and fixtures, pool, and landscape.

Current Trends in Sales and Financial Performance: San Antonio county has been growing in population over the years. Within ten years, from 1978 to 1988, there was a 46.7 percent growth rate in the population. The service industry employs the largest number of people in Texas with 377,862 employees. The average weekly wage for service employees is $359.89 (Exhibit I-E).

The 1990 trends forecast that the U.S. economy will steadily rise in the next few years. Travel volume is continually rising, along with hotel supply, at 2 percent and demand of 3.5 percent. Room rates should increase 3 percent to 4 percent to offset occupancy rates. Leisure and international travel are expected to grow, while commercial travel is expected to decrease because of rising airfares and company cutbacks. The Southwest will be the main place for people to relocate to through the year 2000. Mature households (members age 50 and older) will travel the most because of higher discretionary income, and there will be growth for minority travelers. There are many factors that will affect travel in the future, including technology, global economy, environment, population growth, and other international trends. The key to success is to keep up with the changing trends, but not give in to one fad (see Exhibit I-G).

Travel Trends for San Antonio:

Purpose of Visit: In 1986, 48 percent of travelers visited San Antonio for business or convention reasons; 47 percent visited for discretionary purposes (Exhibit I-H).

Transportation: 75 percent of travelers visit San Antonio by air and 19 percent visit by car (Exhibit I-I).

Transportation by accommodation: 86 percent of air travelers and 10 percent of car travelers stay in a hotel (Exhibit I-J).

Visitor Accommodation: 54 percent of visitors stay in hotel/resort/motel (Exhibit I-K).

Visitors' Residence: San Antonio attracts visitors from the Western United States and the North Central United States. Southern Texas represents 11 percent of the visitors to San Antonio (Exhibit I-L).

Visitors' Residence by Accommodation: Northeast and southern residents prefer to stay in hotels rather than in private households, condos, and campgrounds (Exhibit I-M).

Visitors' Residence by Transportation: Southern Texas residents travel mostly by car, and those from the Northeast, South, and North Central areas travel mostly by air (Exhibit I-N).

Spending per Group per Day in Selected Categories: The average room rate is $78 per day. People average $15 a day on alcoholic beverages (Exhibit I-O).

Summary of Visitors' Spending: See Exhibit I-P for a complete overview of San Antonio visitors.

Strategic Analysis of the Lodging Industry: Internal and external factors that affect the hotel industry's competitive advantage:

Overbuilding: The occupancy demand will catch up with the overbuilding of hotels. A favorable balance between supply and demand is expected.

External Factors:

Finance: Long-term financing coming from foreign sources and U.S. insurance agencies. The current yield of the dollar compared to foreign markets will encourage travel in and to the United States.

Factors affecting travel: Competition of airlines will encourage international travel. Interest in foreign places will increase tourism. Constraints on travel will be environmental degradation and a strained infrastructure.

Giving pause: Average nights stayed on a trip have declined 2 percent. Business trip nights have increased 6 percent.

Labor: The hotel industry is competing for unskilled labor and graduates of college hospitality programs.

Technology: Computerized technology will become more prevalent due to decreasing labor.

Competitive advantage: Differentiation and low costs are key factors in success.

Strategies: To target specific markets with new products or extensions of existing products. Technology will also gain advantage.

Success: Key factors to success are the products offered, marketing tactics, operations of maintaining standards, ongoing research and development, and a stable cash flow to cover all expenses (See Exhibit I-Q).

Product: The service offered will be a one-hundred-room hotel with upgraded amenities at fair room rates. The hotel will have meeting rooms for small conventions and parties available for the use of guests and the local community at rates comparable to those of the competition. The conventions will be served beverages and food at an extra cost. There will be a lounge on the premises to serve guests and the local community. It will provide cocktails and menu items to the bar and pool area. A nightly room service menu will be provided for the guests to receive meals in their room. A continental breakfast will be served each morning from 7 a.m. to 10 a.m., consisting of rolls and morning beverages. Vending machines including nonalcoholic beverages and snacks will be located on each floor. Ice machines will also be on each floor.

The hotel will have a pool and Jacuzzi for guests. The grounds will be kept up to excellent standards. The rooms will be completely clean and ready for the guests. Guestroom supplies will be restocked daily and when a guest requests more supplies. Lower than competition rates will be available to guests of the hotel to provide nice rooms to business and vacation travelers at affordable prices.

The hotel will accommodate each guest with a clean, friendly, and relaxing atmosphere. The three basic principles of the hotel are (1) to encourage respect for the individual; (2) to provide the best guest service in the hospitality industry; (3) to instill a commitment to excellence.

Markets: The hotel plans to divide its market into segments specific to the guestrooms, lounge, and meeting facilities.

Guest Rooms: The target markets for the guestrooms will be business persons and vacationers visiting the San Antonio area. The hotel will be located on Katy Highway and Highway I-10, so it will be easily accessible from San Antonio Airport for tourists who fly to San Antonio. The hotel will also target tourists driving by car from Southern Texas on the I-10 freeway. The basic characteristics of the business markets will be people who need to commute to downtown San Antonio for business meetings. The vacationers will mostly be people flying to San Antonio for an extended stay or people driving from the Texas area for a short vacation. The rooms will be affordable for most patrons and provide upgraded amenities to provide a pleasurable stay.

Lounge: The lounge will target the local community market and the hotel guests. The local community will be mostly professionals living in the vicinity of the hotel who want to have cocktails with friends after work in a relaxing atmosphere. The hotel guests will use the lounge to escape their rooms and have cocktails during the day or evening hours as part of their vacation. The lounge has happy hour from 4 p.m. to 7 p.m. daily, during which it serves cocktails at a low price and has a free hors d'oeuvre bar.

Meeting Rooms: The meeting room facilities will target local businesses and organizations, and visiting groups and conventions that are staying at the hotel and need a place to hold meetings. The sales department will promote the facilities for banquets and conventions. The facilities will provide food and beverages along with banquet service. The cost will be less than the other local hotels, but the service and atmosphere will be comparable.

Target Marketing: West Hotel conducts two types of marketing research studies to remain competitive in the USA. One is the Monthly Opinion Survey to discover the way consumers perceive and what they want and need of West Hotel. The other is the monthly Member Occupancy Study, which has properties that provide Best Western with information on key travel markets (Exhibit I-R).

Customers: The major customers will be business persons, vacationers, and family travelers. They will come either by car from Southern Texas or into San Antonio Airport by plane.

Technology Position: West Hotel International opened a new reservation center in 1990 to meet the hotel needs through 1997. It is also training reservations agents to answer more information about each property to improve sales. West Hotel offers a toll-free reservations line available around the clock. They also offer a telecommunications device for the deaf to book reservations. Worldwide expansion has made West Hotel a global competitor, and reservations can be booked through overseas affiliate offices. The STAR program allows computers to book reservations throughout the world in 30 seconds and it keeps accurate records for referral. A STAR III program is a management system that allows hoteliers to enact rate changes instantaneously in any room category (Exhibit I-S).

Research done by the American Hotel and Motel Association (AH&MA) shows that hotel service can be enhanced with automation. Many hotels are behind in technology because of a lack of understanding of it. Education and tracking of developments in technology are needed to show how valuable it can be. Technology should be used for three main purposes: service, productivity improvement, and office operations (Exhibit I-T).

Cost Analysis: Based on industry figures provided by Bob Sharky (Exhibit U), a San Antonio architect, the building and startup costs would equal $4,168,371 and operating costs are expected to be $649,375 in the first year for a 100-room hotel of this type (Exhibits V and I-W). The figures for the Alamo Park Hotel are operating costs of $551,190 the first year and a total investment of $5.5 million (increasing the total investment over the projected cost of $4,168,371 because of inflation, emergency, financing costs, and to have excess cash to get through the first year). The cost per room to build and start up would be $55,000 for the 100-room hotel with a lobby, lounge, meeting rooms, and kitchen.

Licensing: A hotel with a lounge requires a Class-six liquor license. This is fairly easy to obtain over any other liquor license, because the bar is located in a hotel and serves food.

Other licenses and requirements to adhere to are a business license, county and city health codes, zoning requirements, federal and state taxes, workers' compensation laws, building requirements, and safety regulations.

Location: The hotel will be located on the south side of I-10 and the east corner of the Highway. The hotel will be seen from the freeway and easily accessible from either direction on the freeway.

Use and Size: The hotel will have 100 guestrooms: 8 guest suites, 16 king guest suites, 75 double-double guest suites, and 1 manager's apartment. It will have four floors: first floor has lobby, lounge, administrative offices, corridors, meeting facilities, kitchen, pool area and covered parking. There are 27 covered parking spaces and 75 uncovered spaces, totaling 102 parking spaces. The lot area will be 6 lots equaling 42,000 sq. ft. The total building area will equal 57,748 sq. ft. (Exhibits I-X1, X2, and X3 floor plan).

Capacity: Each guestroom will be at least 12' by 26' including the bath, entry, and dressing areas (312 sq. ft.). The ceiling height will be 8', measured from the floor. There will be two handicapped rooms located on the second floor. The interior finish will include wall-to-wall carpeting, vinyl wall covering, and ceilings with a textured finish. Furniture, fixtures, and equipment will include beds, bed frames, headboards, mattresses, boxsprings, bedspreads, one nightstand, one credenza, luggage shelf, desk, mirror, desk chair, two lounge chairs, round activity table, light fixtures, draperies, television, two framed pictures, two wastepaper baskets, telephone, and hanging clothes storage.

Bathrooms will be 40 sq. ft., including the vanity area. The floor will be ceramic tile and the walls will be covered with enamel paint. Furniture, fixtures, and equipment will include tub/shower combinations with soap holder and grab bar, high quality toilet seats, mirror over the vanity, and guest bath lighting. Chrome-plated accessories will include tissue dispenser, facial tissue dispenser, 24" towel bar, one robe hook, and a heavy duty shower curtain.

Guestroom corridors will be 6' wide, ceilings 8' high, well lighted, have signs to indicate room location, etc., and have carpeting and vinyl wall finish.

The lobby will be 1,028 sq. ft., soundproofed, have high-quality static-resistant carpet, high-quality wall covering, 8' high ceiling, dated light fixtures, and seating for at least 10 persons. Fixtures and equipment will include reservation terminal, postage stamp machine, two house phones, and two pay phones.

The front desk will be 10' long, with key storage accessible only to front desk personnel while working behind the desk. Safety deposit boxes and a mail-drop box will be located behind the desk.

The public rest rooms will be located in the lobby close to the lounge and meeting facilities. The lavatories will contain all the standard furniture, fixtures, and equipment.

There will be one vending area located on each floor containing one self-service ice machine, one soft drink machine, and one candy machine.

The cocktail lounge is easily accessible to the rest rooms, has dimmer-controlled lighting, concealed waitress stations, high-quality carpeting, and accessibility for the handicapped. There will be a long bar with 10 to 15 stools, 8 four-seated booths, and 8 four-seated tables. High quality silk plants and flowers will surround the room.

The meeting room will be 792 sq. ft. with dimmer-controlled lighting, padded chairs, movable tables, high-grade carpet, individually controlled heat and air conditioning, vinyl wall covering, and one folding partition (see Exhibition I-Y, West Hotel New Construction Guidelines).

The kitchen will be 375 sq. ft., including pantry storage and refrigeration. It will contain three sinks, a commercial stove with two ovens, a grill and four burners, a large countertop, and dishes and kitchen utensils.

There will be two offices, one for the general manager and one for the other two administrators. They will contain high-quality desks, high-back chairs, filing cabinets, one PC per office, and general office supplies.

The housekeeping area will have three commercial washing machines and three commercial dryers. All cleaning swipes, cleaning carts, and linens will be stored there.

The hotel will have two elevators for easy accessibility to the four floors of the hotel.

All equipment will be purchased by the contractor new at the time of construction. Equipment, fixtures, and furniture will be replaced as needed when it is outdated, nonrepairable, or obsolete.

Capacity Utilization: Guestrooms need a 35 percent occupancy rate to break even. The expected capacity is 80 percent or over in the winter and 60 percent in the summer. The lounge is expected to be 50 percent full each weekday evening and 80 percent full on the weekends. The meeting facilities should be utilized 80 percent of the time, depending on season and demand. Room service will be utilized by 25 percent of the guests and 30 percent of the lounge patrons.

Acquisition: The hotel will be built by a subcontractor named Bob Stark. He is a long-time friend and business partner of Jerry Knife. Bob will help obtain financing for the hotel and will be in complete control of construction and purchasing of furniture, equipment, and fixtures. He will have a major investment interest in the hotel and be generously compensated for his involvement in its development. Color schemes will be chosen by an interior designer. The land will be purchased for $700,000 in the summer of 1991, while the real estate market price for buying is low. Building costs will equal $2,592,968; development costs will equal $282,778; furniture, fixtures, equipment, and preopening costs will equal $380,000; and financing costs will equal $212,625. The total project breakdown costs will equal $4,168,371 (Exhibit I-V, project breakdown).

Company Strengths:

West Hotel Membership Advantages:

1. *Low cost and no long-time commitment:* Annual fees cost one-quarter of other lodging franchises. Franchise agreements renewable every year.

2. *Name recognizable by guests:* Guests know they will have attractive rooms and good service.

3. *International reservation system:* Available to guests 24 hours a day.

4. *STAR-plus marketing programs:* The reservation system can build and sell promotional rate programs.

5. *Airline reservations systems:* Travel agencies and airline companies have direct links with West Hotel.

6. *B-H insurance:* B-H Insurance agency, affiliated with Best Western, provides members with better insurance coverage with lower premiums.

7. *B-H Supply:* Designs programs to allow members to buy quality hotel supplies and services at low costs.

8. *Quality assurance:* Field inspection teams inspect property to help improve deficiencies.

9. *West Hotel Design:* Design staff helps with refurbishment or hotel design.

10. *Camaraderie:* Independent ownership and common goal of mutual success.

11. *STAR III:* Computer system provides operations and management functions.

12. *Technical services:* Property automation consulting services, telecommunications consulting, and satellite services.

13. *Credit cards:* West Hotel's national contacts with credit card services provide lower discount rates.

14. *Advertising:* Extensive international advertising programs, discount travel and trade advertising, cooperative advertising, advertising and promotional materials are available:

    a. Road atlas and travel guide and travel agent edition.

    b. Eleven regional sales offices target major markets.

    c. Meeting and conference services guide—hotel can be placed in this book for added awareness.

    d. Fly/Drive Kit: Package deals sold by airlines, travel agents, etc., that include B-H lodging.

15. *International operations:* B-H promotes sales to overseas tourists to the United States.

16. *International commission payment and foreign check conversion:* Program to pay travel agents in local currency.

17. *Reservations traffic bulletin:* Monthly reports of each property's reservations activity.

18. *Corporate communications:* Answers questions and advises members.

19. *Education and training:* Ongoing educational programs available to B-H members. (Exhibit I-Y, B-H membership advantages)

Marketing: The hotel will have an administrative person working on the promotion and sales of the rooms, lounge, and meeting rooms.

Finance: Some investment capital will be raised from personal funds and reliable investment sources.

Purchasing: The land will be acquired at a low market cost in times of a suffering economy.

Distribution: The service offered will be available to consumers on an ongoing basis.

Information Systems: Updated computer systems and software will be available from West Hotel.

Policies and Procedures: Each administrative department will have set objectives, but will work with the other departments' goals as well.

Management: Experienced management personnel will be operating the hotel and making important decisions.

Employees: Growing number of administrative employees will provide excellent service.

Location: Traffic area, accessible from downtown, airport, and freeways.

Company Weaknesses:

Finance: Large amount of capital needs to be raised to build and start up the hotel. Must find interested investment capitalists to help finance venture.

Sales: The hotel business depends on the U.S. economy and lodging demand.

Franchise: Must abide by West Hotel standards and pay annual membership fees (Exhibits I-Y, B-H Rules and Regulations, Bylaws and Articles, membership fees).

Bases of Competition: Direct competition comes from Motel 66, Chariot Fairview, and Andrew Park, all located in the same area on the I-10 freeway. Having all of these hotels together can be an advantage to the West Hotel because people will know where hotel rooms are available. There is enough demand to support all of these hotels.

Rates:
Motel 66, budget
Chariot, medium
Andrew Park, high

West Hotel, medium

Amenities:
Motel 66, very few
Chariot, hotel services, pool, bar
Andrew Park, hotel services, pool, lounge, restaurant, conference facilities
West Hotel, hotel services, pool, bar, meeting rooms

Quality:
Motel 66, fair
Chariot, good
Andrew Park, excellent
West Hotel, excellent

Reputation:
Motel 66, low
Chariot, very good
Andrew Park, excellent
West Hotel, very good

Service:
Motel 66, low
Chariot, good
Andrew Park, very good
West Hotel, very good

The Alamo Park Hotel, West Hotel, is comparable to Andrew Park in service and reputation but has lower rates. This will give the hotel a better market advantage over the surrounding area hotels.

Key Success Factors: The West Hotel will focus on competitive rates with high-quality lodging, service, and atmosphere. The West Hotel name will provide a well-established reputation for the hotel.

II. Industry Analysis

Definition: The hotel industry is mainly a service industry. The services offered by the hotel industry include lodging, entertainment (televisions, cable, swimming pool, Jacuzzi, relaxation), banquet facilities, meeting rooms, restaurants, lounges, food and beverages, room service, concierge service, free transportation, housekeeping, telephone service.

Full-service hotels are located throughout the world in all countries. Foreigners own hotels in the United States, as Americans own hotels in foreign countries. It is an ongoing industry that will continue to grow and be used by people forever.

The market segments that use hotels are divided into people who travel for pleasure/vacation, visiting friends, conventions, and business.

The first-class/full-service hotel industry competes directly with resorts and economy/limited-service hotels. The hotel industry competes indirectly with camping, mobile homes and travel trailers, apartments/condos, and private homes.

Industry Size: In Texas there were 41,657 rooms in 1989 (Exhibit II-A). In Metropolitan San Antonio in 1989 there were 12,264 first-class/full-service hotel rooms (Exhibit II-B, page

6). The forecast predicts 38,837 total rooms in the Metropolitan San Antonio area by 1994. (Exhibit II-B, page 10).

The total industry size in annual dollars is summarized in the tables from *Trends* magazine (Exhibit II-C). They are divided by size, rates, city size and property age, and geographic divisions. (See the income before other fixed charges on these tables for 1989.)

1. Dollars per available room: $44,858

   Alamo Park Hotel: $6,631.02

2. Dollars per available room by rate groups: For over $42.50, $5,467.

3. Dollars per available room by size classifications: For fewer than 125 rooms, $3,220.

4. Dollars per available room by city size and property age: For large city, $5,424; for hotels built within last 15 years with fewer than 200 rooms, $3,850.

Industry Growth Rate: In Texas the number of lodging rooms has increased 32.2 percent, from 31,508 in 1989 to 41,657 in 1992. Demand for hotel rooms has increased at a compound annual rate of 10.1 percent over the same period. This has caused occupancy levels to remain stable at levels of 59 percent to 61.2 percent (Exhibit II-A). The national percentage of occupancy in 1992 was 64.8 percent for full-service hotels (Exhibit II-C, page 39).

Texas had 9,306,176 room nights in 1992, which was a 7.8 percent increase over 1991 (Exhibit II-A).

According to Accorn Kerr Forester (AKF), the average room rate has been increasing steadily each year at a rate of 3.8 percent since 1986. This rate is below the inflation rate. The growth is slow because the increase in the number of hotels being built causes the operators to discount rates in order to keep market share. In 1992 the average room rate was $74.28 (Exhibit II-A). The full-service hotel average room rate in 1992 was $70.71 (Exhibit II-B). The national average daily room rate in 1989 was $76.41 for a full-service hotel (Exhibit II-C, page 39).

AKF forecasts that the average occupancy level in Texas will increase to 63.3 percent and the average room rate will increase 4.9, percent to $69.96. The reason is that in 1990 fewer rooms were being added to the supply (Exhibit II-A).

The average price of a Metropolitan San Antonio room was $80.52 in 1992. In 1994 the rate is expected to increase to $84.46, or 4.9 percent above 1992 levels (Exhibit II-A).

The Metropolitan San Antonio market demand continued its growth at a healthy 10.3 percent level in 1992. In 1992 the San Antonio hotels captured 6,002,814 room nights of demand.

The addition of 1,876 rooms was outpaced by a 10.3 percent growth in demand in 1992, resulting in an increase in occupancy levels during 1992. This growth in occupancy levels, even though there was an increase in room supply during 1992, reflects the strength of lodging demand and the ability to absorb the large increase in rooms supply over the past few years (Exhibit II-A). In 1992 six hotels with 100 rooms or more were added to the Metropolitan San Antonio area. In 1993 also there were six hotels added. This is much less than in 1988, when twelve hotels were added in that one year alone (Exhibit II-B).

The decline in new hotel development during 1992 was caused by the lagging market performance in the San Antonio area or the inability to obtain sufficient financing. AKF forecasts 694 new rooms will enter the San Antonio market in 1994, a 2 percent increase in rooms over 1993 (Exhibit II-A).

A 5.9 percent increase in demand is expected in 1994 to outpace the 2.5 percent increase in room supply, resulting in a 61.8 percent occupancy level (up two points from 1989) (Exhibit II-A).

The average room rate was $80.52 in 1992 for the Metropolitan San Antonio area. AKF forecasts the market will increase to $84.46, a 4.9 percent increase over 1992 (Exhibit II-A).

Company Size and Growth Rate: The Alamo Park Hotel, West Hotel, will have 100 rooms and run at a 45 percent to 80 percent occupancy rate in the first year (depending on season). A steady growth rate of 2 percent to 5 percent in occupancy is expected after each year until the rate catches up with the industry average occupancy rate. Special promotions and a slightly lower room rate than the industry will give the hotel a higher occupancy level than the industry overall. The hotel room rates will be different according to season and will range from $42 to $65 in the first year.

Key Growth Factors: There are many significant factors that affect the industry's market size and level of demand.

1. *International affairs and peace:* Foreign travelers are less likely to visit the United States in times of war or when there are negative feelings toward the U.S. government, people, or lifestyles. When the United States does something favorable for other nations, foreigners are more likely to visit.

2. *Economic conditions:* When discretionary income is high, people travel more often. In times of recession, travel is down because it is not a necessity and people save their money to survive.

3. *Weather conditions:* Specifically, the San Antonio area attracts many tourists.

4. *Transportation factors:* The airline industry fares and service have a great impact on whether people visit the San Antonio area. Automobile transportation is affected by the price of gasoline.

5. *Tourist attractions:* San Antonio area expansion of tourist attractions and events results in more visitors to the area. There are many major downtown San Antonio projects being developed that are easily accessible from the hotel (Exhibit II-B, page 23).

Seasonality: The seasonality throughout the industry is different, according to the city each hotel is located in. The hotel will be located in the San Antonio area, so the industry figures will be specific to San Antonio. Occupancy rates are the best measure in the hotel industry to determine seasonality.

The warmer temperature months have the higher occupancy rates in San Antonio, while the cooler months have lower occupancy rates. People like to visit San Antonio when the weather is comfortable for them (usually to get away from snow and cold areas) and not too hot. According to *Trends* and Smith Travel Research, the two highest occupancy months were June (76 percent and 81.8 percent) and July (84% percent and 89.1 percent) in 1992. The winter months still have some occupancy with the lowest month being January (40.5 percent and 43 percent) (Exhibit II-C, page 10, and Exhibit II-B, page 8).

Industry Life Cycles: The hotel industry as a whole is between the growth and mature stages. There are new hotels being built and demand is still increasing, but there are a lot of already existing hotels that are in the mature stage. New hotels enter the market, while old or poorly managed and financed hotels leave the market. The hotel industry is an ongoing one that will not enter the aging cycle. The criteria for the industry life cycle are summarized in the table (Exhibit II-D).

Industry life cycle criteria:

1. *Growth rate:* Increasing steadily.

2. *Market share:* Hotels have large market.

3. *Product line:* Generally not changing, but new services and technology do have effect.

4. *Financial:* Cash rich, medium debt.

5. *Number of competitors:* Stable and shakeout.

6. *Market share stability:* Solid to entrenched.

7. *Purchasing patterns:* Moderate loyalty.

8. *Ease of entry:* Difficult (financing).

9. *Technology:* Performance very important.

10. *Typical volume growth rate:* Stable, but growing slowly (about 5 percent yearly).

11. *Managerial style:* Sophisticated manager.

12. *Overall stage:* Between growth and maturity.

Financial Operating Characteristics: The financial data for the hotel are based on percentage increases. Occupancy rates are increased 2 percent compounded annually and room rates are increased 4 percent annually. These percentages are done on a monthly basis because seasonality affects the rates. In a five-year period occupancy rates are expected to rise a total of 4 percent and room rates are expected to rise about $9. Room income after expenses (based on a percentage of room revenue) is expected to be $443,102 (before fixed) (Exhibits II-E and II-F).

III. Market Analysis

Market Scope: The market scope for the hotel will be international. West Hotel franchises are located throughout the world, and this hotel will be able to take advantage of the franchise name. The hotel will specifically advertise to the regional market scope, but West Hotel International advertises internationally for its member hotels.

Market Distribution: The franchise hotel industry advertises for its members by television commercials, promotions, airline magazines, travel magazines, travel agents, etc. This is provided to the members for an advertising fee, which must be paid under the franchise contract. The individual hotel will also place advertisements in other city's newspapers, telephone directories, and radio.

Market Segmentation: The characteristics of tourists visiting San Antonio are best described by the San Antonio & Texas Convention & Visitor Bureau for 1992.

Most visitors come to San Antonio for pleasure/vacation, being 38 percent of the market. Business visitors make up 21 percent of the market and convention travelers make up 18 percent of the market. Thirty-seven percent of the San Antonio visitors stay in hotel accommodations and stay an average of 10.7 days, over twice as long as in many other western cities; 82 percent of these people will return to San Antonio within the next 2 years.

The demographic characteristics of the tourist market are as follows: The median age of San Antonio visitors is 46 years, higher than that of Oklahoma visitors. Because the age is higher, so is the median income, $59,507. Most people come to San Antonio to go sightseeing.

San Antonio visitors come from all over the country, but most live in the North Central region (27%). Next are the Northeast, South, and other Western regions, all at 16 percent (Exhibit II-B, visitor profile).

Metropolitan San Antonio Lodging Markets: According to Accorn Kerr Forester, there are eight specific hotel markets in Metropolitan San Antonio. This hotel will be located in the West San Antonio market area (map location 1 in Exhibit II-A). The surrounding markets are Bowie Grande (map location 2) and Downtown San Antonio (map location 3).

West San Antonio: Residential in nature, but has key transportation corridors. Key hotel demand generators include Interstate 10, San Antonio Air Force Base, Retirement City, and Retirement West.

Forecast: New properties have been developed, adding 338 rooms to the market. In 1993 one hotel opened, the Sunset Inn, and one closed, the Jacks Inn. Demand for hotel rooms in the West San Antonio market increased 10.5 percent from 1989 to 1992. In 1994 the forecast predicts a 3.6 percent increase over 1992 levels. The highest demand for rooms is by tourists at 46 percent, then commercial at 35 percent.

Occupancy Performance: Demand grew at an average rate of 10.5 percent during 1986 through 1989 and the supply of rooms increased 14.8 percent over the same period. Occupancy rates are expected to grow because of the moderate growth in demand.

Average Room Rate: Budget-oriented rooms are entering the West San Antonio market, causing a fluctuation of room rates. The forecast for 1994 is a $53.06 average daily rate, a 4.3 percent increase over 1992 (Exhibit II-A). (See Exhibit II-A for West San Antonio market table for summary of market performance.)

Surrounding Markets: See tables for summary of market performance for the central market, downtown San Antonio market, and the total Metropolitan San Antonio market (Exhibit II-A).

Market Demand Changes and Trends: The total demand for hotel rooms in the Metropolitan San Antonio market has been steadily increasing, from 5.9 percent to 12.7 percent each year for the past four years. Room rates are continuing to increase each year. The average daily room rate was expected to reach $84.46 in 1994. These figures show that demand for rooms increases each year, so the hotel industry is still in strong demand.

The hotel market surrounding Interstate 10 has been growing in demand and supply. Many new hotels have been built there recently to capture the market driving in from out of state. The site is also centrally located and easily accessible to downtown San Antonio without having to lodge in the heart of downtown San Antonio. It is more open and relaxing for visitors.

According to the San Antonio Department of Transportation, the traffic in the area of Interstate 10 and Katy Highway is as follows:

Katy Highway westbound, 49,128 cars

Katy Highway eastbound, 49,965 cars

3rd Avenue to 14th Avenue westbound, 50,985 cars

3rd Avenue to 19th Avenue eastbound, 51,985 cars

Katy Highway & I-10 southbound, 25,953 cars

All of these travelers would see the hotel sign from the road and some may be looking for a hotel to stay at.

Another trend toward tourism and business travel is reduced spending. Economic conditions and recession have caused businesses to cut down on company spending and travel expenses. Fewer people are going on vacations, and when they do they are more careful about how they spend their money.

The (total trip) average spending per person per day is $84, of which 44 percent is spent on lodging. People staying at a hotel/resort/motel spend, on average, $99 per day. People visiting for a convention spend an average of $106 per day per person, business spending averages $112, and vacation, $92 (Exhibit II-B, page 35).

There is a trend toward budget-oriented hotel lodging. Many people discover that some budget hotels provide the same quality of service as do higher priced hotels, so they tend to stay where the rates are cheaper. Many people are rate sensitive.

Some hotels change owners or go out of business. John Q. Jones, owner of Easy Lodge of Dallas, Texas, said: "Sixty percent of new hotels built change owners three times before they start making a healthy profit. The reason being that the original owner doesn't have enough capital to keep it going between the initial start up costs to when they start building a reputation for themselves and turning a profit."

Major Customers:

Vacationers/Pleasure: There are many types of customers who visit the hotel for vacations.

1. *Older age group:* Retired couples will stay at the hotel to get away from cold weather back home. They will be age 54 and up and have a fairly healthy income.

2. *Couples with children:* Ten percent of the visitors will have children. They will be married couples age 25–45 and generally have a budgeted income.

3. *Young couples without children:* They will either be married or not married and range in age from 25 to 50. They will spend a lot of money for a vacation and want to have a good time. They may or may not have a high income, but they will have sufficient funds for the trip.

4. *Single people:* They may be traveling alone or with a group of friends. Some single men prefer to have their own rooms when traveling with other men, while most women don't mind sharing the room with other women friends. This group will include all single people, any age. Most will have a medium to high income, because they probably live alone and have only themselves to support.

Business/Convention Travelers:

1. *Business/convention—traveling alone:* People traveling on business alone will usually have a travel expense account provided by the company they work for. They will usually have a rental car, and be away from their rooms a lot on business. They will be all ages and have a middle to high income.

2. *Business/convention—traveling in groups:* These people are either traveling for business conventions or social conventions. They may travel to the area alone (not knowing anyone when they arrive and meet the others), or they may travel in groups to get to the convention site. In both cases, the whole group will usually stay in the same hotel with

reservations organized by the host of the convention. These people will do a lot of things together. They can be any age group, depending on the purpose of the convention. Their incomes can range from low to high, also depending on the function.

Percentage of Sales:

Major Customers	% of Total Sales
Vacation/Pleasure	38
Business	21
Convention	18

Sales Tactics:

Advertising: The hotel rooms will be sold by international, regional, and local advertising methods provided by West Hotel.

International: West Hotel International has an advertising mix that includes radio, television, popular consumer magazines, and trade publications, as well as outdoor advertising and direct marketing. There is a discount travel trade advertising program which allows members to use the B-H in-house advertising agency and receive discounts on advertising in *Hotel and Travel Index, Official Airlines Guide and Travel Planner, AAA Tour Books,* and *AH&MA Redbook.*

Regional and local: A cooperative advertising program is also offered by B-H regional sales offices that targets potential guests through direct sales calls in all major market segments, attendance at all major trade shows, and special sales blitzes.

Individual advertising will also be implemented using San Antonio and outside of San Antonio city newspapers, yellow pages, and local magazines and shoppers.

Sales Force: The Sales and Marketing Department will sell rooms by targeting businesses and organizations that will be needing facilities for conventions and meetings and need hotel rooms for the attendees.

Sales Promotions: The hotel will offer sales promotions and special rate discounts.

Reservations System: West Hotel reservation system will refer and make reservations for the guests.

Travel Agencies: A 10 percent commission rate will be given to all travel agencies that make reservations for their clients at the hotel.

Repeat Customers: Guests who like the hotel property, services, and amenities will return to the hotel and refer the hotel to others.

Company Policies:

1. The hotel will not offer discounts above 25 percent of the room rates.

2. There will be an extra charge of $6.00 per person for more than two people, except for children under 18.

The normal sales terms will include payment when the guest checks in. They can pay by cash, check, Visa card or Mastercard. They can pay for days ahead of time or on the day before they stay over. Extra charges such as telephone will require payment when guests check out. Other services such as the bar, room service, etc., will be paid at time of the sale; no tabs are allowed.

Distribution Channels: The middlemen of the hotel will be:

1. *Travel agents:* They will sell directly to their clients and will account for 20 percent of market sales.

2. *Sales force:* They will target markets and convince them to stay at the hotel. This market will account for 20 percent of sales.

3. *Word of mouth:* People who have already stayed at the hotel will refer us to others. This market will account for 10 percent of sales.

4. *West Hotel reservation system:* Guests will contact the reservation system on their own. They will account for 30 percent of the market sales.

5. *Advertising:* The only method of sales that doesn't have a middle link is direct advertising, which will capture the remaining 20 percent of market sales.

Seventy percent to 80 percent of the market sales will depend on middlemen. Travel agents will be compensated by 10 percent of the sale. The sales force will be paid a salary, because they will have other duties to perform in the organization. The reservation system is provided by West Hotel in the contract for the annual membership fees.

Pricing Trends: The average daily room rates increase 3.8 percent to 4.9 percent each year. This is below the inflation rate of 6 percent. The hotel plans to keep up with competition by providing an average room rate for the area. It will be higher than the budget hotels and comparable to the same grade hotels.

The rates will be different according to the season. The monthly competition report provided by Sherman Inn tells the average daily rates for competitive hotels (Exhibit III-A).

The hotel will increase its average daily rate an average of 4 percent per year. It will directly compete with other area hotels by offering sales and promotions and added services. It will also watch surrounding hotels' occupancy rates and average daily rates to make sure they are comparable.

Promotion and Advertising: The hotel plans to spend 4 percent to 5 percent of overall sales on advertising. This will be allocated to different sales media.

Advertising Strategy: The hotel will place ads locally in San Antonio and regionally in large cities like Dallas and other Texas and out-of-state cities. The advertising mix will consist of Yellow Pages, newspapers, local magazines, and shoppers.

Yellow Pages: Yellow Page ads capture 9 percent of the hotel market. It is a directional medium and points willing consumers in the direction where a purchase can be made. If someone is looking for a hotel and doesn't know the area they will look in the phone book for something close. Because the hotel has the West Hotel name, which is familiar to people, they will be more likely to choose that hotel. There are more than 17.4 billion references to the Yellow Pages annually. For consumer use, 63 percent of adults and 48 percent of business people refer to the Yellow Pages in a one-month period. Most of the people have incomes over $30,000 per year. The hotel will budget 1 percent of sales per year for Yellow Pages ads in cities in Texas and other states.

Newspapers: The hotel will place ads and sales promotions in state newspapers like the *Texas Republic* and other major newspapers. Newspapers reach 11.2 percent of the market for the hotel industry. Along with the Yellow Pages, they reach 20.3 percent of the market. The hotel advertising can be targeted to people interested in travel by placing it in the Travel or Leisure sections of the paper. Newspapers attract all age groups and income levels and are read an average of 44 minutes a day. The strengths of the newspaper include:

1. Wide availability: Many cities to choose from.

2. Immediacy: Can place ad and see results quickly.

3. Flexibility: Can cancel or repeat ads.

4. Choice of advertising formats: Can change ads to suit different needs.

5. Reader loyalty: Will be seen by many people.

Their weaknesses are:

1. High cost: Can be controlled by placing coupons or promotions to see immediate reactions.

2. Short lifespan: Read once and thrown out.

3. Need for repetition: Raises costs.

4. Low recall of ads among consumers: If placed in the right sections will attract attention.

The budget for newspaper ads and newspaper promotions will be 1.5% of sales per year.

Shoppers and Local Magazines: Occasionally the hotel will place some advertisements in local papers like the *Dynamic News, MONY Saver,* and *Texas* magazines. These will be to advertise special events at the hotel, the lounge, the meeting facilities for parties, etc. The hotel will budget 1 percent of sales per year for this ad media.

Gifts, Contributions, and Promotions: The hotel will give free lodging certificates and other giveaways to sponsor charity events, organizations, and clubs for added advertising and recognition. The budget will allocate 0.5 percent of sales to these events.

Total Advertising Budget:

Yellow Pages, 1 percent

Newspapers, 1.5 percent

Shoppers and local magazines, 1 percent

Gifts, contributions, and promotions, 0.5 percent

Total budget, 4 percent

Each advertising area will be boosted 0.2 percent whenever there is a need for special promotions.

West Hotel Advertisements: West Hotel International will also help the local, regional, and international advertising by its regional sales offices, reservations system, discount travel trade advertising, cooperative advertising, and advertising and promotional materials (see Sales Tactics, above).

Sales Force: The sales department will market mostly to businesses, organizations, and conventions. It will send out letters to repeat customers to let them know they have facilities available (remind them to use the hotel). It will also call local and regional large companies and organizations and try to sell the facilities and rooms. It will set up convention deals for groups, including rooms, meetings, charter buses, and meals.

Promotions: There are various sales promotions that will be implemented in the company:

Supersaver Weekend Program: Competitive weekend rate program: regionally determined for Friday, Saturday, and/or Sunday nights; available on a space-available basis.

Target Market: All leisure travelers, including extended business trips and amateur and professional athletes.

Guest Benefits: Low supersaver rate.

Corporate Rate Program: Provides corporate travelers with favorable fixed rates, guaranteed for the full calendar year.

Target market: Individual and corporate business travelers.

Consumer Benefits: Guaranteed room rate fixed for full calendar year, last room availability.

Promotional Program: A 10 percent discount off applicable rates (rack) to approved affiliated organizations.

Target market: Leisure travelers marketed through affiliated organizations via travel clubs, coupon books, and newsletters.

Senior Citizens Program: A 25 percent off applicable room rates (rack) available on a limited space basis; proof of age 60 or older or membership ID from seniors' association.

Target Market: Leisure travelers, 60 years of age or older. These promotions are based on Corona Inn's new sales promotions for 1993 (Exhibit III-A). All promotions have a commission policy of 10 percent to travel agents, and third party (airline) booking fees apply.

Market Share and Sales: There are 59 first-class full-service hotels and 12,264 rooms as of 1992 located in Metropolitan San Antonio. Five of these are located in the eastern area, totaling 608 rooms. The forecast for 1994 states that there will be an increase of 400 first-class/full-service rooms in the total San Antonio area (Exhibit II-B). The hotel will take up 1/60 of the hotel market and 1/127 of the room market (based on a 100-room hotel and an industry of 12,700 rooms).

The customer bases for sales will be as follows:

      Commercial, 35 percent

      Group, 12 percent

      Tourist, 47 percent

      Other, 6 percent

      Total: 100 percent

These customer bases will not change too much over the years. They will generally stay the same or change very little.

The growth of sales will increase with the industry. This growth rate will include occupancy rate growth of 2 percent per year and room rate growth of 4 percent per year. The total increase in demand averages 10 percent. The hotel will base its growth rate on an average of 6 percent per year, about the same as the inflation rate. See the market analysis chart (Exhibit III-B) to show the growth rate of revenue.

IV. Management Analysis

Management Objectives: Responsibility of management is to:

1. Develop marketing programs that will increase room sales, particularly in periods of low occupancy.

2. Create favorable market awareness in the minds of the public by providing friendly service, personal attention, and clean, quality accommodations at a reasonable price.

3. Be aware of economic, business, and social changes that affect industry travel patterns and profits.

Management Team:

Administrative Positions: There will be three administrative positions in the startup of this company. They will include the owner, Jerry Knife, as the chief financial officer and purchasing agent; Carrie Snow as the sales and marketing manager and the human resource director; and June Knife as the guest service and conference service manager. Other managers will consist of a top person in each department to oversee the daily operations in the lounge, housekeeping, front desk, maintenance, and room service. Accounting and legal operations will be provided by outside services.

All the administrative officers and managers from each department will conduct weekly (or as needed) meetings. Each department will have its own weekly meeting conducted by the manager of the department, then each week all department and administrative heads will meet to discuss what is happening in each department. Everyone will listen to others' suggestions and have an influence on the final decisions.

Functions of Key Personnel: The job duties will be broken up according to departments.

Job Descriptions: The hotel will have 18 to 22 employees, depending on season. The departments and job duties are as follows:

Owner, Chief Financial Officer, and Purchasing Agent: Jerry Knife. Duties include making the final decisions for management and operations; in charge of paying debts and collecting accounts receivable; dealing with investors; purchasing hotel supplies, lounge swipes, and vending.

Sales and Marketing Manager, Human Resource Director: Carrie Snow (see resume). Duties include selling guestrooms to business travelers, conventions, vacationers, and setting promotions. Placing ads and promotions for the hotel rooms, lounge, meeting rooms, and special functions in the hotel. Hiring employees, managing employees, and overseeing the general day-to-day operations of the hotel. Department managers will come to her to discuss department operations, problems, and decisions.

Guest Service and Conference Service Manager: June Knife. Duties include attending to guests' needs, complaints, and requests when above the manager's responsibilities. Setting up conference meetings and the food and beverage for the meetings.

Legal and Accounting: All accounting duties will be performed by a Certified Public Accountant. Duties include monthly financial statements, cash flow analysis, profit-and-loss statements, and tax preparation. A lawyer will be contacted when the need arises.

Front Desk Manager: The front desk manager will also be a front desk clerk. The manager will work Monday through Friday, 7 a.m. to 3 p.m., and will tend to the front desk duties. (See job descriptions in Company Analysis.) He or she will also conduct department meetings, attend management meetings, attend to any employee problems or discussions.

Housekeeping Manager: The manager of the housekeeping department will schedule employees, order supplies, maintain equipment, inspect cleanings, attend meetings, and attend to employee matters.

Bar Manager: The bar manager will schedule employees, hire bar personnel, order liquor and bar supplies, attend meetings, attend to customer complaints, etc., and tend the bar during the day hours.

Room Service Manager: Because the room service manager's job is small, he or she will be an assistant to June Knife, the Conference service and Guest Service Manager. The room service manager is in charge only of the kitchen menu, ordering of food, preparation of food, and the scheduling of the small number of kitchen cooks. He or she will work directly with June to make and prepare the menus for the banquets. June will be in charge of the meeting facilities and their operations.

Manpower Milestones: There will be about 22 employees, depending on the season. All administrative positions will remain the same, but line positions may increase in the years to come. After one year, more sales, banquet, and housekeeping personnel may be needed to compensate for the added occupancy once the hotel has an established name and clientele.

V. Strategic Planning Analysis

Long-Term Goals:

The management of the Alamo Park Hotel plans to keep the hotel at 100 rooms. The size of the bar, meeting rooms, etc., will all be kept the same for at least 5 to 10 years after the opening. The only restructuring of the hotel will be remodeling on a frequent basis of every 7 to 9 years. The reason the hotel will not be expanded is that the owners are planning on this hotel as a first of many properties. They will be in the hotel business as an investment opportunity and this first hotel will be a starting block.

The owner, Jerry Knife, and his daughter, Carrie Snow, will start up the hotel and manage and operate for a period of 5 to 10 years. At that time Jerry will be approximately 57 years old and ready to retire by either selling the business to an outside party or selling his shares to Carrie. She will be around 33 years old at this time.

Carrie's long-term goals for the company are to expand into new hotel ventures. She plans to take over full ownership of the Alamo Park Hotel 10 years after its opening. She then wants to hire a reliable general manager who will manage and operate the hotel under her ownership. Her next plan is to start up a multimillion-dollar resort hotel either in El Paso or Houston (where new development is occurring in the 1990s). Jerry Knife will help with the financing and development of this venture, but the principal owner will be Carrie Snow. Owning these two hotels will be Carrie's long-term goal for the next 25 years. Thereafter, she may decide to sell the Alamo Park Hotel to devote all of her time to the resort. The specific goals for the Alamo Park Hotel are as follows:

1. To raise room rates from startup rates by 10 percent within two years, not including the 4 percent increase due to inflation each year.

2. To have a good and reliable staff to give the guests excellent service. To have enough employees to fulfill the guests' needs in a timely and efficient manner.

3. To refurbish the hotel periodically to keep up with the changing trends in the industry.

4. To offer new services and new technology to the guests and the employees.

5. To increase the occupancy rates over the industry competition and industry growth rate of 2 percent per year.

6. To increase overall sales in all departments (rooms, lounge, meeting rooms) 10 percent per year.

7. To offer a complete benefits package to all full-time employees after the first year of operation.

8. To increase salaries 16 percent per year to existing employees: 10 percent raise and 6 percent to keep up with inflation.

Milestone Schedule: The month-by-month schedule shows when and how long it will take for the critical deadlines and essential activities to be completed (see Milestone Schedule, Exhibit V-A).

Plan Assumptions: Expected external conditions under which the hotel will execute its plan.

Economy: The economy is currently in a recessionary period. Inflation rates are increasing 5 percent to 6 percent per year and hotel rates only 4 percent per year. The service industry and wage rates are increasing, and minimum wage has increased to $4.25 per hour.

Industry: Industry trends are discussed in detail in the industry analysis.

Market: Market trends are discussed in detail in the market analysis.

Outside Influences: There are no government regulations that will be a threat to the hotel. All government regulations will be adhered to, due to the outstanding service and quality of the hotel.

Red Flag: Problems that will need to be addressed or reexamined in the future:

1. Ability to raise the investment capital of the hotel.

2. Consideration of buying an existing hotel.

3. Market research on the specific location of existing Katy Highway and Interstate 10.

4. Market research on specific occupancy rates of this hotel and hotel location.

5. Consideration of what franchise will accept the Alamo Park Hotel and what franchise company the hotel wishes to operate under.

6. Reexamination of the tourist industry in San Antonio.

7. Economic conditions affecting the lodging industry.

Company Strengths to Exploit:

Franchise: Using the West Hotel franchisor offers many advantages to the Alamo Park Hotel. By taking advantage of all the membership benefits (company analysis), the hotel will receive:

1. A recognizable name with which to draw in more customers.

2. A national reservation system to receive more customers from all over the world.

3. Lower costs for insurance, supplies, membership fees, advertising and training programs.

4. Ability to independently own hotel while using the West Hotel name.

Marketing: The strong marketing program of the hotel will provide increased sales due to:

1. Advertising: Yellow Pages, newspapers, publicity, shoppers, and magazines.

2. An increased number of salespersons to sell the facilities to businesses, groups, and organizations.

3. Sales promotions offered to promote and maintain competitive sales of the hotel.

Finance: The hotel plans to incorporate to raise sufficient capital to finance the venture. The hotel plans to raise more than the projected amount of money to cover any un-planned or emergency expenses.

Purchasing: The land will be purchased during a recession of real estate property. The hotel will be designed and built by a business partner and associate of Jerry Knife. This will ensure fair building costs because he will be given shares in the company along with money for his services. Supplies for the hotel can be purchased at lower costs from the West Hotel franchisor.

Location: The hotel location will be in a high-traffic area, which can exploit awareness and hotel and sign visibility.

Management: The administration will be mostly family for at least the first year, so they can assist each other without fear of making mistakes.

Employee Expansion: The hotel will be adding administrative positions and line employees. This will provide customers with added service and a reason to return.

Exhibits

Author's Note

List all supporting documentation in the appendix / exhibit section as noted and referenced throughout your business plan.

Remember, this information should be clearly and neatly presented so the reader of your business plan can easily reference and understand the data being provided.

A Business Plan For:

Al's Sandwich Shop

January 1, 1992

Table of Contents

Page

1. Identifying Information about Business

Al's Sandwich Shop maintains its principal business address at 777 Bob Street, Phoenix, AZ 85032. Pursuant to the Franchise Agreement, Al's Sandwich Shop authorizes its Franchisees to operate sandwich restaurants under the name "Al's Sandwich Shop." The Franchisee is also authorized to use the Al's Sandwich Shop trademarks, service marks, trade names, advertising, or other commercial symbols.

Franchisor is currently seeking name and registration approval for the service mark Al's Sandwich Shop. Franchisor is not aware of any current infringing uses of the marks stated above, nor is any litigation pending with respect to these marks. Should service mark registration be denied for any reason, Franchisor reserves right to apply any name to the franchise it so chooses and Franchisee agrees to comply with use and display of any such name.

2. Business Experience of Franchisor's Directors and Executive Officers

A. Al Smith—President

Mr. Smith has been in the sandwich business since 1970. Prior to that he worked for Greyhound Bus Lines. Investing in other businesses has been a strong interest for Mr. Smith. In 1970 Mr. Smith purchased John's Sandwich Shop name and recipe from John Jones who operated John's Sandwich Shop for about 15 years in the Phoenix area of Maricopa County.

In 1970 Mr. Smith opened the Phoenix location, and has since opened other locations.

B. Bob Smith—Vice President

Mr. Smith entered the sandwich business in 1965, working and training with his uncle. He has developed an excellent business background and a strong management knowledge, working at all levels of Al's Sandwich Shop business. He graduated from Phoenix High School in 1960. Mr. Smith has since operated the Phoenix location along with 2 other full-time managers and 4 part-time managers. He supervises the additional Al's Sandwich Shop locations under corporate control. Mr. Smith is also training coordinator for franchise and management trainees. He has also been working on obtaining his Master's degree at Arizona State University.

3. Business Experience of the Franchisor

The Franchisor, Al's Sandwich Shop, was incorporated in January 1970 in Maricopa County, Arizona. Prior to the date of incorporation, the principals owned and operated 3 Al's Sandwich Shops, beginning in 1970 with the original Al's Sandwich Shop located in Phoenix, Arizona. The name *Al's Sandwich Shop* had been in existence for nearly 22 years in the area, and the rights to this name were purchased by Mr. Smith in 1970. Since the Franchisor's incorporation, it has been developing its franchise program and is now currently offering franchises for the first time. Neither the Franchisor nor its principals have offered, nor do they now offer, franchises in any other business. Neither Franchisor nor its parent company has previously offered franchises in any other business nor do they at the current time.

4. Litigation History

Neither Franchisor nor any individuals identified in Section 2 of this disclosure document have at any time during the previous seven fiscal years been convicted of a felony or pleaded *no lo contendere* to a felony charge involving fraud, embezzlement, fraudulent conversion, misappropriation of property, or restraint of trade.

Neither Franchisor nor any individuals identified in Section 2 of this disclosure document have at any time during the previous seven fiscal years been held liable in a civil action resulting in a final judgment or have settled out of court any civil action, or are currently a party to any civil action involving allegations of fraud, embezzlement, fraudulent conversion, misappropriation of property, or restraint of trade brought by a present or former Franchisee or Franchisees or that involves or involved the franchise relationship.

Franchisor is not subject to any currently effective state or federal agency or court injunction or restrictive order, nor is it a party to a proceeding currently pending in which such an order is sought, relating to or affecting franchise activities or the Franchisor-Franchisee relationship, or involving fraud, embezzlement, fraudulent conversion, misappropriation of property, or restraint of trade.

5. Bankruptcy History

Neither Franchisor nor any individuals identified in Section 2 of this disclosure document have filed for bankruptcy, been adjudged bankrupt, reorganized due to insolvency, or been a principal, director, executive officer, or partner of any other person or company that has so filed or was so adjudged or reorganized during or within 1 year after the period that such person held such position with such other person or company.

6. Description of Franchise

The Franchisor develops, operates, trains, and authorizes others to operate sandwich restaurants specializing in sub-sandwiches and pocket sandwiches to company specifications. The concept of Al's Sandwich Shop is to market delicious sandwiches, made with quality ingredients and a unique blend of spices, to customers who may eat in or take the product home.

Franchisees also derive income from sales of products such as breadsticks, salads, and soft drinks. Al's Sandwich Shop is approximately 3000 sq. ft. in size and has a seating area of approximately 85 seats. An ideal location is an end unit in a strip shopping center which can be set up with drive-through window. Typically 50 percent or more of the business is with "takeout" customers, who may purchase sandwiches to go or may purchase pocket-sandwiches either inside the restaurant or from the drive-through window. Al's Sandwich Shop does not deliver to homes and normally requires 3 full-time employees and 5 part-time employees.

Sales will be to the general public who frequent the retail area and to others who become aware of the store through advertising, etc. The Franchisee is not restricted in the clients with whom it may do business.

7. Initial Funds Required

Franchisee is required to make the following nonrefundable initial payments to the persons identified*:

Item	Amount	To Whom Paid	Time of Payment
Initial Franchise Fee	$16,000	Franchisor	At signing of Franchise Agreement
Signs, Fixtures, Equipment	$65,000	Purveyors	90 days before scheduled date of opening
Food Inventory/ Packaging Supplies	$10,000	Franchisor	90 days before scheduled date of opening
Lease Deposits, First Month's Rent	From $5,000 to $9,000	Landlord	At signing of lease
Leasehold	$35,000	Contractors	As necessary during construction beginning 60 days before opening
Grand Opening Advertising	$2,200	Franchisor	30 days prior to opening
Printing/Supplies	$600	Franchisor	30 days prior to opening
Insurance, Licenses	$2,200	Insurance, Utility Companies, Government	Two weeks before opening
Total	$136,000 –$140,000		

8. Recurring Funds Required

Advertising Fees

Franchisee shall be required to pay 4 percent of monthly gross sales to Franchisor or Franchisor's approved advertising agency with payments due on the first day of each month. Advertising fees shall be utilized by Franchisor to purchase advertising on behalf of Franchisee within Franchisee's regional area or as determined by Franchisor. Typical media purchased will include local newspapers, direct mail coupons, and handouts. Franchisor has final approval on all ad copy and promotional campaigns initiated by Franchisee, which must be approved in advance by Franchisor. Franchisor will have the authority to preclude Franchisee from utilizing media that overlap the territory of another franchisee.

Fixed Monthly Expenses

Franchisee should expect $2,000 recurring monthly fixed costs such as rent, estimated to be in the range of $750 to $2,000; utilities, estimated in amounts ranging from $500 to $1,300; inventory purchases, estimated in amounts ranging from $6,000 to $11,000; payroll, estimated

* All amounts other than initial franchise fee are approximate and represent best estimates of beginning expenditures. Costs may vary based on size of store, amount of inventory, etc. Capital requirements may be adjusted as necessary but will not exceed those listed herein without approval from Franchisee. A Franchisee may require $35,000 or more in additional working capital for the first 12 months to cover operating costs. *Note:* Franchisee should also have adequate funds available to cover living expenses in addition to adequate operating capital. The amount necessary shall vary according to each Franchisee's personal needs, mode, and source of living.

in amounts ranging from $4,500 to $7,000; telephone, estimated in amounts ranging from $50 to $250; and supplies, estimated in amounts ranging from $40 to $150.

Recurring Expenses

Franchisee may anticipate the following recurring expenses*:

Item	Amount	To Whom Paid	How Often
Store Rent	$750 to $2,000	Landlord	Monthly
Insurance	$1,000 to $2,000	Agent	Yearly
Utilities	$500 to $1,300	Utility Co.	Monthly
Telephone	$50 to $250	Telephone Co.	Monthly
Supplies	$40 to $150	Purveyors	Monthly
Inventory	$6,000 to $11,000 (24% of gross)	Franchisor	Monthly
Payroll/Taxes	$4,500 to $7,000	Employees	Monthly

9. Affiliated Persons the Franchisee Is Required or Advised to Do Business with

Franchisor does not require Franchisee to do business with any person(s) affiliated with the Franchisor. However, Al's Sandwich Shop will recommend suppliers because of the selection and service available through these suppliers.

10. Obligations to Purchase

To maintain the goodwill and prestige of the business and to maintain uniformly high levels of quality service and products sold through Franchise outlets, Franchisee is required to purchase all products related to Al's Sandwich Shop system of conducting business from Al's Sandwich Shop of Phoenix, Arizona. Franchisee may purchase goods not available from Al's Sandwich Shop from other suppliers, provided those suppliers meet the specifications of the Franchisor and are approved in writing, in advance, by Franchisor. Franchisee will purchase required equipment from any supplier, provided that supplier meets the specifications of the Franchisor and is approved in advance and in writing by Franchisor. Initial inventory will include all goods and commodities required to open and operate Al's Sandwich Shop according to the Al's Sandwich Shop system, including dough, cheese, special patented sauces, herbs, and spices. Startup equipment will include oven, mixer, walk-in refrigerator, counter, tables, and chairs.

Franchisor may require Franchisee to modify equipment, fixtures, and inventory from time to time, and Franchisee will be expected to comply with such modifications within 12 months from the date of notification of modifications.

*The amounts and frequency of payments are best estimates of continuing costs and will vary from one franchise to the next, depending on volume of business, amounts ordered and needed for replacement, location of business, regional variations, etc.

11. Revenues Received by the Franchisor in Consideration of Purchases by Franchisee

The Franchisor will derive revenue from the sale/distribution of products purchased by Franchisee from Al's Sandwich Shop.

12. Financing Arrangements

The Franchisor does not provide financing to Franchisee, but will provide its assistance to Franchisee in obtaining financing. The Franchisor receives no payment from any person offering financing, or arranging for the placement of financing, for a prospective Franchisee. Franchisee is responsible for obtaining financing from third-party sources in any amounts necessary to fulfill capital requirements to open an Al's Sandwich Shop.

13. Restriction of Sales

The Al's Sandwich Shop Franchise Agreement provides that the Franchisee is precluded from offering any products or services not specifically approved in advance by Franchisor. A violation of this restriction may result in termination of the franchise relationship. This requirement has been imposed to ensure uniformity in services and product quality among all Al's Sandwich Shop franchises.

The Franchisee is not limited to the customers it may sell to, but is restricted to sales from the franchise location and may not, without explicit authorization of the Franchisor, open or operate another location.

A Franchisee is not granted an exclusive area. The Franchisor does not promise or grant any Franchisee the right to operate his or her business on an exclusive or partially exclusive basis in any city, town, township, or area of a state. Although the policy of the Franchisor to date has been to appoint only a limited number of Franchisees per state, each within a distinct market area, the Franchisor makes no guarantees, warranties, or representations that a Franchisee will not be located within the specific geographic proximity of another Franchisee. Any representations to the contrary cannot and must not be considered valid, since these types of representations cannot and will not be honored by the Franchisor. On the other hand, the Franchisee is not restricted as to area in which it may solicit customers. Franchisor assigns franchises at its own discretion and reserves the right to assign as many franchises as are necessary to fulfill the business potential of any geographic area.

14. Personal Participation Required of the Franchisee in the Operation of the Franchise

Franchisor does not require the Franchisee or, in the case of a corporation, any person affiliated with the Franchisee to participate personally in the direct operation of the Franchise.

15. Termination, Cancellation, and Renewal of the Franchise

By Franchisee

The initial term of the Franchise Agreement is for 10 years. At the expiration of the initial Agreement, and if the Franchisee is not in default of the terms of the agreement, the Franchisee shall have the right to renew the Agreement for continuing 10 year terms by executing the then-current standard Franchise Agreement. The Agreement in effect at the renewal period may differ from that presently used by Franchisor. If the Franchisee desires to renew the Franchise Agreement, he must give notice to Franchisor not less than 6 months nor more than 1 year prior to the expiration of the initial Franchise Agreement. In the event that the Franchisee has not elected to renew the Franchise Agreement then in effect, this agreement shall automatically terminate at the end of the franchise term without any further action by either party. Neither the Franchise Agreement nor the relationship between the parties may be modified during the term of the Agreement except in writing and signed by both parties. Should the Franchisee desire to renew the Franchise Agreement, he or she must not be in default under any of the provisions of the then-existing Franchise Agreement. If Franchisee desires, he or she may sell the Franchise. Franchisee may transfer the Franchise Agreement under the following terms and conditions:

a. Franchisee shall give at least 30 days prior written notice of Franchisee's intention to effect any such transfer.

b. Franchisor approves the buyer in writing; such approvals will not be unreasonably withheld.

c. Franchisee pays to Franchisor all monies due prior to completion of the sale.

d. Buyer agrees to complete the training program required by Franchisor and to pay the expenses as specified in Section 18.

e. Buyer signs a current Franchise Agreement, and Buyer will not be required to pay an "Initial Franchise Fee."

f. Franchisor receives the sum of $2,500 to cover the Franchisor's expenses in connection with the transfer.

g. Franchisee grants to Franchisor a "First Right of Refusal" in which Franchisor may match the buyer's offer and purchase the business; and Franchisee by the Franchise Agreement will offer a "First Right of Refusal" to Franchisor, which allows 30 days for Franchisor to match the assignee's offer and notify Franchisee of intent to purchase the franchise. Franchisee shall provide, in written form, the offer of the proposed assignee for Franchisor's review. Same shall be done *in writing* and shall be sent *certified mail, return receipt requested.* Franchisor may then purchase the franchise upon the same terms and conditions offered by the proposed assignee. Failure of Franchisor to exercise this right within 30 days following receipt of the written offer shall thereafter permit Franchisee to proceed with the sale to the proposed assignee. Any change in the terms between the proposed assignee and the Franchisee shall be considered a new offer that must be submitted to the Franchisor subject to the procedures set forth herein. In the event Franchisor wishes to exercise his right of first refusal, Franchisor shall notify the Franchisee *in writing, certified mail, return receipt requested,* or by in-person notification.

h. In the event of the death or incapacity of the Franchisee this Franchise Agreement shall be assigned to the Franchisee's heirs, who would be required to complete the Franchisor's then-current training program at the costs specified in Section 18.

By Franchisor

Franchisor may terminate the Franchise Agreement if Franchisee does not abide by all the terms and conditions of the Franchise Agreement, and if in default, does not correct same within 15 days of written notification by Franchisor. The Franchisor will also terminate the

Franchisee in the event that the Franchisee declares bankruptcy, becomes insolvent, or appoints a receiver for any portion of his property. Upon termination of the Agreement, Franchisee shall cease to be a Franchisee and will:

    i.   Promptly pay Franchisor all monies due.

    j.   Immediately stop using all Franchisor's signs, names, logos, marks, colors, telephone listings, advertising, and all other materials, systems, and methods identified with Franchisor.

It should be noted that a covenant not to compete is part of the Franchise Agreement and prohibits a Franchisee from engaging in any retail sandwich business during the term of the Agreement.

Covenant of Nondisclosure

The Franchisee, in the course of association with Al's Sandwich Shop, will obtain knowledge of valuable information, trade secrets, marketing methods, business affairs, recipes, and methods of doing business. The Franchise Agreement will require that all information transferred from Franchisor to Franchisee be considered strictly confidential and that Franchisee shall not, directly or indirectly, make available to any person, firm, corporation, or association such confidential information as described in this paragraph without the specific written consent of the Franchisor. This covenant of nondisclosure extends only to that information and those methods of doing business that are not known by independent third parties. A Franchisee will agree not to circumvent, bypass, or obviate the rights of the Franchisor by doing business directly with any supplier to whom Franchisee has been introduced by Franchisor without the advance written consent of the Franchisor. Failure to comply with this provision will be grounds for immediate termination of the Franchise Agreement.

16. Statistical Information Concerning the Number of Franchises (and Company-Owned Outlets)

With respect to the Franchisor and as to the particular names and business being offered, the following statistical information is offered:

    a.   2 franchises were in operation at the end of the preceding fiscal year.

    b.   1 company-owned outlet was operated at the end of the preceding fiscal year; the company as of this date has awarded 2 franchises.

    c.   Names, addresses of Franchisees, and telephone numbers of Franchise units.

    d.   No franchises were voluntarily terminated or not renewed by Franchisees within or at the conclusion of the term of the Franchise Agreement, during the preceding fiscal year.

    e.   No franchises were reacquired by purchase by the Franchisor during the term of the Franchise Agreement, and upon the conclusion of the term of the Franchise Agreement, during the preceding fiscal year.

    f.   No franchises were otherwise reacquired by the Franchisor during the term of the Franchise Agreement, and upon the conclusions of the term of the Franchise Agreement, during the preceding fiscal year.

    g.   No franchises were refused renewal of the Franchise Agreement or other agreements relating to the franchise during the preceding fiscal year by the Franchisor.

h. No franchises were canceled or terminated by Franchisor during the term of the Franchise Agreement, and upon conclusion of the term of the Franchise Agreement, during the preceding fiscal year.

17. Site Selection

The Franchise Agreement provides that the Franchisee is precluded from establishing a Franchise in a territory not specifically approved by the Franchisor. The site selection process is assisted by the Franchisor and must be approved by the Franchisor and the Franchisee.

The proposed location for the Franchisee's Al's Sandwich Shop and the terms of the lease, sublease, or other document pursuant to which it is acquired must be approved in writing by Franchisor prior to the Franchisee entering into the lease, sublease, or other agreement pursuant to which the Franchisee is given the right to use the premises.

The lapse of time between the signing of the Franchise Agreement or the agreements relating to the franchise and commencement of the Franchisee's business is best estimated by the Franchisor to be 3 to 6 months. Obtaining zoning permits, variances, etc., will be the responsibility of Franchisee, should such permits not be in place or not be handled by landlord. Although the Franchisor does provide substantial site location assistance, the ultimate responsibility for securing a location/lease is that of the Franchisee. Franchisee may not hold the Franchisor responsible for failure to secure a location/lease. In any event Franchisee shall be required to open his or her business no later than 12 months after the signing of the Franchise Agreement. If the franchise unit has not been opened within 12 months, the Franchisor may, at its sole discretion, elect to terminate this agreement, and return to Franchisee the franchise fee minus reasonable expenses incurred in assisting the Franchisee over that time period. The Franchisor assists the Franchisee in site locating and lease negotiation but does not warrant any amount of earnings in association with any specific site.

The signing of the Franchise Agreement does not restrict Franchisor from assigning other applicants' rights to open Al's Sandwich Shop within the general geographic area designated in the Franchise Agreement. The geographic area designation and the signing of the Franchise Agreement simply reserves space for one franchise unit for the Franchisee within the general geographic area selected by Franchisee and permits the Franchisee to go forward with attempting to locate a site for the Franchisee's store within the designated area. Other Franchisees of Franchisor may have the right to open Al's Sandwich Shops within the same geographic area as the Franchisee. The first Franchisee to sign a lease for a site acceptable to Franchisor will be allowed to open that store. Neither the date of the receipt of franchise deposit by franchisor, the date the application is approved by Franchisor, the date of the signing of the Franchise Agreement, nor any other event gives any Franchisee exclusive rights, priority, or other preferences in locating a store site or in connection with the timing of the opening of the Franchisee's Al's Sandwich Shop. Should Franchisor present to the Franchisee a prospective store location within the geographic area approved for the Franchisee, Franchisor is free to offer the location to other Franchisees until such time as Franchisee has signed a lease or option to lease drafted by the landlord specific to the site presented to Franchisee.

18. Training Programs

A 12-day training program for Franchisees will be conducted at the Corporate Headquarters, and continuing support is provided for Franchisees during the grand opening at the franchise location. Al's Sandwich Shop requires all new Franchisees to complete the training program prior to opening the business. The Franchisee may designate a manager of the business to attend and complete the training program in lieu of the Franchisee's personally attending.

Instruction will be given by Al Smith and/or his authorized representatives. Instruction will cover but not be limited to management and training in dough preparation, special patented sauce preparation, pie making, oven operation, operation, inventory control, advertising, accounting, displays, employee relations, basic techniques of management, and other skills. Franchisee shall be responsible for all transportation, meals, and living expenses incurred in attending the program. A night in a hotel in the Phoenix, Arizona, area will require approximately $50 to $55 in costs. The Franchisee should expect to spend approximately $15 to $20 per day for meals.

Franchisee agrees to attend any and all pre-opening meetings required by Franchisor in Franchisee's local area. Schedules and duration of training visits to Franchisee's business location will be determined at Franchisor's sole discretion.

19. Public Figure Involvement in the Franchise

The name of a public figure is not used in connection with a recommendation to purchase this franchise, nor as a part of the name of the franchise operation. No public figure is involved with the management of the Franchisor.

20. Financial Information Concerning the Franchisor

A financial statement is attached.

Franchise Agreement

Agreement made this_____day of _____, 19   , by Al's Sandwich Shop under the laws of the State of Arizona located at 777 Bob Street, Phoenix, AZ 85032 (hereinafter called

Franchisor) and _____

whose principal address is: _____

(hereinafter called Franchisee) as follows:

Recitals

Franchisor is the owner of the service mark Al's Sandwich Shop and is the Franchisor and operator of sandwich restaurants specializing in sub-sandwich and pocket sandwiches. Franchisor has developed valuable products, formats, procedures, and practices used in the operation of those restaurants in which the Franchisee will receive complete training. The Franchisee is hereby granted the right to use the Al's Sandwich Shop name and the marks and designs associated therewith. Franchisor is developing a chain of units bearing the Franchise name and which are designed, built, decorated, and operated in accordance with Franchisor's requirements and format in order to create and maintain a unique image and appeal to the public. In this regard, Franchisor must maintain control over the format, design, decor, equipping, fixturing, stocking, sales practices and procedures, advertising and promotion of the operation of Al's Sandwich Shops.

All trademarks, trade names, service marks, logotypes, and other commercial symbols as well as processes, trade secrets, trade practices, copyrights, patents, manuals, forms, formats, advertising and promotional material and practices, operating practices and procedures, training materials, goodwill, and all other items, tangible or intangible, used presently or in the future in connection with this franchise and with Al's Sandwich Shop units are referred to in this Franchise Agreement as *"the assets"* and shall remain the property of Franchisor.

1. Grant of Franchisee

Upon payment of the "Initial Franchise Fee" described in Appendix A, attached to and made part of this Agreement, as well as the other fees set forth therein, Franchisee shall have the right, subject to the terms and conditions of this Agreement, to operate an Al's Sandwich Shop (the Franchise).

2. Term

This agreement is for an initial term of ten (10) years. If Franchisee is not then in default, Franchisee shall have the right to renew this Agreement for additional ten (10) year consecutive terms. Renewal must be executed in writing and signed at least six (6) months but not more than one (1) year prior to expiration of each term. Renewal shall be accomplished by signing the Franchisor's then current Franchise Agreement. At the time of renewal, there shall be no additional "Initial Franchise Fee" payable by current Franchisee. If, at least six (6) months before the expiration of any term, Franchisee has not executed Franchisor's then current Franchise Agreement, the existing Agreement shall automatically terminate as its own conclusion without the need for any further writing between the parties.

3. Territory

Franchisee is awarded the right to operate the Franchise from within the following general marketing area and no other, the specific restaurant location to be within said territory.

_____

_____

The address of the restaurant location shall be inserted herein upon Franchisee signing a lease for said location.

A Franchisee is not granted an exclusive area. The Franchisor, does not promise or grant any franchisee the right to operate their business on an exclusive or partially exclusive basis in any city, town, township, or area of a state. Although the policy of the Franchisor to date has been to appoint only a limited number of franchisees per state, each within a distinct market area, the Franchisor makes no guarantees, warranties, or representations that a franchisee will not be located within a specific geographic proximity of another franchisee. Any representations to the contrary must not be considered valid since these types of representations cannot and will not be honored by the Franchisor. On the other hand, the Franchisee is not restricted as to area in which it may solicit customers. Franchisor assigns franchises at its own discretion and reserves the right to assign as many franchises as are necessary to fulfill the business potential of any geographic area.

Franchisee agrees to open his franchise unit no later than twelve (12) months following the date of this agreement except for delays beyond the control of Franchisee. In the event same is not opened within said time, Franchisor, at its sole discretion, may elect to terminate this agreement and return to Franchisee his Franchise fee, minus reasonable expenses incurred in assisting the franchisee over the same time period. Franchisor shall then be free to assume the lease for the location in question and either operate or resell same. In the event Franchisor elects to exercise this option, Franchisee's sole entitlement shall be the refund of this franchise fee.

The proposed location for the Franchisee's Al Sandwich Shop and the terms of the lease, sublease, or other document pursuant to which the location is acquired must be approved in writing by Franchisor prior to the Franchisee entering into the lease, sublease, or other agreement pursuant to which the Franchisee is given the right to use the premises. Approval of the lease and location are not to be considered guarantee of success. Franchisee is responsible to satisfy himself as to the choice of the location. Approval by the Franchisor is only to the fact that the location will satisfactorily accommodate Al's Sandwich Shop.

Franchisee understands and agrees that although the Franchisor does offer site location assistance, the representatives or agents of the Franchisor have represented to the Franchisee that the ultimate responsibility for securing and maintaining retail leases or locations for the Franchisee's business is the sole responsibility of the Franchisee; and that neither Al's Sandwich Shop nor its representatives or agents can be held responsible for the failure of the Franchisee to secure a retail location/lease in his own behalf. Franchisee also understands that any retail lease secured through the direct efforts of the Franchisor, carries no representation or warrant of earnings on the part of the Franchisor.

4. Obligations of Franchisor

In return for payment of the franchise fee and so long as no default by Franchisee has occurred, the Franchisor shall provide, at times and in methods and manners as determined by Franchisor in its discretion, the following services to the Franchisee:

    a.   Use of the names, marks, logos and copyrighted materials of the Franchisor for the duration of this agreement;

b.   Operations Manual;

c.   Training at Franchisor's location;

d.   Lease negotiation and guidelines;

e.   Restaurant layout and equipment selection, pre-opening assistance;

f.   Trade and operating procedures and methods (which are to be maintained confidential and secret by the Franchisee);

g.   Ongoing telephone support and assistance;

h.   Continuing research and development;

i.   Marketing assistance;

j.   Regional advertising program(s) (utilizing funds provided by Franchisees);

k.   Making available printing and supplies.

5. Advertising Fees

Franchisee shall pay 4% of his monthly gross sales to Franchisor or Franchisor's approved advertising agency with payments due on the first day of each month. Late charges will be assessed for each day for which the advertising fee is late beyond the due date in the amount of ten dollars per day or 5% per day of the advertising fee due. Franchisor shall collect the late fee which is greater and will advise Franchisee which sum is due. Failure of the Franchisee to pay the late fee may be grounds for termination of this Agreement. Franchisee shall be considered in default of this agreement should payment of this advertising fee not be received ten days after the date due. The Company makes no guarantees and does not insure that any particular Franchisee will benefit directly or pro-rate from its contributions to the Al's Sandwich Shop Corporate Advertising Fund.

Franchisee agrees to conduct all advertising and promotional activities in accordance with the requirements of Franchisor, as reflected in its directives or as otherwise communicated to Franchisee. Franchisor has final approval on all ad copy and promotional campaigns initiated by Franchisee which must be approved in writing, in advance by Franchisor. Failure by Franchisee to fulfill advertising requirements of Franchisor or to submit advertising copy prior to its use shall constitute a violation of this agreement and be grounds for immediate termination as no cure of this breach is possible. It is agreed and understood that all service marks and trademarks are the property of the Franchisor and that, therefore the Franchisor must control all use of such marks. Franchisor will have the authority to preclude franchisee from utilizing media which overlap on the territory of another franchisee or to require franchisees with adjoining or near territories to cooperate in their advertising efforts/programs.

6. Standardization of Franchisee's Organization

In order to promote uniformity and excellence of products and services within the franchised system, Franchisee agrees to operate its franchise in accordance with the following standard terms and conditions:

A.   Standard Product Line: Franchisee agrees to sell only those items or products specified by Franchisor and in the manner and method specified by Franchisor. In the event that Franchisor wishes to expand or modify the products or services offered for sale within the system, upon written notice from Franchisor, Franchisee agrees to expand or modify the products or services offered for sale and agrees to acquire the equipment necessary for such change or modification within one hundred eighty (180) days of written notification by Franchisor. To maintain standardization and high quality of the Al's Sandwich Shop product, the Franchisee agrees to purchase all products and supplies from the Franchisor. Violation of this provision, and all provisions requiring pre-approval by Franchisor of advertising, constitutes grounds for immediate termination as Franchisee is incapable of curing such a default.

B. Standard Equipment and Supplies: Franchisee agrees to operate the franchise in accordance with standards established by Franchisor, to include, but not limited to, facility cleanliness and maintenance, hours of operation, signs, equipment, replaceable supplies and in compliance with all applicable Federal, State and local laws, ordinances and regulations. To promote uniformity throughout the system, Franchisee agrees to use only those displays, signs, equipment and products and services approved in advance and in writing by Franchisor.

All required equipment must be purchased by Franchisee from any source so long as said equipment meets current standards and specifications of Franchisor, and is in compliance with all applicable Federal, State and local laws and health codes. The supplier of said equipment shall be approved in advance and in writing by Franchisor, which approval shall not be unreasonably withheld.

C. Standard Service: Franchisee agrees to maintain the quality of service in his franchise in accordance with the high standards established by Franchisor and in compliance with all applicable Federal, State and local laws, ordinances and regulations.

D. Standard Franchise Center: Franchisee agrees to abide by Franchisor's standards of maintenance and cleanliness and to maintain Al's Sandwich Shop in good condition and with a clean and neat appearance. Franchisee shall not undertake any alterations, modifications, or additions to Al's Sandwich Shop which would materially alter its appearance or function without the prior written consent from Franchisor. Failure to give written approval within 45 days after receipt of notice from Franchisee, which notice shall be sent certified mail, return receipt requested, shall constitute approval of the proposed plans. Routine repairs shall not require such approval of Franchisor.

E. Standard Business Weeks, Hours, Etc.: Franchisee shall maintain sufficient inventory, supplies, and staff to keep its franchise in normal operation to satisfy local customer demand for fifty-two (52) weeks per year, seven (7) days per week in a retail location (except such periods as it may be required by law or permitted by Franchisor to be closed).

F. Management and Employee Standards:

1. Franchisee will assure that all employees, engaged in the operation of this Franchise during working hours shall dress conforming to Franchisor's standards, shall present a neat and clean appearance in conformance with reasonable standards of Franchisor and shall render competent, efficient service to the customers of the Franchise.

2. Franchisee agrees that it shall devote best efforts in directing the day-to-day operations and development of the Franchise. Franchisee may, however, delegate the day-to-day operation of the Franchise to a manager so long as said manager is approved by the Franchisor in advance and said manager successfully completes the training program offered by the Franchisor.

G. Standard Operation Procedures and Reports:

1. Books and Accounts: Franchisee agrees to establish and maintain books, accounts, records, order receipts, etc. required by Franchisor and by good business procedures and particularly to keep and maintain accurate records of purchases, gross and net sales in a manner designated by Franchisor. To promote the standardization and uniformity of all franchise units and such good business procedures, Franchisee agrees that such books, accounts, records, etc., shall be open for inspection and audit by Franchisor or its representative at all reasonable times. In the event Franchisor conducts an audit of Franchisee's operations, and finds that Franchisee has failed, for whatever reason(s), to properly report its sales to Franchisor then Franchisee shall pay the cost of said audit. Franchisee shall pay any deficiency within 15 days of the completion of said audit in the event the error is 3% or greater.

2. Standard Advertising and Promotion: Franchisee agrees that all local advertising and promotional plans or programs if other than those provided by Franchisor, which feature the use of franchisor's trademark, service marks, slogans or trade names, and any other trademarks, service marks, slogans or trade names, which may hereafter be used by Franchisor shall be submitted to and approved in writing by Franchisor before release or use thereof.

3. Standard Systems: Franchisee agrees to follow all Al's Sandwich Shop marketing and operating systems in their entirety and with no deviations from these formats unless approved in advance by Franchisor.

Franchisee agrees that the violation of any such standards or requirements enumerated under this paragraph or elsewhere within this Agreement shall be deemed to be a material breach of this Agreement and shall give Franchisor the right to terminate this Agreement according to the provision of paragraphs 9 and 10 below.

Franchisee further agrees that, in order to maintain the high quality and uniform standards associated with the Franchise and to protect its good will and reputation, to permit Franchisor during business hours, to inspect the Franchise facility, confer with Franchisee and Franchisee's employees and customers, check inventories, methods, books and records, and perform any other inspection deemed by Franchisor to be necessary to protect the standards of quality and uniformity of the Franchise and Franchisee's performance under this Agreement.

4. Insurance: Franchisee agrees to procure and maintain public liability and property damage insurance covering the operation of the business and the location where the business is conducted, with insurance carriers reasonably acceptable to Franchisor in a minimum amount of one million dollars ($1,000,000) combined single limit and real and personal property insurance including fire and extended coverage on an all risk replacement cost basis. Franchisee agrees to carry such insurance as may be required by the lease of Franchisee's location or by any lender or equipment lessor of Franchisee and such workers compensation insurance as may be required by applicable law. Franchisee shall, if requested by Franchisor, add Franchisor to all insurance contracts as an additional insured under the insurance policies, the cost of which to be paid by Franchisee.

7. Indemnity

Franchisee agrees that it will indemnify and hold harmless Franchisor from all fines, suits, proceedings, claims, demands, judgments, or other liability or costs of any kind arising from or otherwise connected with Franchisee's operation of its franchise, except for such liability or costs arising from actions or activities of Franchisor.

8. *Change of Ownership*

Franchisee may, with Franchisor's prior written approval, assign this Agreement if:

a. Franchisee agrees to give at least thirty (30) days prior written notice of Franchisee's intention to effect any such transfer.

b. Assignee submits Franchisor's then current franchise application and Franchisor approves assignee in writing, which approval will not be unreasonably withheld. For the assignee to receive approval he must be financially capable of purchasing and operating the franchise.

c. Assignee agrees to successfully complete the training program required of all new Franchisees.

d. Franchisee pays to Franchisor all monies due and cures any existing defaults with regard to this Agreement or the relationship between the parties or otherwise makes arrangements for same, said arrangements to be made in writing and signed by all parties hereto.

e. Franchisor receives the sum of Two Thousand Five Hundred ($2,500) Dollars to cover the Franchisor's expenses in connection with the transfer.

f. Upon the death or incapacity of Franchisee this agreement may be assigned to the heirs of the Franchisee so long as the heirs complete the training program offered by the Franchisor according to this agreement.

g. Franchisee by this agreement has offered a "First Right of Refusal" to Franchisor which allows 30 days for Franchisor to match the assignee's offer and notify Franchisee of intent to purchase the franchise. Franchisee shall provide, in written form, the offer of the proposed assignee for Franchisor's review. Same shall be done in writing and shall be sent certified mail, return receipt requested. Franchisor may then purchase the franchise upon the same terms and conditions offered by the proposed assignee. Failure of Franchisor to exercise this right within 30 days following receipt of the written offer shall thereafter permit Franchisee to proceed with the sale to the proposed assignee. Any change in the terms between the proposed assignee and the Franchisee shall be considered a new offer which must be submitted to the Franchisor subject to the procedures set forth herein. In the event Franchisor wishes to exercise his right of first refusal, Franchisor shall notify the Franchisee in writing, certified mail, return receipt requested, or by in-person notification.

9. *Cancellation or Termination*

Neither this agreement nor the relationship between the parties may be modified during the term of this Agreement unless such modifications are set forth in writing and signed by both parties. Franchisor may terminate this Agreement in the event Franchisee is in default of any of the provisions hereof and, with the exceptions hereinafter noted shall justify immediate termination, in the event that default is not remedied within 60 days following receipt of written notice, served by certified mail, return receipt requested. The following shall in Franchisor's discretion, justify immediate termination: (1) If Franchisee shall declare bankruptcy, voluntary or involuntary, or shall become insolvent, shall have a receiver appointed for any portion of its property, shall make general assignment for the benefit of its creditors; (2) If Franchisee shall voluntarily abandon this Agreement; (3) If Franchisee shall perform such act of default, or otherwise be in violation of this Agreement, which act cannot be cured within the 60 day notice period; (4) If Franchisee shall violate any of the advertising policies of the

Franchisor. Franchisor reserves the right to sell or assign, in whole or in part, its interests and/or obligations to the Franchisee under this Agreement.

Non-Disclosure

The Franchisee, in the course of its association with Al's Sandwich Shop, will obtain knowledge of valuable information, trade secrets, marketing methods, business affairs, recipes and methods of doing business. All information transferred from Franchisor to Franchisee shall be considered strictly confidential and Franchisee agrees that it shall not, directly or indirectly, make available to any person, firm, corporation or association such confidential information as described in this paragraph without the specific written consent of the Franchisor. This covenant of non-disclosure extends only to that information and those methods of doing business which are not known by independent third parties. Franchisee agrees not to circumvent, bypass or obviate the rights of the Franchisor by doing business directly with any supplier to whom Franchisee has been introduced by Franchisor without the advance written consent of the Franchisor. Failure to comply with this provision will be grounds for immediate termination of the Franchise Agreement.

10. Obligations of the Franchisee upon Termination

In the event of termination or non-renewal of this Agreement, Franchisee shall immediately upon the effective date of termination or non-renewal:

A. Discontinue the use and practice of any and all of Franchisor's proprietary and confidential information including methods, designs, marketing techniques, etc., in connection with the operation of the business.

B. Discontinue the use of any and all of Franchisor's trademarks, service marks, slogans and trade names and any other trademarks, service marks, slogans or trade names which may hereafter be used by Franchisor, or any colorable imitations or variations thereof. This shall include the immediate cessation of use of all telephone numbers, advertising products, signs and other materials which bear such trademarks, service marks, slogans and trade names. All telephone numbers used by Franchisee shall, at Franchisor's discretion, be assigned to Franchisor should Franchisor elect to take the telephone numbers. Franchisor shall pay the cost of same from the date of assignment.

C. Cease from representing to the public and trade contacts that Franchisee is or was a member of the Franchisor's systems.

D. Have a full audited accounting prepared within thirty (30) days of the effective date of non-renewal or termination and submitted to Franchisor, detailing all monies due Franchisor pursuant to any requirement under this Agreement and to make payment in full.

11. Relationship of the Parties

Franchisor and Franchisee are strictly Franchisor and Franchisee. Franchisee is an independent contractor, and any act of omission by either party shall not obligate the other. Franchisee shall protect, indemnify and save Franchisor harmless against any and all claims (including punitive damages), costs and liabilities of any kind in connection with Franchisee's operation of the Franchise. Franchisee shall, upon Franchisor's request, post notice that Franchisee is a Franchisee of Al's Sandwich Shop.

Franchisee understands and agrees that fulfillment of any and all obligations of Franchisor based on any and all written understandings or based on any oral understandings adjudged to be binding shall be the sole responsibility of Al's Sandwich Shop and no agent, representative, nor any individual associated with Franchisor shall be held responsible. This is an integral part of this Agreement. No oral representations of Franchisor, or its agents shall be binding. This written agreement incorporates all representations between the parties. Do not sign this Agreement if there is any question concerning its contents or any representations made.

12. Covenant Not to Compete

Franchisee acknowledges that as a participant in the Franchise System, Franchisee will receive confidential information and materials, trade secrets, and the unique methods, procedures and techniques developed by Franchisor. Therefore to protect Franchisor and all Franchisees of the Franchisor, Franchisee represents and warrants: that while a Franchisee of Franchisor, and for a period of three years thereafter, Franchisee shall not engage in any retail sandwich business other than the one in this Agreement. Engaging shall include, but not be limited to, activities whether direct or indirect, as an individual proprietor, partner, stockholder, director, officer, principal, broker, agent, employee, consultant, lender or otherwise. If Franchisee is found to be engaging in a similar endeavor while a Franchisee, Franchisee agrees to pay to Franchisor, damages equal to 15% of the Gross Sales generated by the endeavor. Payment of said damages shall not preclude Franchisor from filing any other claims it believes is appropriate, to include injunctive relief in the event of a violation of this provision.

13. Waiver

A.   A waiver of any violation of this Agreement shall not impair Franchisor's or Franchisee's rights with respect to any further violations; and

B.   No delay or omission on the part of Franchisor or Franchisee to exercise any right arising from any violation of this Agreement shall impair their rights as to any future violations.

14. Arbitration

Any unresolved controversy arising out of this Agreement will be, if either party requests, decided by Arbitration in the County of Maricopa, State of Arizona, by a panel of three (3) independent Arbitrators in accordance with the rules then in effect, of the American Arbitration Association, with both parties sharing equally the total payment of all fees and expenses of the arbitrators. The decision of the Arbitrators may be filed as a judgment in the Superior Court of Maricopa and shall be binding in any other jurisdiction.

15. Notice

All notices under this Agreement shall be in writing and delivered by registered or certified mail, return receipt requested, addressed to the party's last known address and shall be considered lawful and valid process.

16. Severability

If any portion of this Agreement is held to be invalid or unenforceable, the remaining portion shall remain in full force and effect as if it has been signed with the invalid portion omitted.

17. *Jurisdiction, Venue and Controlling Law*

This Agreement shall be governed by and enforced in accordance with the laws of the State of Arizona. Franchisee and Franchisor consent to the jurisdiction and venue of any court of general jurisdiction, County of Maricopa, State of Arizona and any legal proceedings arising out of this Agreement shall be brought only in such court. This is an integral part of this Agreement.

18. *Entire Agreement*

This Franchise Agreement contains the entire Agreement of the parties. There are no representations either oral or written, except those contained in this Agreement.

Franchisee understands, acknowledges, and agrees that Al's Sandwich Shop as well as any and all representatives and/or agents with whom Franchisee has met have not and are not making any guarantees as to the extent of the Franchisee's success, and have not and are not in any way representing or promising any specific amounts of earnings or profits in association with the Franchisee's new business.

Franchisee acknowledges that he has received and reviewed, at least ten (10) business days prior to entering into this Agreement, Franchisor's FTC Disclosure Statements or such other disclosure statements as required by applicable state law.

19. *Place of Execution*

It is agreed that this Agreement was executed at the Franchisor's place of business in Maricopa County, Arizona.

Date: _____   _____

                                   Al's Sandwich Shop, Inc.

Date: _____   _____

                                   (Franchisee)

Date: _____   _____

                                   (Franchisee)

I, Franchisee hereby acknowledge that I have read this franchise agreement completely and fully understand its requirements and obligations.

Date: _____   (Franchisee) _____

Appendix A

Standard Program*

A.	Initial Franchisee Fee	$16,000
B.	Fixtures, signs, equipment	$65,000 supplies
C.	Inventory	$10,000
D.	Lease deposits and 1st month's rent	From $5,000 to $10,000
E.	Supplies	$600
F.	Grand Opening Advertising	$2,200
G.	Insurance, Licenses Utility Deposits	$2,200
H.	Buildout and leasehold design and improvements	$35,000
		From $136,000 to $140,000†

It is recommended that Franchisee have at least an additional $35,000 available as reserve capital after the business opens. Allowable storefront signage will vary greatly from one site to the next due to township requirements, zoning, etc. All signs must conform to Franchisor's approved standards regarding design, logos, colors, etc. Note: Franchisee should also have adequate funds available to cover living and household expenses in addition to adequate operating capital. The amount necessary shall vary according to each Franchisee's personal needs, mode and manner of living.

Receipt for Initial Franchise Fee

Franchisor acknowledges receipt of the sum of _____as full and total payment of the initial Franchise Fee. The Initial Franchise Fee is deemed earned by Franchisor upon receipt and acceptance of Franchisee's application by Franchisor and the execution of this Agreement. Should Franchisee be disapproved for any reason, Franchisor agrees to refund the initial Franchise Fee. Execution of this agreement by Franchisor shall constitute acceptance of Franchisee's application. The balance of equipment, signs, supplies, fixtures, inventory and deposit payments is payable by Franchisee to Franchisor, landlord and purveyors as needed to meet grand opening and leasehold deadlines and as otherwise requested by Franchisor.

Al's Sandwich Shop _____

Franchisee Address _____Franchisee _____

Date _____Franchisee _____

*All amounts other than initial franchise fee are approximate and represent best estimates of opening expenditures. Cost may vary based on size of restaurant, rents, amount of inventory, etc. Capital requirements may be adjusted as necessary but will not exceed those listed herein without approval from Franchisee.

†If Franchisee has indicated on the Franchise Application that the full amount of the investment is not readily available, it is the sole responsibility of Franchisee to secure any financing necessary from third party lending sources in order to satisfy capital requirements of opening an Al's Sandwich Shop. Franchisee hereby agrees to secure such financing. This is an integral part of this agreement.

Appendix B

Equipment Package

Al's Sandwich Shop

Item	Quantity	Model	Description
1.	1	AB540	Oven
2.	1	Custom	10' x 12' Walk-in Cooler w/floor storage rack one side
3.	1	M22	3/4 HP Outdoor Pre-assembled Refrigerator
4.	1	492H	Traulsen 2 Door Refrigerator w/tray slides
5.	1	P49	Table
6.	1	HH22	Eagle 3 bowl S/S sink & Faucet
7.	1	P940	Quart Mixer w/ss bowl, bowl cover and dough hook
8.	1	941	Cheese Shredder Attachment
9.	1	77766	S/S Work Table w/back Splash &S/S Shelf under table
10.	1	BH123	Work Table w/ss top 8 ft.
11.	70		Anodized Bun Pans
12.	1	H40	50# Scale
13.	1	55091	See/Thru Counter Case
14.	1	64222	ICE Machine
15.	2	Custom	2' x 5' Sandwich Holding Cabinets
16.	4	19H2	10 Gal. White Buckets
17.	4	19H3	Lids for above
18.	2	2120	Rolling Pins
19.	2	1460	1/2 Qt. Measuring Cups
20.	15	1691	60 oz. Plastic Pitchers
21.	2	2222	Upright Brooms
22.	1	22223	Lobby Dust Pan
23.	1	33312	Lobby Brooms
24.	1	76767	26 Qt. Combo Mop Bucket
25.	2 DZ.	611	2 oz. Salt & Peppers
26.	3 DZ.	540	6 oz. Slotted Mason Jars

Item	Quantity	Model	Description
27.	1	1298	16 Qt. S/S Bowl
28.	4	2190	Dough Scraper
29.	2	2220	4" Plastic Handle Dough Cutter
30.	12 EA.		Pans 9", 12", & 14" Square Pans Stackable
31.	10	TBases	Standard Table Bases (Black)
32.	36 Chairs	#588	Banquet Chairs Silvertone(SB)
33.	12		Napkin Holders Mini-Mor Nap 13" x 13"
34.	1	Board	MENU Sign (MainStreet) Lited
35.	2	0001	Pot Forks 20"
36.	2	0002	Pot Fork 15"
37.	4	686	8 oz. Ladles
38.	2	684	4 oz. Ladles
39.	1	1084	#1 Can Opener
40.	1	1330	Potato Peeler
41.	1	1542	64 oz. Plastic Scoop
42.	1	3217	10" White Handle Knife
43.	1	3217	6" White Boning Knife
44.	4	2192	Sandwich Server
45.	2	1582	23 Cap Trash Cans
46.	2	1584	Lids for above
47.	8	0022	5 Gal. Clear Buckets
48.	8	0023	Lids for Above
49.	8		Cantilevers Brackets, Supporting Booth Top
50.	9		3' x 3' Table Tops
51.	8		Booth Tops
52.	1		Booster Seat
53.	1		High Chair
54.			Sign Package/Drive-Thru Canopy
55.	2		Cup Dispensers/Spring Loaded

Equipment Package Total Cost.....................$65,000.00

A Business Plan For:

American Medical Insurance Services, Inc.

February 1994

Ms. Julia Smith President

(555) 555-5555

Business Plan Copy Number _____

The following Business Plan is an example of a plan that may be used to aid in the sale of an existing business. Financial projections are not included. From a liability standpoint, we do not recommend that an existing owner attempt to calculate or project what the new owner will achieve. It should be left up to the new owners to calculate their own Financial Projections.

The main emphasis should be on past performance and practices that made the business successful and desirable for purchase. A reference may be made to the fact that if these practices continue, similar results may be expected.

Table of Contents

Executive Summary

In 1981, AMI Services, Inc., was formed to offer quality insurance products to the Florida market. The primary purpose of AMI is to provide elderly individuals with Medicare Supplement and Nursing Home insurance policies. As an additional service, Health insurance and Life insurance products are also offered to persons under Medicare age.

AMI is now at a stage where its owner and president, Julia Smith, is ready to sell the business. Ms. Smith is 70 years of age and is at the point where she feels it is time to settle down and retire from the insurance industry.

Background

For many years people have relied on AMI Services, Inc., to provide them with quality insurance products and superior customer service. This has been of utmost importance to Ms. Smith. The additional services provided by AMI were not required or even expected. However, Ms. Smith would have it no other way.

There are many general insurance agents and insurance agencies in the Metropolitan Florida Beach market that offer a good product and service. However, there are very few agents who will go the extra mile by performing acts of service that are not part of the "job description." For example, it has always been a strict policy of AMI Services, Inc., to submit claims for and on behalf of the Medicare Supplement policy holder, or to make copies of the "Explanation of Medicare Benefits" and enter them in a personal logbook.

This book contains a log of each claim submitted to Medicare and the insurance company. This log also contains the name of the attending physician or hospital, actual amount submitted, amount approved, and amount paid to the patient. These are only a few samples of the superior services that are part of the daily routine offered by Ms. Smith.

Annual growth for the insurance products that AMI specializes in is projected to be steady each year of operation.

Concept

The condition of the industry today is such that more and more elderly people understand the necessity for Medicare Supplements, Nursing Home Policies, and Home Health Policies. Each year medical costs are rising, so are other alarming statistics.

Statistics show that one in four senior citizens will be confined to a nursing home sometime during their lifetime! Medicare will only cover a portion of these enormous medical costs.*

The federal government does not cover all of these medical expenses for the elderly through Medicare. In fact, it covers only a small portion of medical and doctor bills, yet the medical personnel and facilities expect payment for their services. Where will this money come from? It should be coming from supplemental policies that are available through agencies like AMI.

Compared to competitive services, AMI's services are not currently being matched or duplicated. A quick glance at the Letters of Recommendation in the Appendix will give a clear understanding of how important Ms. Smith's services and products are to the clients of AMI. The new owner(s) of the business can enjoy as much success, but only if the new management is capable of interacting well with clients and providing superior customer service, is willing to do so, and has the desire to work.

* Source: Department of Health and Human Services

The ability to provide all these important services is a capability unique to AMI Services, Inc. Current clients judge the insurance products and services provided through AMI as superior to those of competitors.

The strategy for meeting the competition is very simple: Offer a competitive, high-quality insurance product, and package it with the type of professional service that you would want in return for your dollars spent.

AMI's target market includes existing customers who do not presently have Nursing Home policies or Home Health Policies and persons over the age of 65 who do not have adequate Medicare Supplement coverage.

AMI is rapidly moving into its expansion marketing phase by directing efforts to the Nursing Home policy market. This approach is generating a tremendous amount of interest throughout the insurance industry, because it is virtually an untapped area for generating business.

Other products/services include Health and Life insurance policies from A+-rated companies.

Responses from customers indicate that AMI Services, Inc., enjoys an excellent reputation. Letters and telephone calls from existing customers come in on a weekly basis, thanking Ms. Smith for her compassion and professionalism. Inquiries from prospective customers also suggest that there is considerable demand for Nursing Home policies.

Objectives

Our objective at this time is to maintain the company in a prominent market position after the business is sold. We feel that within two years the business will be in a suitable condition to increase current sales and commissions into an even greater, more profitable position.

A great opportunity exists to build an agency with several agents. Management can develop a sales force and receive an override of commissions for each sale made by agents. The potential is virtually unlimited. Because of Ms. Smith's severe leg injury, she decided not to take on the additional responsibilities.

The accomplishment of this goal will depend on the new management's ability to intensify and accelerate marketing activities and maintain customer service.

To implement plans for the transfer of ownership to new management, AMI requires an investment of $275,000.

Management

The management team consists of one woman, whose background includes 15 years of sales and marketing within the insurance industry. Ms. Smith has received awards and honors too numerous to list, but they include Top Sales Representative in the Western Region and in the United States with various insurance companies.

Before starting in the insurance industry, Ms. Smith moved into a prominent position with the Avon Sales Company, as the Top Regional and National Sales Representative. She has also operated several other businesses in a profitable fashion.

She was hired by a large manufacturing company to open sales operations in Australia, but turned down the offer and started in the insurance business. Since that day, Ms. Smith has never looked back. She has demonstrated that anyone with drive and determination can succeed, no matter what the obstacles are.

Marketing

The fundamental thrust of AMI's current marketing strategy consists of three important elements: (1) telemarketing leads generated by a sophisticated computer dialing system, (2) quality referrals from trusted clients, and (3) leads generated from Ms. Smith's networking with other professionals.

The new owners of the business should expect to maintain a reasonable amount of personal involvement to continue receiving referrals and leads. Ms. Smith spends three days a week, primarily in the afternoons, going on scheduled appointments. The other days of the week are spent taking care of administrative duties.

AMI Services can be characterized as a business offering a service that clients cannot live without. The image for customers to see is a professional, courteous, honest insurance representative, who really does care for their needs and security.

AMI enjoys an established track record of excellent support for its customers. Their expressions of satisfaction and encouragement are numerous, and we expect the new owners of the business to continue these efforts of quality, honesty, and courtesy. Insurance buyers don't always buy the product for its price only. The clients must feel, especially in the age group most of our current business comes from, that they will not have to worry about who will take care of them.

Ms. Smith will turn her client lists, which will consist of names, addresses, phone numbers, and the type of insurance policy each client has, over to the new owner(s). There are more than 300 clients, and each will need to be acclimated to the new owner(s). This transfer of ownership will need to be handled in a personal fashion by Ms. Smith. She will send a formal letter to each of her clients to introduce the new owner(s) and make the new owner(s) feel welcome.

Finance

Actual gross receipts for the past five years, which include new commissions and renewals, are as follows:

1989	$250,139
1990	$225,999
1991	$176,998
1992	$223,908
1993	$261,123

Actual amounts paid to AMI Services, Inc., from the various insurance carriers it represents (i.e., 1099s issued at year end) are as follows:

1989	$201,346
1990	$209,963
1991	$123,987
1992	$210,000
1993	$221,084

Reflected on the annual tax returns for each year are additional business expenses, which are not accounted for here.

Present Situation

Products and Services

Presently, the products and services offered by AMI Services, Inc., are in the mature stage. Medicare Supplements, Nursing Home Policies, and Health insurance products have been in the marketplace for several years.

Typical customers are aware of these types of policies. Sometimes they do not understand the importance of such products. An educational process is often required by the selling agent to help and assist in the understanding of the powerful importance of these and other insurance products.

Pricing and Profitability

Current prices are increasing because medical expenses keep rising. Profits, or commissions, are increasing with the premiums, because a fixed percentage is associated with the sale of such products.

Customers

Current customers are purchasing our products for peace of mind. Customers are of all ages and come from diverse backgrounds. However, our primary market is within the age group of 65 to 80. This age group represents the majority of our current clients.

Objectives

The primary objectives of our organization are to:

a. offer a quality insurance product that will benefit the client when the need arises;

b. sell only products that have a good solid history behind them;

c. provide a service to each client that we would want provided to us and our loved ones; and

d. allow the new owners the opportunity to take advantage of Ms. Smith's expertise and hard work, buy a business that enjoys a very good reputation, and obtain a profitable income.

Business Goals

Customers	Integrity
Products	Profits
Quality	People
Growth	Management

This is a list of business priorities that have always been the foundation of AMI's success.

Compared to past performance of AMI, the new management should be capable of achieving a similar or a greater income level. This will depend on attitude toward successful achievements, a positive mental attitude, and the personal services rendered to clients.

Bear in mind that Ms. Smith is 70 years old, and does not always enjoy the best of health, due to her leg injury. However, she is still capable of making a six-figure income with her current clients and marketing strategies. This income has been derived from an average work-week of three to four afternoons per week.

Return on Investment

Based on financial figures presented and produced in the past by AMI, we estimate that new management will begin to realize a return on investment by the second year of operation. This is a conservative estimate, but takes into consideration that the new owner(s) may not have any insurance-, sales-, or marketing-related experience.

Position for Growth

1. Understand customers, competition, and industry.

2. Product/service/channel/customer congruency.

3. Product/service life cycles.

4. Growth by fields of interest.

5. Balance people/management/business goals.

6. Transition from single-point to distributed management.

7. Develop values and culture.

The previous list of activities and priorities should be considered for planning and future growth.

Training

The following training procedures will be offered by Ms. Smith for a period of 30 days following the purchase of the business. This training package will be comprehensive and time-consuming, and will be part of the total purchase price. The training will be offered for 40 hours a week for four weeks—a total of 160 hours—and will consist of the following elements:

I. Insurance School

    A. Enroll buyer in insurance school and pay for entrance and exam fees for the necessary insurance licenses required by the state of Arizona.

    B. Offer any assistance to help pass the state insurance exam.

II. Marketing

    A. Show the new owner how and where to obtain names and addresses of potential clients.

    B. Explain how to select the geographic areas that have the best possible potential clients.

    C. Show how to determine when and how to contact potential clients.

III. Computer Training

    A. Show how to operate computer system by loading names and phone numbers of persons over age 65 years into the computer.

    B. File names by area and zip code.

    C. Thoroughly explain how to cover the area in a systematic way.

    D. Show how to load phone numbers from the master copy into the computer.

    E. Explain how to have computer call potential clients and record their response.

    F. Explain how to set up lead (prospect) book and record names and addresses of potential clients.

IV. Product Knowledge

    A. Medicare

        1. Who is eligible.

        2. How to apply for Medicare.

        3. When client will receive Medicare.

        4. What the Medicare benefits are.

        5. The difference between A and B benefits.

        6. Explain how to fill out Medicare forms.

    B. Major Medical Insurance

        1. Who is eligible.

        2. How they qualify for major medical insurance.

        3. Explain how to read the benefits for different insurance plans.

        4. Explain how to help clients select the best insurance plan for their needs and pocketbooks.

        5. Explain how to tell the difference between a good insurance company and a poor one.

    C. Nursing Home Policy

        1. Teach how to qualify clients.

        2. Explain how to check medical records.

        3. Show clients what the best policy will be for their individual situations.

        4. Explain what to do if you are not sure a client will qualify.

        5. Assist clients with the following:

            a. amount of insurance needed

b. benefit period

c. amount of benefits needed.

6. Teach how to calculate premium by mode.

7. Teach how to fill out application properly.

D. Home Health Care

1. Explain how to determine who will qualify.

2. Explain amount insurance company will pay per hour for services.

3. Explain who the benefits are paid to.

4. Teach how to help client decide which kind of benefits he or she will need (e.g., nursing home, home health).

5. Explain how to determine which company is best suited for a client's health and pocketbook.

6. Explain how to compare one policy against another, and assist the client in deciding which coverage will be best for their needs.

7. Teach how to calculate premiums.

8. Teach how to use bank drafts.

V. How to Obtain General Agent's License

A. The new owner(s) will need to decide which companies will be best suited for his or her personal needs. Ms. Smith will assist in making this decision. Her experience with several insurance companies will be of great benefit. Ms. Smith will assist new owner(s) to obtain General Agents contracts with the insurance companies that pay the highest commissions.

VI. Telephone Techniques

A. Many techniques are necessary for a successful enterprise to operate. The following items are a representation of some of the skills and "tricks of the trade" to help the new owner(s) accomplish these objectives.

1. When to call potential clients to set up an appointment (e.g. the best time of the day, specific days that are better than others).

2. What to say to obtain an appointment.

3. What to say when clients are not interested.

4. How to listen to what the person on the phone tells you, and how to offer the best insurance plan for his or her needs.

5. How to reconfirm specific points of conversation (e.g., appointment time, address, telephone number, name, directions).

6. Learn when not to make an appointment.

VII. Making the Sale

    A. Ms. Smith will teach and thoroughly explain all the important factors that help solidify a sale for this specific industry. This will be a comprehensive training package by itself. There are many factors to be considered here; however, the following items will give you a good understanding of what to expect in this area:

        1. Tell prospective clients how much they will pay in premiums.

        2. Tell them when they will pay—monthly, quarterly, or annual premiums.

        3. Give a comparison of the policy they have with the one you are offering.

        4. Know how to present a Nursing Home policy or Medicare Supplement policy.

        5. Help the client decide which policy will benefit him or her the most.

        6. Learn when to stop talking and ask for the sale.

        7. Learn how to ask for the sale.

        8. Learn how to close the sale.

VIII. Submitting the Application

    A. Making copies.

    B. Calculating amount of premium.

    C. How to submit net amount.

    D. How to use the bank draft forms.

    E. How to make a transmittal properly.

    F. How to figure your commission.

IX. Record Keeping

There are too many components of proper record keeping to mention in this section. Ms. Smith will help the new owner(s) set up a proved, successful filing system that will allow him or her to keep accurate records and indexes of all current and potential clients. This comprehensive system will include ways to keep track of purchasing supplies, recording transmittals, a detailed card index, individual insurance companies the new owner(s) will be licensed with, thank-you cards to current and new clients, commissions earned, etc.

X. Handling Cancellations

    A. Learn when a client may cancel a policy.

    B. Learn what the requirements are to cancel.

    C. Learn what statements are required to cancel.

    D. Learn how to get a refund for the client.

    E. Learn how to adjust your files.

    F. Learn how to get a refund for a client if a loved one dies.

There are many other areas that will be covered by Ms. Smith in training and development of the new owner(s). These items are listed as an overview of what the new management can expect.

Customers

Basic Characteristics

The typical customer for our product/service is someone who is 65 to 80 years of age. Their *needs* will vary, but these are the typical ages of our customers.

It is likely that potential customers are going to be retired individuals who are familiar with the products and services AMI offers, and that they will readily accept the products provided. It is important to approach and educate potential customers on what they are considering for their financial security.

Insurance coverage already in use by our customers is primarily Medicare Supplemental insurance, which is seen as a tremendous help in convincing present customers to purchase Nursing Home policies as well. This is a ripe market that is ready to be approached. A large majority of AMI's clients do not own a Nursing Home policy.

It is easy to understand why the principal buying motives are financial security for themselves and their loved ones in the event of required professional assistance. A fair question to be asked is "How sensitive are they to pricing differences?" Most of Ms. Smith's customers are on a fixed income, and therefore cannot afford to purchase the most expensive insurance product on the market. For this reason, AMI offers affordable, top-rated insurance products.

In reality, when prices are fairly competitive, the people will buy from the person they are most comfortable with. That is why Ms. Smith has been so successful in her industry. People simply like her and appreciate her professional service. And in her words, she has a purpose each day to get up for!

Customer List

Due to the extremely confidential nature of the agent/client relationship, and as a form of protection to Ms. Smith, the names of the clients are not listed in this publication. However, once an escrow account is established for the purchase of the business, Ms. Smith will release a complete list of her clients to the new owner(s).

This also applies to the insurance companies. Their names, addresses, phone numbers, and contact persons will be released upon the opening of an escrow account. Ms. Smith has formed some very important relationships with major insurance companies. These relationships are critical to the success of a general agent in the insurance industry. A smooth transition from Ms. Smith to the new owner(s) must be handled in a personal and professional manner.

Conclusions and Summary

The plan and outline that have been presented represent a small portion of the enormous potential of this business. The insurance market is a wide-open industry that has made many agents, general agents, and insurance companies very wealthy.

The services that have been provided by AMI Services, Inc., have always been honest, fair, and ethical. This will be expected from the new owner(s) of the business, and will hopefully be of utmost importance to him or her, as it has been for Ms. Smith.

The particular market niche that has been carved out by AMI serves as a strong foundation for the new owner(s) to consider. Medicare Supplements and Nursing Home policies are a necessity for thousands of people in this area.

The capital required to purchase AMI Services, Inc., is $275,000. The total balance is due and payable within 7 days of signing the Agreement of Sale. AMI will not finance any portion of the sale price. Once the financing is in place, training will commence and continue for a total of 160 hours, over a 4-week period, 40 hours per week.

Renewals that are currently coming in to AMI Services, Inc., as a result of sales over the years will be turned over to the new owner(s). This represents an average range of $2,000 to $3,000 per month in renewal commissions. The new owner(s), then, will realize an immediate return on the investment. This will give the new owner(s) a chance to begin training, contacting current clients, and developing new clients, without having to worry about generating immediate business.

Ms. Smith has devoted many years of her life to building AMI Services, Inc., into a reputable, money-making business. It is her desire and objective to sell her insurance agency to someone who will continue to enlarge the business and take care of the existing clientele.

Whoever has the proper work ethics, vision, and desire to succeed in the insurance industry will reap the rewards more quickly with a sound business already in operation. AMI Services, Inc., offers this type of luxury to the person(s) who wants to operate his or her own insurance agency.

Appendix

Author's Note:

List all supporting documentation in the appendix section as noted and referenced throughout your business plan.

Remember, this information should be clearly and neatly presented so the reader of your business plan can easily reference and understand the data being provided.

Business Plan For:

CC DAY CARE CENTER

Lili Lako

June 15, 1994

Index

Summary

CC Day Care Center (CC) will be formed in July 1995 in the city of South Orange, New Jersey, as a partnership. The dynamic team that will be responsible for the daily operations of the day-care center will be the manager director (Lili Lako), a personal assistant, an accounts clerk, an administrative staff, three lead teachers, and two teachers' aides. CC will hire professional company secretaries, auditors, and maintenance personnel to handle these three aspects of the business. This business promises to be very lucrative for the following reasons:

1. There is a great need for an excellent day-care center in the city; at present there are none. The actual market for this service is substantial (the child population is 87,570), and has a potential 20 percent annual growth in the next two to three years.

2. The initial target market, which is only 2 percent of the ultimate target market, has virtually no competitors, and this gives CC the easy entrance it needs at the start.

3. The prime location in the upper class, Kenny Hills area is ideal for a center of this nature, and the residents are willing to pay for the services that will be offered.

4. CC's ability to accomplish its goals and lead in the industry is significantly related to the know-how and ability of the management to recognize the great need of the area and seize the opportunity to capitalize on it. The high standards that CC will set will make it difficult for unscrupulous competitors to enter the market. This will reduce the competition to only those who can match the high quality of service set by CC and still be able to make a profit.

As a result of these conditions, CC believes that it has a unique opportunity to provide the best quality of service in the city at very appealing prices and capture a sizable portion of the whole market in five years.

Company Analysis

Background of the Company

CC Day Care Center will be the name of the child-care service to be started in South Orange, New Jersey, in 1995. The company is named after Lili Lako's (LL) three-year-old daughter, Carol.

Carol's Carousel (CC) will be a partnership. LL's husband, Stuart Lako (ST), will be the other partner, who will initially assist in setting up the business. ST is a business major who has vast experience as an entrepreneur. Currently ST is the owner of a medium-sized advertising agency in South Orange. ST wants to broaden his business base and is therefore looking to invest in other services. ST also has a wide network of business associates who are looking for lucrative businesses to invest in; this will be extremely useful in the near future, should the need arise for more capital!

LL will be responsible for the daily running of the business. The main purpose of the company is to provide an all-day child-care service to the upper-class community of *Kenny Hills* in South Orange. The average income in Kenny Hills is about $100,000 annually. There is currently no such service being offered in this area.

Initially, there will be one personal assistant, at least one administrative and accounting staff member, and the other personnel will consist of lead teachers (Masters in Education) and teachers' aides (i.e., teaching certified but trained by CC,s own lead teachers). The number of personnel will grow with the increase in the number of children per day. The ratio of teachers to children will be about 1 to 15, and this is to be the initial selling point. The wealthy are very concerned about the personal attention their kids are receiving; they do not mind at all paying for this attention.

Service Offered

The philosophy of CC is based on the following:

a. Children between the ages of three and six cannot stand conformity, so their work will be less structured. However, their curriculum will include Math, English, Science, Social Studies, and an additional language taught through the latest methods (through games, cooperative learning, etc.).

b. Children should be self-directed. This concept teaches the children to work independently of the teacher. This will be preparation for the future when the company has grown. This new concept that "a small class does not necessarily mean better" will have to be introduced with utmost care, because we began with just the reverse as our marketing strategy.

c. The children here will be taught to be self-motivated, to survive in any environment, and to have positive self-images. Positive reinforcement will be highlighted!

d. The service should meet high standards, which will be monitored closely; the "homey" yet professional educational support provided will be the key ingredient.

The service CC will be offering will be aimed at rich families where the parents are occupied with their own careers and need to be assured that their children are safe while being educated. Many rich wives may not have careers of their own but may have social obligations that take them away from their homes. They, too, need to be confident that their kids' needs are well taken care of!

Market and Customers

The major market that CC will serve will be the wealthy community of the Kenny Hills region in the heart of South Orange. There are many such rich communities in the city, but this will be the first group focused on. The total population of this area is approximately 3,600; however, CC initially will be addressing only about 10 percent of this market. This is mainly due to the limited capital; CC's owners will "dig deep into their pockets" because they do not want to start the business with the heavy burden of debt.

Capital

The capital that has been set aside for the business is between $65,000 and $75,000; this will include the initial start-up cost plus the cost of all the necessary equipment that is required of a business of this nature (see list under "Operation Resources"). The return on investment that is expected of CC is 30 percent per year.

Customers

Although the principal customers will be those whose annual income is $100,000 and above, the *upper middle class* will be CC's peripheral customers. These people also want the best for their children and will strive to achieve this. The common denominator among these customers will be their concern for reliability and professionalism coupled with the latest teaching techniques.

Competition and Location

The fact that the closest day-care center of any kind is 10 miles away is also a point in CC's favor. The other centers are mainly for the lower income groups of people. There are other, smaller, private centers but they are all mediocre, not very reputable, and are located on the far side of town. CC will be strategically located in a building that is already being reserved for 1995; the contract is currently being drawn up by our lawyers. This building has been examined by the local authorities and is deemed fit for a child-care service business.

According to a national survey, more than 57 percent of men and 85 percent of women have trouble finding child-care facilities. This need for more child-care facilities has been brought to the attention of state legislatures, many of which—along with the federal government — provide subsidies for low-income families in need of baby-sitting services. However, most parents realize that baby sitters cannot provide the structured learning activities necessary in early childhood development.

Strengths

The primary strength will be its location and the fact that it will be one of the first preschools of such caliber in the city of South Orange. The child-care center will be nearer the parents' homes. Studies show that parents prefer to leave their children nearer their homes than their offices, and for this reason, centers do better in or near residential areas. Also, mothers need to feel that their kids are close by, should the occasion arise that the mothers need to see them.

The other fact is that there are no other competitors in this lucrative segment of the market. The preschool population (i.e., children between the ages of three and six) is rising, up by 10.2 percent in the past few years. Current projections call for the population of children under the age of six to increase by a further 8 percent.

Weaknesses

Because this will be a new setup, it will take some time before the center will be able to rely on word-of-mouth as its dominant marketing tool. The company will have to use the Yellow Pages and other advertising devices to make CC known. However, the establishment will be able to use both LL's and ST's networks to reach many potential customers. Because LL will be the only one providing a service of this nature in this location, achieving recognition should not pose much of a problem. As the venture takes off and the company establishes its reputation, the *parents* of the enrolled kids will be the company's salespeople.

The advertising costs are expected to be high initially, because the company will have to depend on a good "media mix" to enhance the business and reach all the potential customers. Fortunately, this will last only until the reputation of CC is established; this is expected to take between six and eight months.

Technology and Backward Integration

The most dominant feature here will be the latest teaching methods incorporated in the school curriculum. CC will have to update its facilities and mode of instruction by regularly sending its teachers for training. The director will also have to go abroad to find new ways of tapping the young minds at CC. The use of computers in the classroom will definitely be a must.

Farther down the line, CC will be a backward-integrated company—it will control some of its supply systems (e.g., the company that supplies all the stationary and elementary supplies necessary for schools). It may even go into the nutrition business and supply all meals made available at CC.

Operation Resource

The facility that will house the business allows for 35 square feet per child indoors and 50 to 70 square feet per child outdoors. Because the teachers will probably never have all the children outside at once, it is required that LL designate the play space per child for only the children who will be outdoors at any given time. (See Appendix B for "child oriented environment.") There will also be ample parking space. The minimum requirement for 30 children will be two toilets and basins for boys and the same for girls. To save on plumbing costs, the bathrooms will be located adjacent to existing adult-sized bathrooms.

Since all children will be assigned a cot, they can store their personal belongings on their cots to eliminate the need for a special storage area. Below is a list of some of the equipment CC will need:

1. Classroom stacking chairs

2. Round and rectangular tables

3. Cots, pillows, cot sheets, cot blankets

4. Storage cabinets (for toys and educational materials)

5. Tape dispensers

6. Set of state-approved swings

7. Slides

8. Sandboxes

9. Set of monkey bars

10. Stove, oven, other kitchen utensils

11. Refrigerators, freezers

12. Dishwashers, electric-mixer

13. Three-compartment sink

Office equipment also will be necessary. The installion of a computerized record-keeping system will be a necessary down-the-road move, too.

LL will provide snacks and main meals if they are requested by the parents. There will be an extra charge for these meals. (See Appendix C for a guide to child care food.) Though LL will have a few suppliers to buy from, she will run checks on the food to ensure that high standards of safety, hygiene, and balanced meals are maintained. There are many savings that can be obtained by making orders in large quantities. Because CC is an all-day child-care service, most parents will opt for the full-meal plan as opposed to the partial-meal plan. The additional cost per child will be between $5 and $10 per child per day.

Costs

The initial capital LL will need to start this business is $65,000, which will come from family savings. The service CC is offering will cost the customer between $400 and $500 per month. This payment will cover the cost of rental, equipment, advertising, utilities, professional services, owner salary, payroll, supplies, insurance, and other expenses. The projected gross sales will be between $144,000 and $180,000 (depending on whether the fee is $400 or $500 per child per month). The fee charged initially will be $400, and after six months (after market penetration) the fee will be increased to $500. This increase will be simultaneous with CC's new requirement for higher qualified teachers. The lead that CC will take in raising the standards of day-care centers in the region will justify the increase in the price.

The main costs that can deplete the finances will be the purchase of equipment. Therefore, LL will have to take great care in monitoring this element. To curb wastage, it is imperative that LL first decide on the teaching activities before ordering the needed tools. The other element that should be handled with care is the payroll—CC will need the best teachers and yet LL will have to watch the costs, too. If LL is able to keep the costs low and yet maintain high teaching standards, CC will definitely be assured of success. The self-motivated, confident, and intelligent children will be CC's best advertisers.

Industry Analysis

The Child-Care Industry Definition, Size, and Growth

The child-care industry includes all child-care services for children between the ages of three and six; this includes *all-day care* and *education*. For a start, CC will be appealing to those parents who are earning $100,000 and more per year—the upper-class community of Kenny Hills.

The actual size of the entire child population of South Orange is 87,570. The eventual target market is about 21,892 children (1990 figures from the Bureau of the Census) who will be able to afford to attend CC DAY CARE CENTER (CC). However, the current target market will be just 2 percent (439 kids in the Kenny Hills area) of the ultimate target market. This market is expected to grow by at least 20 percent in the next two to three years due to the growth in the economy; this growth is also based on the assumption that people will become more affluent and that more parents will migrate to this city because of the better, more lucrative job opportunities in South Orange.

Currently, CC has no competitors in this industry (that is, in the Kenny Hills location). This residential area is ideal for a child-care center of this nature. It is also opportune because the government will be launching a nationwide "Educational Awareness Program" in 1995. Presently, there are no special (qualification) requirements for teachers in these centers. LL will begin to set some standards by ensuring that the teachers have a minimum qualification of an undergraduate degree in Early Childhood Education. There are many well-trained teachers who are currently employed by the public sector because there are no lucrative job offers in the private sector. CC will begin the trend and allow teachers more job opportunities while raising the standards of day-care centers. Later (i.e., January 1995), CC will raise the requirements further by insisting that lead teachers have a Master's degree in Early Childhood Education.

The forward trend in this industry is that day-care centers are expected to "mushroom" everywhere because the standards of education are rising, and parents want to give their children the competitive edge. There are no startling trends in technology, except for personal computers to maintain the database of students. The prevailing preschools, kindergartens, and day-centers are synonymous and are just play schools for the kids to pass their time in safety while their parents are busy with their own careers. Some of the better centers do offer rudimentary teaching of the alphabet, but only one offers the basics of "READING, WRITING and 'RITHMATIC." This one is called "Marguerite" and is 10 miles away from CC's location.

The statistical arm of the government reports that all the government-sponsored centers are welfare-oriented, that is, they cater to the lower income bracket.

Cyclical Influences and Seasonality

LL believes that CC's long-term performance will not rise and fall as a result of the external economic cycles. There will always be a need for a good school like CC, regardless of how good or how poor the economy is; during good times the parents can afford and want to give the best to their kids; during bad times both parents may need to work to supplement their income, but they invariably want the best for their children. Generally, this type of business should do well, especially since CC's target is the very rich. Also, CC should do very well since it has no competitors in this locality.

The distribution of business activity throughout the year will not affect CC because the fees (inclusive of registration and all other related fees) for school are paid even if there are holidays. In fact, most parents will pay their registration fees very early to ensure their children are guaranteed a place in the respective schools. All fees fall due on the first of every month.

Financial Operating Characteristics

Through extensive research done by LL's partner, ST, we have arrived at the respective financial (Profit & Loss Account) estimates found in Appendix F.

The Working Paper for Setting Up CC

Assumptions and Notes

The study is limited to the preschool population in the city only. There is no point in going beyond this because the transport problems are tremendous, not to mention other obstacles.

CC will begin by charging a flat fee of $400 until the month of December 1995. This is because the teachers CC will be employing will require only a Bachelor's Degree in Early Childhood Education. Currently, the law does not require these teachers to possess any special qualifications. However, later CC will upgrade its teachers, and in 1996 CC will require lead teachers to have a Masters in Early Childhood Education. Hence, the fee will then be increased to $500.

In 1996 the classes will also get bigger, and CC will change the teaching emphasis. The selling point will be the independent learning abilities of the children. The children will be taught to be self-motivated and excel in any environment—this will be the new marketing strategy.

Sales

Purchases relate to those expenses that can be directly charged to CC's clients, that is, the students. For example, it may cost $7.50 per day to feed each child. The other costs will be called "overheads." Overhead costs are incurred in the running of the school but can only be "apportioned" to each pupil on a per-head basis. This is because the cost is usually "indirectly" incurred.

The formula is Cost per Student x Number of Children x Number of Days in the Month.

Bank Charges

A fixed figure for the charges will be assumed because of the service charges and interest rates levied by the bank on any overdrafts that CC may apply for. To be conservative, LL has provided for $200 per month.

Director's Salary

LL will assume a director's salary of $3,000 per month.

Entertainment and Refreshments

The budget for the monthly entertainment and refreshment expenditure will be $1,000. This refers to the expense involved in going out to meet prospective students and their parents.

Insurance

The going rate for a general liability medical/accident policy for the children is $10 per child.

Formula: Insurance Rate x Number of Children per Month.

Medical Fees

CC will provide some medical benefits for the staff—this covers only minor ailments. A rough estimate based on recent estimates of medical costs is $150 per month.

Newspapers and Periodicals

CC will subscribe to daily newspapers and other relevant periodicals that enable the center to keep up with the latest developments in the industry and in the city. This will cost $200 per month.

Postage

This is directly related to administration and is expected to increase with the number of children.

Printing and Stationery

Documents like letterheads and invoices have to be printed. Other office supplies are also included and the total cost is estimated to be $5,000, which will be paid for at the start of the business.

Rental

This expense will form the largest single item of overhead. Sufficiently large premises must be rented to accommodate at least 500 kids—this allows for predetermined expansion. The contract is currently being examined by our lawyers, and cost of renting the premises is expected to be $10,000 per month.

Salaries

Salaries are forecast to be as follows:

- 1 personal assistant at $2,000 per month
- 1 teacher ($900 per month initially; later, in 1994, $1,800)
- 1 administrative clerk
- 1 accounts clerk at $800 per month

Secretarial and Accounting Fee

The company will use outside professional company secretaries and auditors to manage these two aspect respectively. The present rate for these services is $1,800 per year. It can be apportioned over the period of 12 months, thus making a monthly fee of $150.

Telephone

Telephone charges fluctuate from month to month. As there is no precedent for estimating such charges, CC would be wise to provide a "safe" amount to cover any contingencies that may arise. $500 per month should be adequate.

Maintenance

The center will use an outside professional maintenance company to ensure the premises are clean. The going rate is $350 per month.

Utilities

The utilities will increase with the enrollment. The increase is projected at 10 percent per month based on the figures provided by the city utilities department.

Advertisement

Advertisements will be essential at the outset. Since the reputation of the establishment will not have been established, selection of a "media mix" is essential to the center. The medium that CC will select will be TV and radio. The local newspaper (rates of the major newspaper are seen in Appendix G) and the Yellow Pages will be the other advertising media. Hence, the initial cost of $10,000.

Leasing

The capital expenditure for this business will be mainly on the equipment required; this will, however, be leased at the rate of 8 percent over 3 years. Thus, these payments work out to be $2,584 per month.

Break-Even for July 1995:

$S = FC + VC$

$1000S = 38,609,000 = 405S$

$S = \$64,889$

Break-Even for June 1996:

$S = FC + VC$

$595S = 52,451,000$

$S = \$88,153$

Therefore, it is projected that CC will need $88,153 in sales to break even and anything more will be a profit. It can be seen that at the end of the first year CC should have $137,888 (accumulated profit/loss).

Market Analysis

Market/Location

Recent studies have shown that more than 50 percent of children are in need of day care. The need is even greater among the wealthy. There is a dire need for excellent child-care facilities, and this has been brought to the attention of the federal government. Home baby-sitting services have been sprouting around the city, but most parents realize that these baby sitters cannot provide the structured learning activities necessary in early childhood development. Besides, the authorities have also exposed some of these services as "scams." There also have been some cases of child abuse brought to light in connection with these home businesses, which has caused many parents to be skeptical about such setups.

Consequently, a more structured and professionally run day-care center will be received very well, especially by the wealthy populace. One of the most significant trends is the increase of women in the work force. As such, CC will be a welcome relief to these career-conscious women. The actual size of the entire market is 87,570 (i.e., children between the ages of three and six). The company's target market is the 21,892 kids (1990 figures from the Bureau of the Census) whose parents will be able to afford to send their children to CC. However, the initial market will be just 2 percent (439 kids in the wealthy Kenny Hills area) of the ultimate target market. This market is expected to grow by at least 20 percent within the next three years for reasons mentioned in the Industry Analysis section.

Studies show that working parents prefer to leave their children nearer home than office. For this reason, CC will do better in this residential area. The rich in this neighborhood have at least one maid per household. These maids will be able to tend to the needs of the kids more readily if the children are located near their homes. The parents in this region tend to be very well educated and in one of the highest income brackets in the country. Generally, these people are young to middle-aged CEOs of huge corporations, and own homes worth more than $500,000. Many of these residents have inherited much of their wealth from affluent ancestors.

The wealthy community of Kenny Hills is situated in the heart of South Orange and is very strategically located—it is within easy reach of all the modern conveniences: communication centers, transportation, commercial and banking centers, shopping centers, etc. Its central location makes Kenny Hills easily accessible, and yet this unique, mature dwelling of the rich is very private in its layout.

Economic Base

The wealth of this community has already been determined and mentioned in the Company Analysis section. Hence, with an average family income of $100,000 per year, CC's opportunities seem very bright. The houses here are valued at a minimum of $500,000 and the percentage of ownership is 95 percent.

Important Factors for Site Selection

Accessibility

The parents will have easy access to CC's site when dropping their children off. The center is situated on a corner location at the end of a two-lane street; it is a private road that does not have a heavy flow of traffic since it is in a private residential area. However, it is easily accessible, because there are "feeder" roads that turn off into the main street. Therefore, congestion is reduced and, because the speed of traffic is not more than 20 miles an hour, drivers will not have difficulty entering or leaving the site.

Rent

The working paper with the sales-and-profit projection for the first year of operation was discussed in the Industry Analysis. It was clearly shown how CC forecasted a gradual increase of sales (from $12,000 to $180,000) through the first year of operation. A Market Analysis of the Forecast Monthly Sales is shown in Appendix F.

The rental is seen (in Appendix F) to be as high as 80 percent of total sales in the beginning of the business, but by the end of the first 12 months it is projected to be just 5 percent of total sales. This is because the rental is quite high in this premium rental area. It is also observed that the enrollment will begin with just 12 kids and increase to 360 (30 times the initial number) by the end of the first year. As this flat rent is for two years, it will remain as a fixed cost of $10,000 throughout the contractual period.

Parking

CC will provide easy, adequate parking and access for its customers. Since this building used to be a Finishing School for girls, it has a parking area that is relatively new and does not need resurfacing; this means no additional costs to CC.

History of the Site

This building used to be a "Finishing School" for wealthy girls, but the school has been relocated to smaller premises, and has been changed to a holiday camp because the needs of its customers have changed.

Advertising

At the beginning CC will have to select a good "media mix" to enhance the business as the reputation of the center has not yet been established. The medium that CC will select in which to place its commercials will be TV and radio. The local premier daily (the rates of this major newspaper are displayed in Appendix G) and the Yellow Pages will be the other advertising media.

". . . An effective media mix should have a synergistic effect on its components . . ." (*Yellow Pages and the Media Mix,* p.1). CC's potential customers must see a newspaper ad, hear a radio spot, and see a TV commercial to reinforce the company's message at the outset of business. The impact on these potential consumers will be far greater if CC uses the "media-mix" rather than just one of these media.

Television

Television is the second largest advertising medium. It is the most dynamic of all forms of advertising because it combines visual activity and sound. Its broad appeal and large audience will definitely work for the center. However, CC has a relatively small audience, so the company will only advertise in the immediate area. TV is relatively expensive, so the spots will be selected very carefully to capture the right audience at prime time.

Radio

This is the most universal of all media. The average American has three radios per household and most cars also are equipped with one. The air times will be selected carefully because the target audience is very important to the organization. The cost for radio advertising is relatively low and is usually within the reach of many small businesses. The major drawback of radio advertising is the absolute need for repetition.

Newspapers

There are six main newspapers in the area and the Survey Research Department maintains that *The New York Times* is most widely read and circulated. This is the newspaper that is read by every household in the Kenny Hills area. The cost is relatively low and there is reader loyalty. However, because the life span is very short there will be a need for repeat ads. However, CC will be able to take advantage of the discounts being offered for "run-ons" (i.e., discounts for ads running 3 days in a row). The detailed advertising rates are listed in Appendix G.

Newspapers appeal to a diverse range of age groups and income levels; however, since this is the main publication distributed in the area it will assist CC to expand its market in later years. Newspapers, like the radio, can offer advertisers the ability to target their audiences with precision (*Yellow Pages and the Media Mix*, pp. 3, 4). The greatest advantage of this medium of advertising is flexibility; the amount of advertising is not limited, as in TV or radio, by the constraints of time. Advertisers are not limited to just one format—they can choose a full page, a two-page spread, or even buy space by the column-inch. On the other hand, newspapers have a very short life span and, like the radio, need a high degree of repetition to be effective.

The Yellow Pages

The Yellow Pages is a fast-growing advertising medium. The advertising functions of this medium are different from the other media. It does not work by creating an awareness of or a demand for CC's services; instead, it points willing customers in the direction of where this service can be had. The Yellow Pages is a "directional" medium. CC will use this medium to attract new customers who are willing to spend their money.

CC will be highly successful in the Yellow Pages because currently, it has no competitors in its niche of the market. The users of this directory are, generally, young to middle-aged, relatively well-educated, employed professionally or as managers, living in metropolitan areas, and financially well off. The Yellow Pages are in great demand and are used both at home and at places of business.

Eventually, the most important marketing tool will be by word-of-mouth. CC will inevitably concentrate on this tool. As the company's reputation grows, CC will move away from all other modes of advertising and the advertising cost will be lowered considerably. In this line of business when one is dealing with parents (who are almost always concerned with the reliability and reputation of the school and its staff), all other marketing devices will not work. Eventually, most, if not all, of the children enrolled at CC will be as a result of positive referrals. The parents of these kids will be CC's true salespeople.

Management Team

Employee Qualifications

Currently, the law requires only minimum qualifications for the staff in day-care centers. However, when CC first goes into business there will be a general requirement demanded of all the personnel. The staff will be screened carefully to ensure that CC secures the best "help" to ensure that the center will be able to offer the best service in the area.

Before hiring, the two partners will write down the following: (1) a job description, including the objectives of the job, the work performed, responsibilities, working conditions, and relationships to other jobs; and (2) the job specifications, that is, a description of the qualifications required to fill the particular job, including experience, education, special skills, and any physical requirements. See Appendix A for a sample to be adapted for CC's use.

Because CC will be taking care of children, the interview of the potential employee will be conducted in a manner that will enable the interviewer to learn as much as possible about the interviewee. CC will employ only the "trouble-free" applicants.

Duties

The Director

As the owner/director, LL's job will include almost everything initially. The director will provide the necessary hiring, training, supervising, planning the curriculum and scheduling, budgeting, making purchases, promoting the business, setting up the books, handling enrollments, solving problems, etc. Fortunately, the other partner, Mr. Stuart Lako, will help in this area, too. They will employ professional help in many of the above areas to ensure that the company starts off on its best foot.

There will be a personal assistant to help with the running of the business. This person will have a degree in education or early childhood development, and will also have good communication skills, able to relate equally well to both parents and children. There are many retired teachers with both organizational ability and expertise in dealing with young children. These retirees are currently unable to find any useful employment. It will be relatively easy to get the "cream of the crop" now.

Staff

CC will start with one college-trained teacher for every 15 children, as mentioned in the Company Analysis. CC will set the standards for quality. To ensure that this center will be the leader in this industry, it will maintain very high standards as it becomes more established—always ahead, always getting better. The center will begin with just college-trained teachers, and later as mentioned in the Industry Analysis, will hire Graduate lead teachers and under-graduate teachers' aides.

The monthly salary was taken care of in the Industry Analysis. As the profits increase and the requirements change, so will the salaries (from $900 to $1,800). Children are fragile people, so the people handling them will have to be loving, mature, and healthy, with positive attitudes about life, love, sex, and interpersonal relations. It must be noted that kids are very intelligent and extremely impressionable and will pick up attitudes and behaviors of the adults around them with amazing accuracy. The aides must also be instinctively adept at disciplining children fairly without traumatizing them. Finally, they must have the skills to implement play and instructional activity for groups of disorganized, rambunctious, strong-willed youngsters.

Other Employees

The company will hire professional company secretaries and auditors to manage these two aspects of the business. The present rate is a monthly fee of $150. There will also be an accounts clerk and an administrative staff member, who will each be paid $400 per month. The center will be maintained by professional maintenance personnel to ensure the premises are clean. The going rate is $350 per month.

Recruiting employees for this business will be limited by geography. There is no competition currently, so there will not be much competition to contend with in regards to "pinching" good staff members. However, as the company grows, CC will ensure that it shares its profits with the staff to ensure that the better members will remain with the organization. We will pay them what the market requires—with significant increases once they have proved themselves, because "two motivated, well-paid, capable employees will serve one better than three medio-cre, lackadaisical, underpaid ones . . . " Weak employees hurt the morale of the others, so they will have to go.

Good Personnel Policies

CC will go out and recruit staff at universities and schools, at established government and private employment agencies, through referrals from friends and other business firms. Adver-tising in the local daily publications can also be effective, but only if advertising expense is reasonable or the position requires special training.

References will have to be checked carefully, and extended interviews will be conducted to *weed out the undesirable*. Initially, salaries will reflect market rates or better, if this can be justified. There will be an annual review of each employee's progress and productivity. These reviews will be discussed with the employees so that they will know where they stand with the company.

Fringe benefits, health and hospital insurance, profit-sharing plans, pensions, and paid vacations will all be part of a complete personnel program. All successful business owners recognize that fair wages, attractive fringe benefits, desirable working conditions, and concern for employees are important in building a dedicated, efficient staff. Such staff will advance CC's goals and, by word-of-mouth, create an image of this company as a good place to work.

Build Employee Morale

CC will accept and use the ideas of the company's employees, and give them full credit if the idea is successful. This will definitely encourage employee contributions and cooperation and create a true spirit of aggressiveness and accomplishment. Employee morale and team spirit are important to the success of this company. Regulations with regards to salaries and minimum work hours will be strictly adhered to.

Hidden Costs of Employment

CC figures that 12 percent above total salaries will cover payroll taxes, worker's insurance, and paid vacation. There is also a portion that has to be paid into the employee retirement fund to take care of their retirement benefits and this amount is around 8 percent at present.

The failure or degree of success will often be related to the quality of employees in the organization. CC will develop professional and psychological techniques to use in the interviews to ferret out hard, smart workers. *(AEA Business Manual #X1058, Business Startup Guide.)*

Strategic Planning

Goals of the Company

CC Day Care Center will make its debut in the Kenny Hills area as the first excellent day-care center in South Orange. As it becomes a more established organization throughout the city, it will branch out into other similar locations. After the third year of operation, CC should have an enrollment of at least 1,080 children (ie., about three times the enrollment at the end of the first year).

After the first three years of operation, CC will be well known for its advanced teaching methods and will expand into other markets. This will be a good time to venture to capture the upper-middle and the middle class. CC will be in a better position to command a bigger share of this market.

In its fourth year of operation, CC will make its facilities available to toddlers from families who are in the lower income bracket. This will be a nonprofit organization and will be run to aid less fortunate children. This will be CC's way of making its contribution to society. This center will be run in conjunction with some of the government programs available, making use of teachers provided by the state but retrained by CC. This project will be done as a separate undertaking to help society and also to gain some goodwill for CC. The center will want to move away from the public image that CC is an organization only for the rich; this, then, will be a good time for CC to move into the bigger market—the entire northern portion of New Jersey.

Operations

Admissions Policies and Procedures

In the initial step of the interview, the parent and the child will be given a guided tour of CC's child-care facility. This gives the director an opportunity to "sell" the advantages of structured play and instruction with other children over simple baby sitting. Simultaneously, the exposure to the equipment, play areas, and other children will excite the child.

Almost all working parents know the need for child care, so CC's sell will be a soft one, allowing the cleanliness, friendliness, and efficiency of the facility to be observed. Next the director will determine the days and the hours that parents will need the child-care services. Monday through Friday will be best, because most parents prefer that their children have the weekends off. The rate schedule will be presented, along with a brochure describing the goals, curriculum, and services of this excellent center.

As part of the contract, the parents pay for the first term (the first three months) in advance, and then the child is scheduled to begin. CC will accept all children between the ages of three and six because this is common practice. The children will then be evaluated and placed in their respective classes; they will be allowed to progress at their own pace.

The children will not be placed in the conventional "A," "B," and "C" classes, as has been the prevalent practice in the past. This categorizing only makes the slower child feel bad and retards rather than advances his or her progress; it reinforces his or her slow capabilities. This labeling has proved to be detrimental to the well-being of such a child. Instead, children at CC will be evaluated according to their skills in reading, writing, arithmetic, etc., and when these classes are scheduled children will be regrouped according to their levels. The older children in the classes will seem to be teaching the younger ones. Children are always learning from each other, and they learn faster this way, too. Of course, this will all be done under the guidance of the teacher.

An enrollment card will be filled out by the parent, stating the child's name, address, names of parents or guardians and their home and office phone numbers, the days and hours of attendance, the child's medical insurer and policy number, and any special conditions regarding the child. A short statement of the limited liabilities and responsibilities of the facility will be printed on the card, read by the parent or guardian, and signed. This will be done in accordance with applicable law.

Food Service

The children at CC will be provided with complete menus for well-balanced meals throughout the week. This will be made possible by engaging one of the many food specialist services in the city. The food costs will be budgeted carefully, keeping a tight range of costs for the feeding of each child. It will cost about $5 per day per child: this will include breakfast, lunch, and a light snack. The light snack will be around 3 p.m., because most parents prefer to have dinner with their children between 7:30 p.m. and 8:30 p.m.

Suggested Daily Program

Schedules will be set up with the help of the directors and in accordance with the relative curriculum. See Appendix E for the guide from which CC will adapt its curriculum. The following schedule shows the kinds of activities that will be organized for the facility:

* 7:00 am to 8:00 am	Arrivals
* 8:00 to 8:30	Breakfast
* 8:30 to 9:00	Show-and-Tell Time
9:00 to 9:30	Individual Projects
9:30 to 10:00	Cooperative Learning
10:00 to 10:30	Snack Time
10:30 to 11:00	Free Play

11:00 to 11:30	Learning Skills
11:30 to 12:00 noon	Fun with Math
12:00 noon to 1:00 pm	Group Singing
1:00 pm to 2:30	Rest Time
2:30 to 3:00	Snack Time
3:00 to 4:00	Learning Skills
4:00 to 5:00	Story Time and pickup at school

The above schedule serves only as a guide; good child-care programs are not as regimented; indeed, they are flexible enough to vary with the day-to-day temperaments of the children. The key here is flexibility—this is essential when handling children.

Transportation

Delivery and pickup of these children will inevitably be done by their parents or their chauffeurs, as they all come from very wealthy households. Therefore, there will not be any extra costs incurred by CC to purchase vans or small school buses to transport the children to and from home.

Medical Problems

If an accident should occur while the child is at the center and immediate treatment is needed, the child will be taken to the emergency room of the nearest hospital, with his medical insurance information and parents' names and numbers. The hospital will inform the parents and obtain a verbal medical release.

All staff members will be required to have first-aid training, with at least one person CPR-certified. A small isolation room for the sick will be made available on the premises. The teachers will be required to give their respective students a quick checkover each morning. Any potentially contagious disease is a danger to the health of other children and employees, hence, care will have to be exercised in this area.

Regulations

CC will meet all regulations affecting the child-care industry. CC will be the leader in this industry and maintain very high standards in the operation of the facility.

Monthly Operating Statement

This is examined in great detail in the Industry Analysis (also refer to Appendix F). It is clear that the average monthly revenue will be $92,250 and the average monthly expenses will be $43,401, therefore making the net profit before tax $48,848. The gross profit will be $54,892. The net profit as a percentage of gross sales in the first year will be 52.95 percent.

Failure Factors

CC will take special care to avoid making the same mistakes that other entrepreneurs have made in the past. Constant market research or seeking help from a consultant will help resolve some of the major problems. Most small-business surveys show that the primary reasons for failure lie in the following areas:

1. Inefficient control over costs and quality of service

2. Bad stock control

3. Underpricing of service

4. Bad customer relations

5. Failure to promote and maintain a favorable public image

6. Bad relations with suppliers

7. Inability to manage efficiently

8. Failure to keep pace with management system

9. Illness of key personnel

10. Reluctance to seek professional assistance

11. Failure to minimize taxation through tax planning

12. Inadequate insurance

13. Loss of impetus in sales

14. Bad personnel relations

15. Loss of key personnel

16. Lack of staff training

17. Lack of knowledge of the service

18. Inability to cope adequately with competition

19. Competition disregarded due to complacency

20. Failure to anticipate relevant market trends

21. Loose control of liquid assets

22. Insufficient working capital

23. Growth without adequate capitalization

24. Bad budgeting

25. Inadequate financial records

26. Extending too much credit

27. Bad credit control

28. Bad control over receivables

29. Overborrowing or using too much credit

30. Loss of control through creditor's demands

Market Opportunities to Exploit

The upper class in Kenny Hills is the market segment that CC will serve as described in the Company Analysis, Industry Analysis, and the Market Analysis sections. Later, in the third year of operation, the company will venture to other geographic areas to widen its market. Here the center will serve different types of customers who will offer new opportunities. As mentioned earlier, these will be middle-class households.

Business Strategies

Market Strategies

The strategies that CC will create initially will be the small student-to-teacher ratio to satisfy the needs of its customers. However, later on, as mentioned in the earlier section, the center will move away from this strategy and focus on the teaching techniques and technology available at the center. The high standards and highly-qualified teaching staff will also be another marketing strategy used (see Appendix H).

The "media mix," as mentioned in the Market Analysis, will also be a part of the marketing strategy that CC will use to make the company a success. Television, radio, newspapers, and the Yellow Pages will be effectively used to capture the right audience and will be to CC's advantage. The most effective marketing tool, word-of-mouth, will only be used when the company has established itself in the industry. At that stage in time, all the other marketing strategies will not be as effective, because most of the enrollment will then be a direct result of positive referrals. The only exception will be new residents of the city.

Financial Analysis

Licenses and Taxes

Licenses

The city requires that the owners of CC obtain a license to show compliance with local regulations. The owners will need to pay a fee to operate the business in the city. There is no additional fee to be paid. Obtaining the license is a simple process, as there are few laws that restrict or hinder the application procedure. CC has had the premises checked by the local authorities for safety and all of the company documentation has already been taken care of by CC's lawyers.

Health-Department Permit

Since CC will not be preparing any food, it will not be necessary to obtain a health-department permit. The company will be purchasing its food supplies from a reputable food specialist (as mentioned in the Company Analysis).

Fire-Department Permit

The city's fire department requires the business to have its premises inspected for safety features. However, it does not require businesses to secure a permit. CC has already been given a "clean bill of health" by the fire department and will be ready to begin operation in July 1995.

Company Taxes

CC will have to pay a 45 percent tax on the profits. The company will be required to estimate its tax liability each year and pay it in installments if it so chooses.

At the end of each year, the organization will be required to file an income tax return for the federal and state governments and compute the tax liability on the profits earned for the year. The tax liability of the business will be calculated on a calendar year basis, and the tax return of CC must be filed with the respective department no later than April 15 of each year.

Startup

The startup expenses and the operating capital of CC were discussed in the Company and Industry Analysis sections.

The Business Plan

The process of creating this business plan has forced the directors of the company to take a realistic, objective, unemotional, more-or-less detached look at the proposed business in its entirety.

This finished business plan will become an operating tool that will help the owners to manage and work toward its success. If financing will ever be needed, this plan will become the basis for CC's loan proposal.

Financial Documentation

CC's key financial document is the profit-and-loss projection for the first five years (refer to Appendix F). This is the financial summary of projected income and expenses. It is clear that with the numerous initial expenses, CC will have to take losses in the first six months of operation. However, because businesses are allowed to accumulate their losses and carry forward for the first three years of operation, it is only in the month of April 1994 that profits are noted. This document shows the profit and loss at the end of each period, but it also shows the amount of money that will be on hand to operate the business. Appendix F also shows all the total expenses as a percentage of the total sales.

Financing

CC will need some financing in the third year of operation, when it plans to expand its market share. The company will get investors from among the directors' acquaintances to be able to arrange a better deal. CC's directors will assess the proposed value of the business in order to determine how much capital will be needed over specific periods of time.

The best source will be the directors themselves, of course. This is the easiest and quickest form of capital, and there is no interest to be paid. (This personal equity is reflected in the Balance Sheet in the amount of $65,000.) In addition, the company will not have to surrender any equity in the child-care center to "outsiders." The profits will also be carefully reinvested in the business.

The next best choice will be friends and relatives of the owners. However, any money raised through this avenue will be treated as a loan. In fact, CC's lawyers will be required to draw up loan papers for each of the contributors. This legality is sought because it will prevent lenders from gaining equity in the business (unless the directors default on the loan) and it will also protect the investor's loan.

Borrowing from Banks

The most visible sources of ready financing are banks; however, they are notoriously conservative. CC will try at all costs to avoid this avenue for various reasons.

Selling Equity

Dividing the ownership of CC among investors is not in the plan of the organization. It is just part of a contingency plan.

Selling Equity would mean that the owners would have to give up some control as well as a portion of the business. The profits would have to be shared with the new partners, depending on the setup of the establishment. The skills of good negotiators would be necessary and the services of a lawyer would be highly essential to the overall "health" of the company. It is usual for the owners to retain a 50 percent equity in the company. While the 50-50 rule is fairly common, everything is negotiable in a deal of this nature.

Appendixes

Author's Note:

List all supporting documentation in the appendix section as noted and referenced throughout your business plan.

Remember, this information should be clearly and neatly presented so the reader of your business plan can easily reference and understand the data being provided.

A Business Plan For:

Costa Pools, Inc.

Index

Introduction

THIS BUSINESS PLAN AND ACCOMPANYING MEMORANDUM MUST BE READ IN THEIR ENTIRETY BY INTERESTED PARTIES. THIS BUSINESS PLAN IS, THEREFORE, QUALIFIED IN ITS ENTIRETY BY REFERENCE TO THE FULL TEXT OF ACCOMPANYING MEMORANDUM.

COSTA POOLS, INC., is a privately owned Arizona corporation formed as a successor to COSTA POOLS, a company that has operated in the metropolitan Phoenix area in the pool service and repair business, with the same principal, since 1966. THE PRINCIPAL OF THE COMPANY HAS CONSTRUCTED APPROXIMATELY 400 POOLS. The recent incorporation of the company has been strengthened with the addition of an experienced director to face the anticipated growth. The principal owners remain the same.

This is a management team and company without a single customer or subcontractor complaint lodged against it in a lucrative industry where such complaints are all too often justified. This speaks highly of the integrity, morals, and ethics of the managing principal.

COSTA POOLS, INC., is in the unique position of not being committed to the metropolitan Phoenix market and, therefore, possesses the flexibility to design its future growth around the less competitive, more profitable, market centers consisting of Arizona's fastest growing master planned communities of CHANDLER and BULLHEAD CITY. The pool construction competition measured in these communities is less than 5 percent of what it is in the Phoenix metropolitan area.

It is the company's plan to take a leadership role in these rapidly-growing, master-planned communities. These communities represent a path of growth with the least resistance for the company, enabling management to utilize capital that normally would be required for competitive advertising programs, for services, and for inventory. Due to the growth and the lack of competitive saturation of these targeted master-planned communities, further opportunity arises in the lucrative ancillary, pool gazebos and outdoor furniture. These markets are at similar low competitive levels. Retail sales of pool supplies and accessories are a natural addition to the company's plans.

Typical of management's thorough planning is the company's plan to house corporate management and accounting in its retail outlet in a high traffic area. This element of planning minimizes overhead, tightens control, and maximizes market exposure.

COSTA POOLS, INC., therefore, has prepared this Business Plan, which is designed to capitalize on its impeccable reputation, and to take the lead in these targeted, high-intensity, low-competition markets.

Summary of Funding Requirements

The company is offering a funding opportunity in the form of a combination capital loan, a line of credit, and a homeowners financing plan to interested financiers and the opportunity to become bankers and secured lenders to the company and a wide range of its homeowner customers. All financial transactions will be secured within the State of Arizona.

Paramount to the successful growth of COSTA POOLS, INC., is the requirement that it be able to grow at a fairly rapid rate to attain a leadership position in these new markets.

Such flexibility can only come from a flexible funding plan comprising a capital loan, a line of credit, and retail financing for the homeowner customers. Some floor-planning credit lines may be required for the company's retail store operation.

Specifically, the funding to be made available through this plan will be utilized as follows:

1. **Capital Loan.**

   To acquire additional equipment.

   To underwrite initial increase in cost of operations and new Chandler facility.

2 . **Line of Credit.**

   To serve as future growth capital if and when required.

3. **Homeowner Financing.**

   To provide a financing package to customer homeowners for financing pools, spas, and patio construction as home improvements.

4. **Floor Planning for Retail Store.**

   To serve as required should retail sales volume of large ancillary items, i.e., gazebos, spas, and outdoor furniture require displays and promotional sales inventories.

These expenditures, together with the results thereof, will:

1. Increase line and volume of service and repair operation by 100 percent in a demand market.

2. Permit the company to realize prudent growth to a leadership role in its marketplace.

3. Increase sales, give the company the competitive edge, provide total service to customers; reciprocate courtesies to company's bank by referring all homeowners to the bank for their banking needs.

4. Enable the company to be the only single source, one-stop retail center for the market community.

The projected results of these financial support functions can be evaluated by examining this Business Plan in its entirety.

This Business Plan essentially involves the development of increased services and products to feed an existing, fast-growing, and underserviced market. To fully capitalize on these plans, the following levels of financial support may be required.

Maximum Amounts of Funding Requirements

Capital Loan (Chandler)	up to $100,000
Credit Line (Growth Capital)	up to $100,000
Floor Planning (Retail)	up to $50,000
Home Owner Finance Plan (Monthly)	up to $75,000

The Corporation

This is a privately owned Arizona Corporation, which began operation in 1966 as an unincorporated entity. The founding principal and current owner is Mr. Donald Shell, who formed the operation during his tenure as a Captain of the Cactus, Arizona, Fire Department. The company was incorporated in October 1993 as part of this Business Plan. The corporation is authorized to issue 10,000,000 shares of common stock and has issued 150,000 shares to Mr. Shell, representing substantial control of the issued and outstanding stock of the corporation. The balance of the shares of the common stock is held in the treasury of the corporation.

The officers, directors, and managers of the company consist of:

Donald Shell, President and Director
Nancy Shell, Secretary and Director
James Shell, Vice-President and Director
W. R. Tercell, Advisor and Director

Commensurate with the implementation of this Business Plan, the company's investment banking firm will appoint one of its senior partners to act in the capacity of director of the corporation and as a full-time advisor to management. This Advisor/Director has more than 30 years of hands-on management experience in the service and contracting fields and has agreed to serve in this capacity for the remuneration of $100 per Director's meeting, plus direct travel expenses as required to assist the corporation in its business affairs.

The corporation is in good standing and is not a party to any legal proceedings at this date, nor has it ever been involved in any form of litigation or adversity. The books of the company have been professionally established by a Certified Public Accountant and will be maintained accordingly, pursuant to this Business Plan.

The books and records of the corporation will be audited by independent auditors on a regular semiannual basis, at which time certified financial statements will be presented to management. All such financial statements will be provided to the corporation's banks.

The corporation utilizes computer accounting for monthly operating statements and management control.

The Management

Mr. Donald Shell, President and Director, has 27 years of management, training, and service-related experience. Thirteen of these twenty-seven years of experience were as a Captain of the Cactus, Arizona Fire Department, where he excelled in management, training personnel, and public relations. He served in each area of work over a sustained and lengthy period of time. Mr. Shell later served as Fire Chief for the City of Thunderbird, Arizona.

His management position with these municipalities in a stress-related field required only four-day workweeks and, therefore, enabled Mr. Shell to found COSTA POOLS in 1966. While operating COSTA POOLS in purely an ancillary position during this period, he still managed to have the company appointed as warranty service agent for the leading pool equipment and construction companies, including Black Hydro, Stay Now Industries, Inc., Northwest Motors, Ltd., Dade's Heaters, Inc., A. Eberling Corporation, and Langone Industries, Inc. The company became recognized as a qualified and reputable expert from the outset as a result of Mr. Shell's efforts.

Separately, and as a result of a personal interest in the projects, Mr. Shell functioned consecutively as Marketing Director and co-owner of electric and computer-oriented companies, wherein he gained six additional years of invaluable management experience.

He was born in 1934, has virtually perfect health, and attended Phoenix College, where he attained a GPA of 3.94—4.0.

It is anticipated that Mr. Shell will manage all of the bidding policy and supervisory field work of COSTA POOLS, INC.

Mrs. Nancy Shell, Secretary and Director, has 8 years of administrative, sales, public relations, and management experience. Three of the 8 years' experience was hands-on line management. Mrs. Shell excels in administration, computer operation, and public relations. She was formerly owner-manager of a computer-oriented company, where she gained extensive experience in the day-to-day operations of a company.

She was born in 1947, is the wife of Mr. Donald Shell, has virtually perfect health, and attended both Scottsdale Community College and Glendale Community College, where she majored in Business.

It is anticipated that Mrs. Shell will manage the administration and public relations of COSTA POOLS, INC.

Mr. James Shell, Vice-President and Director, has 17 years of hands-on experience in the servicing, repair, and sales of pool-oriented supplies. He has played a major role in the service of the company from its inception, beginning at a very early age.

His tenure with the company was temporarily interrupted during his college educational period.

James attended Oral Roberts University and attained a Bachelor of Science degree in Business Management, with a minor in Spanish Language.

His 17 years of hands-on experience in the pool business, coupled with his Business Management degree and management experience, make him a key employee. The family loyalty and first-hand interest further enhance his abilities.

James was born in 1955 and has virtually perfect health. It is anticipated that James will assist in the overall business aspects of the company, with emphasis on proper accounting, service, and planning.

Mr. W. R. Tercell, Advisor and Director, is a senior partner and co-owner in the Investment Banking Company of UNDERWRITERS INVESTMENTS CORP, LTD. He has 33 years of management and financial experience as a principal of various corporations. He is the former President of American Investment Bankers, Inc., Soccer Investment Division, and owner of five operating companies, including a Mortgage Banking and Brokerage firm, an investment management firm, a publishing firm, an energy development firm, and a full-service travel agency. Mr. Tercell previously owned and operated Word Inc. for a period of 10 years. Word Inc. employed 248 employees and operated 34 aircraft for the United States Government Top Secret and "Q" clearance projects throughout the world.

Mr. Tercell began his career as an Industrial Engineer with the Cool Radio Company (Rockcliff Corporation) in 1953 and advanced to marketing management. Later he was employed by Leer Inc. and functioned as head of Leer's Domestic and International commercial marketing operations until he formed his own company in 1968.

Mr. Tercell attended Glendale City College, Los Angeles City College, and the University of California at Los Angeles, where he majored in Business and Industrial Engineering.

Mr. Tercell is the recipient of numerous industry awards; has served as officer, director, committeeman or chairman of nine separate industry organizations; and has lectured before the American Society of Tool Engineers, Association of Airline Presidents, Electronics Manufacturers Association, National Junior Achievement Organization, Mortgage Bankers Association, and others.

Mr. Tercell is known throughout most of the world for various business endeavors. His business biography is listed in *Who's Who in Finance and Industry, Personalities of America, International Who's Who of Intellectuals,* and six other international registries.

He will serve as a full-time advisor to management of the company for an indefinite period of time.

The Products and Services

The company's business consists of marketing both products and services as follows:

1. Pools

The company offers a wide variety of custom pool designs for the pool buyer at an average cost of $15,000, including extras or add-ons, based on a 5-year history of purchases in the Phoenix metropolitan area.

2. Service and Repair

This is perhaps the most active market area of the company, involving hundreds of customers. It is also the original product of the company. The service consists of short- and long-term contracts for maintenance of the pool chemical balance and scheduled cleaning of the pool. The repair portion of this service is a natural extension of pool maintenance.

The repair work consists of warranty work for manufacturers of pool equipment, i.e, pumps, heaters, filters, and other repair work at the request of the pool owners.

3. Decking

Each pool includes standard decking, or a conventional amount of quality decking known as cool decking; however, the company offers expert craftsmanship in designing and constructing custom decking. In some cases, the extra custom deckwork approaches the price of the pool.

4. Spas

The company offers a complete line of spas, both remanufactured and custom-built. Spa sales, installations, and service represent a substantial market of its own. One market for spas is the pool owner who demands the ultimate luxury of the added spa. The second, and very large, market for the spa is the space-limited homeowner, who is unable to purchase a pool due to space restrictions. A third, and ancillary, spa market is the therapeutics and recreational market.

5. Gazebos

This market has steadily increased throughout the Southwest during the past decade. Gazebos are particularly popular in the Arizona area, due to the high temperature ranges. They are often purchased in conjunction with spa purchases and as accessories to patio and pool decor.

6. Patios and Patio Covers

This market is quite often stimulated by the homeowner's purchase of a pool, especially with new homes. The pool builder logically has the inside track to this business. It is a logical and basic extension of the pool and new home. The company designs each custom patio and patio cover to meet the customer's demands.

This product is, however, often acquired by homeowners independent of any purchase of a pool. Patios and patio covers are the number-one home improvement made by owners of older homes. Once again, the vast Arizona market for this product is, in part, due to the extreme heat levels experienced in the area.

7. Outdoor Furniture

This is an annual multimillion-dollar business in the State of Arizona. Not only is it the first accessory purchased by pool, spa, and patio purchasers, but it is expendable due to its direct exposure to weather extremes and rough recreational treatment by homeowners. While customers view this service as a convenience to themselves, it is, in fact, a very large and profitable business.

The company's products are all depicted in a professionally prepared, quality color brochure and other literature issued by the company, together with a price list for all products except custom items. The less costly sales literature is utilized for general distribution in developing interest and sales leads, while the more costly quality color brochure is presented only to known or qualified prospective pool purchasers.

The Facilities

The facilities of the company are considered minimal for the sales volume generated. They consist primarily of:

- A single combination, commercial building, housing a retail sales outlet, warehouse, and corporate and administrative offices. This building consists of approximately 5,000 square feet with 3,000 square feet allocated to retail sales, 1,000 square feet of warehouse, and 1,000 square feet of general offices.

- An exterior display area of approximately 2,000 square feet, together with a security fence, is required directly adjacent to this building. Additionally, and to the rear of the building, is a security-fenced storage lot for company vehicles, equipment, and a chlorination storage tank.

This facility must be located in a high-traffic location of the community. The extended Business Plan calls for a second, self-underwritten, retail outlet during the third year of the plan and a major new building in the Chandler area during the fifth year of the Business Plan.

The Equipment

It is the plan of the company to minimize company-owned equipment related to the pool construction portion of the business. The company will, for several more years, utilize subcontractors in the construction portion of its operation. This method of construction enables the company to parallel its direct expenses with income and, simultaneously, contract multiple jobs without the burden of a major debt service for equipment. This policy will apply to all pool construction, concrete, and patio contracts.

The service and repair operation of the company requires a moderate amount of equipment, including service route vehicles, service tools, chlorination storage facilities, and repair-shop tools. The retail sales operation of the company requires a moderate amount of equipment, including display counters, warehouse and store shelving, outdoor sign, one office set of furniture, cash register, and miscellaneous hand tools.

The general offices of the company, which are housed by the retail sales facility, require two office sets of furniture, a computer, telephone system, and various miscellaneous accessories, including copy machine, calculators, and typewriters.

Summary of Equipment

General Offices:

2 sets, office furniture

1 computer

1 telephone system

1 set, office machines and equipment

1 radio, base communications system

2 executive automobiles for sales and company business

Construction Operations:

1 one-half-ton pickup truck

1 radio mobile system

Service and Repair Operations:

6 one-half-ton minitrucks

4 sets of service tools and equipment

2 sets of repair tools and equipment

1 chlorination, central storage supply tank

1 set of tools and equipment for repair shop

6 radio mobile systems

Retail Sales Operation:

12 sections, display counters

16 sections, steel warehouse shelving

1 outdoor sign

1 cash register

1 set, office furniture

1 set, miscellaneous tools and equipment

The Market

The basic object of this Business Plan is to strategically position the company in a minimum-competition, high-demand market, with ongoing growth. Hence, the markets of Chandler and Bullhead City, Arizona.

In both markets there exists phenomenal growth in housing coupled with virtually nonexistent, local competition in the pool business. This situation exists only as a matter of timing. The pool industry has not yet responded to these vast markets. It is paramount to the company's long-term industry status to immediately establish itself in these available markets. Once established in these markets, it will serve as a deterrent to competition and allow for further penetration of these markets prior to the entry of any measurable competition. The company's impeccable reputation will boost its efforts in establishing itself as the leader in these markets.

The company plans to service the Chandler, Arizona, market as a locally-based, owned, and operated company.

It will service the Bullhead City, Arizona, market through an alliance with home builders in the area and through local sales representation.

The plan is to group Bullhead City contracts, or schedule five or more contracts, for completion during the same period. This plan will be cost-effective and provide adequate service for the immediate market. The company's future plans make provisions for a second autonomous operation to be based at Bullhead City. This operation, although to be separated physically and financially, will be a duplication of the Chandler operations.

The company has made no plans beyond these markets except through its service and repair operations, whereby it will continue to serve existing and new clients located throughout the South Phoenix-Tempe-Gilbert-Mesa market.

Chandler Market

1. There are no pool builders in Chandler or listed in the Chandler telephone directories through 1993.

2. There are only 3 retail pool supply stores in Chandler, serving a population base of more than 80,000, a ratio of 26,666 residents to each retail store.

Sample Comparison:

In the Phoenix metropolitan area there are 155 retail pool supply stores serving a population base of 1,900,000 residents, a ratio of only 12,258 residents to each retail store (approximately 633,333 houses and 158,333 pools).

In metropolitan Phoenix there are approximately 1,022 pool owners to each retail store. In the Chandler area there are approximately 3,111 pool owners to each retail store.

3. There are only 4 pool service and repair firms in Chandler serving the population base of more than 80,000, a ratio of 20,000 residents or 2,333 pool owners, to each service and repair firm.

Sample Comparison:

In the Phoenix metropolitan area there are 236 service and repair firms serving the population base of 1,900,000 residents, a ratio of 8,051 residents, or only 671 pool owners, to each pool service and repair company.

4. In 1980 there were only 29,673 residents of Chandler. This increased to more than 80,000 residents by 1989, an increase of 170 percent, or 21 percent per year. Current studies by the Department of Planning and Development, as approved by Maricopa County Association of Governments, project 93,341 residents by 1994, 104,342 residents by 1995, and 197,288 residents by 2000; a further increase of 147 percent, or 11 percent per year for the future.

5. Chandler is consistently one of the two fastest-growing communities in the State of Arizona (Bullhead City is the other).

6. New housing and new pool starts in Chandler have been:

Houses		Pools	Ratio	Pools/Houses
1990-91	3,548	262		7%
1991-92	1,876	727		39%
1992-93	3,238*	1,184 *		37%

7. The progressive mode of Chandler city officials toward developing the downtown financial district, Chandler Airpark, and Chandler City Center encourages future growth even beyond present rates and projections. The company's plan is to be a vital part of this growth.

8. There are approximately 540 pools constructed each month in the adjacent market of Phoenix. There has been an average of 1,029 new homes constructed each month (12,350 per year) in the Phoenix area since 1975. One out of every three of these new homes receives a pool. One out of every 35,186 older homes receives a pool (or 180 additional pools each month).

9. More than 40 percent of Chandler's residents are between 25 and 44 years of age and more than 75 percent of Chandler's residents have attended college, two important elements related to the pool market.

10. Chandler Airpark alone is projected to produce 22,000 new jobs by 1995 and 45,000 by 2005.

Bullhead City Market

1. The Bullhead City market area consists of 100,000 residents; 42,000 of these residents are located in Bullhead City and Laughlin, Nevada.

2. There are no builders located in Bullhead City or listed in the Bullhead City telephone directory.

3. There are only two retail pool supply stores located in Bullhead City, a ratio of 50,000 residents to each retail store. (See item 7 herein regarding temporary versus permanent housing.)

Sample Comparison:

Phoenix area ratio, 12,258 to 1

Chandler area ratio, 26,666 to 1

4. There are no pool service and repair firms located in the Bullhead City market area.

Sample Comparison:

Phoenix area ratio, 8,051 to 1

Chandler area ratio, 20,000 to 1

5. There are approximately 33,000 single-family dwellings located in the Bullhead City market area. Bullhead City population grew 60 percent from 1980 to 1985. In 1985 there were only 18,000 residents. This is projected to increase to 43,868 residents by 1995, an increase of more than 143 percent or more than 14 percent per year.

6. Bullhead City is consistently one of the two fastest-growing communities in the State of Arizona (Chandler is the other).

* annual rate based upon new starts through June 30, 1993.

7. The rapidly-growing housing requirements of the neighboring Laughlin Hotel and Casino industry are forcing Bullhead City's growth. During 1991 and 1992 there were more than 10,000 new jobs created within the Bullhead City market area. For the same period there were 364 new housing starts and 494 temporary housing (mobile) starts. There was virtually no housing available in Laughlin (in 1992). Laughlin, Nevada, is one of the fastest-growing small cities in the United States and is located across a river bridge from Bullhead City, Arizona.

8. The Arizona Department of Commerce projects 14,294 new housing starts in Bullhead City by 1995.

9. There is no adjacent community or city to compete with Bullhead City (or Laughlin) for the influx of residents. Phoenix is located 204 miles southeast of Bullhead City and Las Vegas is located 73 miles northwest of Laughlin.

10. The new employee/residents are largely transfers from Las Vegas, Nevada, and Phoenix, Arizona, two of the country's most pool-oriented communities.

11. Bullhead City/Laughlin consistently records the highest daily temperatures in the United States (85.4 degrees annual average), the number-one known factor favorable to pool sales.

12. More than 80 percent of Bullhead City's residents (Laughlin employees) are between 25 and 40 years of age, a favorable age range for pool owners.

13. Demographers project that the neighboring Laughlin Hotel and Casino business will create more than 62,500 new jobs in the 1994 through 1997 period (about 11.5 service-oriented jobs for each of the 5,000 Hotel-Casino jobs).

14. New housing construction, as reported by the Bullhead City Planning and Zoning Commission, increased more than 500 percent for the period 1991 through 1992. It increased another 68 percent through July 1993.

The Marketing Program

The company's marketing program is primarily dictated by demand markets as set forth in this Business Plan. Demand markets call for "service marketing" as opposed to sales-oriented marketing. Servicing a demand market drastically reduces the usual costs of competitive advertising and solicitation. It is every company's dream, but few have the insight to plan their company's growth around such markets.

Equally important in the planning and structure of the company's marketing plan is to recognize its competition as it is presently, and as it is anticipated to be at future periods. Therefore, this Business Plan is based upon a portion of known markets that the company can reasonably expect to capture. The conservative projections should in no way be viewed as negative or pessimistic. They are the company's guidelines to financial control, and experienced management knows that it is much less painful (financially) to grow than to recede.

The company's marketing program will consist of six key elements.

1. *One-on-One, Quality Brochure.* This is directed only to the qualified and interested prospective buyer. It consists of an embossed cover and eight full-color pages depicting the company's complete range of products and services. This brochure is comparable in all respects to those utilized by the leaders in the industry. The purposes: to give the company an edge over most competitors, to eliminate questions relative to the company and its products, and to carry forward the company's image of quality and ethics.

Brochures such as this generally eliminate from competition the independent, the unlicensed, and the unscrupulous pool builders that make up a large part of the pool builders serving the Phoenix area. Such brochures also enable the company to sell using representatives who are less than highly paid experts, while maintaining factual and controlled representations of the company products and policies.

2. *Advertising.* The company's media advertising is limited to strategically-positioned listings.

3. *Industry Interface.* Management's association with home builders, real estate agencies, and civic organizations generates a high level of referrals in the market communities.

4. *Vehicular and Facilities Decor.* The company's logo and image is conveyed to hundreds of homeowners every day, making it an acceptable entity in the market communities.

5. *Community Activities.* The company and its principals participate in and support meaningful organizations and functions, including the Chamber of Commerce and business-related organizations.

6. *Select Direct-Mail Brochure.* This envelope-size, foldover, low-cost brochure is an introductory piece only, directed toward generating inquiries from home buyers as recorded in city, county, and other records. It places emphasis on pool service and repair, because of the large number of homes being purchased that already have pools; however, it depicts the company's wide range of product and experience.

The Competition

The company's competition is principally preoccupied with the massive Phoenix Metropolitan Area's 1,900,000 residents. The Chandler and Bullhead City markets are not only remote and bothersome to the metropolitan-based pool builders, but they represent less than 5 percent of their immediate market targets. This will benefit COSTA POOLS, INC.

It is a long-established marketing fact that local residents will trade with local businesses more than 95 percent of the time when an equivalent selection of products, prices, and services is available. The company's plans are to fulfill these requirements.

The known competition is the pool builders of the metropolitan Phoenix area. There were 76 such pool builders operating in 1993. There were 79 in 1992, and 73 during 1988 through 1991.

This establishes a ratio of one pool builder for each 25,000 residents for the metropolitan Phoenix area, compared with COSTA'S position in Chandler of one pool builder to 80,000 residents and in the Bullhead City market area, of one pool builder to 100,000 residents, a 300 to 400 percent advantage with respect to established residents.

The percentage growth rate in new housing construction of both Chandler and Bullhead City far exceeds the metropolitan Phoenix area (Chandler, 58 percent, 1993; Bullhead City, 500 percent, 1992 through 1993; metropolitan Phoenix, 2.9 percent, 1993). However, the overall current size of these markets is dwarfed by the massive metropolitan Phoenix market which is required by the larger pool competitors to sustain their volume and overhead. It is highly unlikely that the major competition will redirect effective efforts toward the markets of Chandler and Bullhead City in the near future.

The unknown competition for these select markets is the second- and third-level, small pool contractors. This is the segment of the industry where integrity and service problems prevail. This is the company's most competitive edge, its impeccable integrity and service. The company has prepared itself for this area of competition by becoming a locally owned and operated business and by the publication of quality literature featuring the company's record. The company projects that this level of competition will initially affect certain sales due to a period of public education; however, such competition generally results in added business for companies such as COSTA POOLS, INC.

The company anticipates the so-called copy-cat competition that traditionally follows any successful program. However, management believes that such competition will not appear until after the second year of the company's plan of operating in these markets.

The company believes that all such competition will serve to stimulate industry growth, more sales, and certainly, more service contracts.

The Financials

Author's Note

As suggested earlier, the financial presentation portion of the business plan needs to be well prepared. If assistance is needed, contact a reputable accounting or other business firm that will be able to provide accurate, reasonable, and meaningful information.

As a general guide, the financial section may include the following data:

- *Notes, definitions, and assumptions used in preparing the financial data.*

- *Profit and loss forecasts:*
  —years one and two by month;
  —years three through five by year.

- *Balance sheet forecasts:*
  —years one and two by quarter;
  —years three through five by year.

- *Cash flow forecasts:*
  —years one and two by quarter;
  —years three through five by year.

The Growth Potential

The growth potential of the company's selective markets is phenomenal. It is one that must be prudently managed, not aggressively attacked for maximum sales. The rate of growth of these markets far exceeds the company's projected growth. The company's plans are deliberately restricted to approximately 2 percent of these markets. This is believed to be an easily attainable objective to reach and maintain with satisfactory profits and minimum risks.

This plan does not preclude the company's automatic growth as a result of its maintaining the 2 percent of these growing markets. As the market grows, so grows the company's position of 2 percent of the market.

The company's secondary plans for growth include a second full-service, autonomous operation at Bullhead City. This is expected to be in place prior to the end of the second year of this Business Plan at a time when the company has surplus capital available.

The growth of the company is limited only by management's conservative approach of slow, profitable growth. It is not within the company's plans to become the "biggest" or "largest," but to always be recognized for its quality and impeccable reputation.

The company believes that reasonable growth is one of manageable reality.

The Diversification Program

The company is fully diversified within the pool construction industry by the product line it markets, which includes pool construction, spas, gazebos, patios, outdoor furniture, pool service, pool repair, and retail sales of supplies and accessories.

Part of the secondary diversification plan of the company is to purchase and own real estate related to its business, specifically, the facilities of its retail outlets and residential properties of the principals.

The long-term plan for diversification calls for the formation of a subsidiary finance company that will enable the company to build contract equities.

Since the company is service-oriented, it is difficult for it to accrue real assets. Therefore, a major effort is being made to increase its real-asset base over the term of this business plan. Management intends to build the company's asset base with:

1. Retained earnings

2. Real estate holdings

3. Contract equities

4. Equipment ownership

5. Inventory investments

These plans should lead the company away from the traditional weaknesses affiliated with service-oriented companies.

Summary of Business Plan

This Business Plan has been developed by management from their more than 20 years of operating experience in the subject industry and with the assistance of professional consultants utilizing 33 independent and authoritative sources of data. Each representation contained herein is believed to be not only factual but conservative.

Emphasis has necessarily been placed on identifying the selected markets. The end results prove beyond a doubt that management has selected the most favorable markets in which to attain the desired profit levels. There are few, if any, markets that possess the attractiveness of the selected markets, which are virtually free of competition and rich with growth. Management properly points out that such market conditions exist only as a result of timing. The company's plan is to immediately assume leadership in these markets.

Paramount to the substance of this Business Plan is management's decision to restrict all projections, current and future, to a nominal, less than 2 percent share of the known markets. It is believed that this portion of the market can be attained with very little cost to the company at a very profitable level. Given all of these favorable factors, management has still compiled all projections herein with less than one-half of the company's normal percentage of profit (28% versus 13%).

Despite the foregoing, a $1,280,000 net profit is anticipated for the projected period.

Receipt for Copy of Business Plan

I acknowledge that I have received a copy of the 1992 through 1996 proprietary Business Plan of COSTA POOLS, INC.

I acknowledge receipt of this Business Plan both as a responsible individual and as an authorized representative of the entity I have listed below.

I understand that this Business Plan is the proprietary property of COSTA POOLS, INC., and must not be shown to others, or reproduced in part or whole, without the express written consent of COSTA POOLS, INC.

I agree to immediately return this Business Plan to the company either upon completing my review or upon terminating further business interest in the plan. Under any circumstance, or event, I agree to return this Business Plan to COSTA POOLS, INC., immediately upon its request.

_____

Company or Entity

_____

Name   Title

_____

Address

_____

Telephone Number

A Business Plan For:

The Diamond Brokers USA

November 1994

President:

Jim Smith

1122 W. Box 123

Fort Lauderdale, FL 88448

Table of Contents

Executive Summary

The Diamond Brokers USA is a small retail jewelry business located in Fort Lauderdale, Fla. It began through the part-time efforts of Mr. Jim Smith. During the early years of growth, the firm had little direction, poor financial reporting, and few efforts in marketing. Mr. Smith has recently received his M.B.A. from Florida State University and is now taking the firm into a new period of growth.

The firm recently moved to a new location on Fifth Avenue, after operating on the sixth floor of a bank building for the past six years. Mr. Smith has hired three additional full-time salespersons to help implement his marketing strategy. With commitment to a direct marketing strategy (personal selling), the firm should increase revenues substantially. To date the firm has steadily increased sales each year as a result of word-of-mouth advertising. Mr. Smith will continue to focus on the strengths of the firm: low overhead, a professional environment, strong clientele base, and an established reputation.

The Diamond Brokers USA will market fine jewelry and incentive and recognition awards. Its target markets include engaged couples, the "professional," insurance companies (insurance replacements), and small to medium-sized corporations. The strategy consists of developing and expanding the current customer base through direct mail and telephone prospecting. Businesses and professionals will be contacted and visited by out-of-store salespeople. A database will be developed and used for marketing to the repeat customer. A newsletter will continue to be sent to the firm's clientele.

The Diamond Brokers USA will need additional capital ($50,000) to finance expansion. Much of these funds will be used to expand inventory. The balance will give the firm the working capital it needs to grow. Projected returns show that the firm should generate a $28,890 profit after one year and $67,802 after the second year.

The Diamond Brokers USA had its beginnings as the part-time endeavor of Jim and Mary Smith. As a student at Florida State, Mr. Smith used his background in diamonds to generate extra income for the family. After graduation, Mr. Smith moved to Fort Lauderdale Fla., as an employee of the L.D.S. Public School System. He continued to wholesale diamonds and jewelry to local jewelers and private individuals. He eventually opened an office on the sixth floor of the First Interstate Bank Plaza in Fort Lauderdale. Over the past five years, his clientele of retail customers has grown and he has discontinued wholesaling.

The Diamond Brokers USA has distinguished itself from conventional jewelry stores. Because it was located on the sixth floor, Mr. Smith kept overhead extremely low. This, combined with his ability to buy from some of the nation's largest manufacturers and suppliers, enabled him to offer diamonds and diamond jewelry at extremely low prices. Marketing consisted of word-of-mouth referrals. The firm employed a small part-time sales force and a part-time office manager. (Most of these have been college students.) Since its beginning, annual sales have increased from $35,000 to over $200,000. The firm is open six hours a day, Monday through Friday. The firm successfully built a loyal following because of personal attention, a professional environment, education given to the customer, and extremely low prices.

The Diamond Brokers USA's sales are in two areas: the diamond and jewelry market and, to a lesser degree, the marketing of incentive and recognition awards to Fort Lauderdale companies. Mr. Smith feels that the latter field has great potential, but has done very little to develop this area. The firm has several major accounts, including the U-Haul Corporation and Benjamin Wholesale.

Another area of success has been among "professionals." The Diamond Brokers USA has a developing network among professionals. This is in part because Mr. Smith is willing to go to their offices.

Sales for the firm are broken down as follows: Diamonds and diamond jewelry, 56 percent of total sales; karat gold rings, 15 percent; karat gold jewelry, 9 percent; custom work and repairs, 12 percent; corporate awards, 6 percent; and other, 2 percent.

To serve customers better, and in an attempt to increase walk-in traffic, the firm recently moved from its sixth floor location to the ground floor of the same bank plaza. The firm has maintained its professional image. There is a small display area, but the majority of the selling takes place in an office setting. The owner has employed a second office staff member. (There are currently four store personnel, and four part-time salespeople, besides the owner.) The firm has production and repair facilities on the premises. D&L Jewelry Repair, an independent goldsmith, sublets space in the office and performs work for The Diamond Brokers USA on a contract basis.

Industry Analysis

Today, the consumer has many options when purchasing fine jewelry. (Fine jewelry is defined as diamond, gemstone, and karat gold jewelry.) Traditional retail outlets, the family-owned stores, are decreasing in number as large retail chains continue to expand. There are more than 24,000 stores in the United States, with about 360 stores in the state of Florida. Small stores with annual sales of less than $100,000 account for 25 percent of all jewelry stores, yet they have less than 4 percent of all sales. By contrast, stores with annual sales of more than $1 million account for 7 percent of the industry and have approximately 35 percent of total sales. Other sources for jewelry include the growing number of "wholesale clubs" and discount department stores, such as Target and K mart. (Catalog sales of fine jewelry have not fared well.) In 1993, as reported by *JCK Almanac*, 70.7 percent of all diamond jewelry purchases were at jewelry stores, 13.4 percent at department stores, 7.3 percent at catalog showrooms and discount stores, and the balance at other sources. Jewelry sales have continued to increase steadily since 1982 and are expected to continue to climb at an annual rate of 9 percent through 1995. In 1993, sales topped $12 billion.

Today's markets are more diversified. Shoppers are more segmented than in the past. Recent surveys published in the *Jewelers Circular Keystone* have indicated that the younger markets are attracted largely by price. More mature jewelry buyers are concerned with quality and service. In an interview with Tracy Larsen of the *Jewelers Circular Keystone* Marketing and Statistical Department, it was noted that wholesale clubs were felt initially in the market, but that the effect has stabilized and jewelers are not reporting any serious threats. (No harder evidence is available at this time.) Ms. Larsen stated that most consumers of fine jewelry want a certain amount of service and education with their purchases, and hesitate to buy from a "warehouse" outlet.

In the latest study of how jewelry sales are distributed, diamond jewelry was the highest category of jewelry sold across the industry. Diamond engagement rings were the top category for most stores, followed by other diamond jewelry. Total diamond jewelry sales for small to medium-sized stores were approximately 30 percent of their total revenues. In larger stores (chain stores), 40 percent of their sales were diamond jewelry. Smaller stores dominate in the area of jewelry repairs. They handle nearly 50 percent of all repairs in the industry, while collecting one fourth of their total revenues for this service.

It appears that the large variety in distributors serves a wide variety of market niches. Large chains and department stores offer the most variety in merchandise. They heavily promote credit purchases. They often use promotional sales, using high markups to allow for promotional markdowns. Another market segment is served by the smaller chains or upper-scale independent jewelers. These stores target the more affluent buyer and focus on quality and service. Still another group are the "mom and pop" operations that rely heavily on years of past performance and an established clientele. These stores offer a variety of services and products at a moderate price. They represent a "vanishing breed," as the previously mentioned groups are taking away their small market share.

The traditional jewelry store works on a high-markup basis. The average markup for chain stores runs between 300 percent and 400 percent. The following information was obtained in an interview with a manager of a Miami-based medium-sized chain. (The interviewee asked to remain anonymous to avoid any problems with his employers.) The firm marks jewelry up an average of 300 percent, striving for a 60 percent gross margin. Twenty-five percent of this margin is for salaries and expenses, and the balance contributes to profit. Many items are marked up much higher than 300 percent to maintain the average. Larger diamonds of 1.5 carats or more are only marked up 60 percent. He stated that the use of even higher markups followed by "50-percent-off sales" used to be a key strategy, but that consumers are much wiser today; thus, the strategy is no longer used. To compensate, this store has kept markups level and decreased its advertising budget considerably. It also has found that putting more of its advertising dollar into increased merchandise has helped improve sales and profits.

The most profitable products in stores are diamond engagement sets (11.4 percent of sales), other diamond jewelry (9.1 percent), and 14-kt. gold jewelry (8.8 percent).

Financial Analysis of the Diamond Consortium

Pertinent financial data on The Diamond Brokers USA is only available for 1989 and later. Previous to 1989, the operation was much smaller and maintained a poor record system. Much of the information available for that period is lost and/or faulty. From 1989, sales have increased steadily, from $151,679 to $210,679. Net income has gone from a $5,000 loss to nearly a $10,000 profit three years later (see Projections and Financials). Currently, sales are about the same as last year at this time but profits are higher. An analysis of The Diamond Brokers USA's financial data shows some interesting comparisons with the industry. Although the industry strives for gross margins of 60 percent, The Diamond Brokers USA has consistently had a gross margin of about 22 percent. Since its move in May 1990, as well as the hiring of two full-time salesmen to pursue out-of-office sales, monthly overhead has increased. At the current level of sales, the firm needs a margin of at least 40 percent to break even. To compensate for this, it has recently raised prices by 20 percent. If sales remain level, this will produce the margin necessary to cover overhead. Any increase in sales over last year as a result of increased marketing efforts or the new location will contribute to profits.

A comparison of inventory with annual sales shows an inventory turnover of 6 compared with an industry average of 2.3. This appears to be good, yet a large percentage of sales are not out of current inventory but out of special orders and custom jobs. This has created a cash-flow problem for the firm and made it difficult to expand inventory or increase marketing efforts.

Although the firm lacks cash, it has managed to maintain a high credit rating with the Jewelers Board of Trade. This has made it possible to purchase from a very wide supplier base and obtain excellent financing arrangements.

Market Conditions

The market for jewelry and related products has been increasing and is projected by most experts to continue. Business Trend Analysts, of Commack, New York, predicts a 9 percent annual growth rate in sales of precious jewelry through 1995. Another indicator is DeBeers, the diamond magnate, which controls 85 percent of the world's diamonds. In its 100-year history of reading the market and its signs, it has an enviable record of being right. DeBeers is convinced that in 1995, demand for diamond jewelry will surpass last year's records. As a result, it increased diamond rough prices by 10 percent last year, followed by an additional 13.5 percent this year. For diamond marketers that is a strong vote of confidence in continuing consumer demand.

Even with the recent slowdown in the economy, The Diamond Brokers USA has maintained sales even with last year. With the new location and with increased marketing efforts, sales should increase.

Target Markets

The Diamond Brokers USA has identified four specific markets that it will target.

Engagement Rings

The engagement ring market has always been The Diamond Brokers USA's "bread and butter." This represents an important area of sales. The average amount spent on an engagement ring has increased 22 percent over the past two years. Diamond engagement rings have accounted for more than 50 percent of The Diamond Brokers USA's sales over the past 5 years. The Diamond Brokers USA has created a referral network that continues to bring in new business.

Incentive and Recognition Awards

The corporate premium awards business will reach nearly $25 billion this year in the United States, according to statistics provided by Premium Awards Publishing Company in Chicago, Ill. This is an increase of nearly 9.3 percent annually over the past 10 years. Of the market, 45 percent of the most popular awards consist of pens and desk sets, watches and clocks, and jewelry. The Diamond Brokers USA specializes in all three of these products. In the past few years, The Diamond Brokers USA has gained a small share of this market with virtually no marketing effort. Mr. Smith has also found that most of the major suppliers of corporate awards market to larger firms, those with 500 employees or more. In the Fort Lauderdale area there is a large market of smaller firms. In 1990 the U.S. Census Bureau reported that Florida had 136 firms with 500 or more employees. On the other hand, there were 3,584 firms with from 50 to 499 employees. The Diamond Brokers USA views marketing to these smaller businesses as a tremendous opportunity. These contacts will also provide the professional market, described below.

The "Professional"

The "professional" is considered to be the business man or woman, generally between the ages of thirty and forty-five. More women are entering the business world and have increasing jewelry needs. *Jeweler Circular Keystone* reports that "professionals" spend more than any other group on each purchase, making them more profitable for service for the time and effort invested. Large jewelry stores are targeting this market; however, The Diamond Brokers USA has a unique advantage in that it will have salespeople that will go to the client. This service has been successful for The Diamond Brokers USA, because the "professional" often does not have "time to shop." (Salespeople are insured up to $10,000 and follow strict guidelines as to the amount of merchandise they may carry and the process of screening potential clients.) Another advantage of targeting this market is that The Diamond Brokers USA salespeople will be actively involved in marketing incentive and recognition awards to these same individuals when appropriate.

Insurance Replacements

The Insurance Replacement market is an area in which the Diamond Brokers USA should be able to excel. Through the use of out-of-store salespersons, the firm will be able to personally call on insurance agents and adjusters to let them know of the firm's services. In the past The Diamond Brokers USA has worked well with insurance companies in settling their clients' losses, and have been encouraged by various agents to expand their services to other agents. Other major metropolitan areas have firms that do nothing other than insurance replacements. In Fort Lauderdale, no one has effectively pursued that market. One local private party has generated sales in excess of $100,000 annually doing insurance replacements on a part-time basis. (Reported by John M. Jensen, Inc., a local diamond wholesaler.)

The Competition

There are many firms that market the same products offered by The Diamond Brokers USA. The Diamond Brokers USA differentiates itself from these in several ways. Low overhead makes it possible to sell at tremendous savings. The "professional" environment helps establish the feeling of "not" buying from a "retailer." The referral system has been spreading for the past 5 years to create the firm's current market, without using any other marketing. The use of out-of-store salespeople and personalized attention are desired by the market.

Market Strategy

The Diamond Brokers USA will use the following marketing strategies:

- Direct Marketing persuaded one in five adults to buy something in 1993, according to a Gallup survey. Mr. Smith will hire one full-time salesperson in the first year (Sept.). This salesperson will be trained by suppliers regarding the products in the first few weeks. He or she will prospect through a program of telemarketing and direct selling supported by mail. Fifty professionals will be contacted each week, first by mail and then by follow-up phone calls. They will be approached for incentive awards as well as personal jewelry purchases. He or she will also contact the Valley's Insurance Adjusters and let them know of the firm's services. In the following year a second salesperson will be added.

- Mr. Smith will continue to recruit young people at valley colleges and universities to act as referents in return for a finder's commission. Five new sales representatives will be added by November 1995, and an additional five in 1996.

- Mr. Smith will develop a customer database to keep track of anniversaries, birthdays, and other occasions that might be an occasion for a jewelry purchase. Reminders will be sent at these times. He will also continue to mail a newsletter, as has been used in the past.

- Moving to the ground floor of the First Interstate Bank building will give The Diamond Brokers USA exposure to some street traffic in the business district of Fort Lauderdale. (This is an area that is being heavily developed at this time. Several new office complexes are currently being built.) Mr. Smith also has arranged for a goldsmith to sublease part of the office space. This will help in serving customers. Frequent displays will be set up in the lobby of the building to attract new business.

The Diamond Brokers USA has had some success with all the strategies mentioned; however, it has not been consistent in implementing any of them. In the last year, Mr. Smith has not fully implemented any of the above strategies because of personal time restrictions. Even without any marketing efforts, the firm has continued to grow. With the addition of a new staff member, Mr. Smith will again concentrate on generating new business.

Financial Needs

Mr. Smith wants to raise $50,000 to help the firm move into a period of growth. These funds will give the firm additional inventory (purchased at reduced cash prices), some needed fixtures for the office, and sufficient operating capital.

Use of Funds (See Cash Flow Projections)

February 1993	$1,000	Furniture
March 1993	$10,000	Inventory
	$2,000	Cases
May 1993	$15,000	Inventory
	$10,000	Accounts payable
	$4,000	Computer and printer
June 1993	$8,000	Inventory (as cash permits)

Projections and Financials

The following Income Statement and Cash Flow Analysis is based on last year's monthly averages. Sales have already increased over last year at this time, so these numbers are felt to be conservative. (Sales were calculated by adjusting for the increase in prices implemented last month to correct the low gross margin.) Sales are projected to increase slowly as the new salesperson develops his or her clientele. Sales again will increase in the second year several months after hiring an additional salesperson.

First Year's Net Income (1995)	$28,890
Second Year's Net Income (1996)	$67,802

(Note: Financials not included with this business plan.)

Supporting Documents

EXHIBITS

AUTHOR'S NOTE:

List all supporting documentation in the appendix/exhibit section as noted and referenced throughout your business plan. Remember, this information should be clearly and neatly presented so the reader of your business plan can easily reference and understand the data being provided. As in the previous business plans, the Financial Sections are primarily the same format.

A Business Plan For:

The Fidelity Group, Inc.

July 1994

Statement of Purpose

THE FIDELITY GROUP, a closely held company incorporated under the laws of Arizona, is seeking investment capital of $150,000 to purchase inventory and office equipment, as well as six months' operating capital. This capital will allow us to maintain sufficient capital to successfully expand an existing consulting firm.

The sum, together with $47,000 equity investment of the principals, will be sufficient to finance the transition through the expansion phase so that this recently started consulting business can operate as an ongoing, profitable enterprise.

Marketing Information

Leaders Development Group (LDG)—The Fidelity Group (TFG) recently purchased LDG in April 1993 to offer our clients an additional dynamic service. With this important acquisition, TFG developed a new system, "Triple-Tiered Corporate Engineering System," which allows us to take a client through the three most important stages of startup or expansion. These phases are (1) marketing; (2) financing; (3) management improvement and sales force training.

The Traveling Associates—TFG developed the business plan and marketing package for funding of a large project in the tour and travel business. To date, we have arranged an investment package of $500,000 with a local investment group. TFG also has consulted with management and members of the sales force and has been instrumental in increasing overall time management and organizational development. TFG is currently still consulting with The Traveling Associates.

Absolute Financial Group (AFG)—As a consultant to AFG, TFG developed a successful marketing campaign that increased sales 18 percent during a twelve-month period. The radio ad campaign and company brochure were instrumental in the increase of sales.

Execubuild, Inc.—The marketing campaign developed for this construction company proved to be very successful. During a 60-day period, our marketing division brought 12 clients to Execubuild for the construction of custom homes.

D.R. Construction—Our marketing division engineered a very successful campaign for Bull-head City, Arizona. This company will build 150 homes during the next year. The business plan developed by TFG enabled D.R. Construction to raise $325,000.

Mesa Chamber of Commerce—TFG helped the Chamber develop a system to increase member-ship sales by fabricating a credit card system for discounts issued to Chamber members by Chamber members.

Business Showcase 1994—The principals of The Fidelity Group serve on the Board of Directors for the Annual Trade Show of the Mesa Chamber of Commerce. Brian Smith is this year's Chairman. Expected attendance in October is 8,000 people. TFG has increased participation for the event by forming a series of committees and subcommittees to handle the enormous task of developing a successful trade show. Due to the influence of TFG, a few members of the Phoenix Cardinals will attend the event.

Chilton Corporation—Brad Stevenson was instrumental in developing a successful marketing campaign for the Short Stop Convenience Stores of Phoenix. Brad's creative expertise helped increase sales 22 percent over the previous year's sales.

Christmas Trade Fair 1994—The product of the creative imagination of The Fidelity Group team of consultants. This trade show will be a "welcome back" to our Winter Visitor Friends.

We will have booth space for 90 participants. The public will enjoy a "one-stop-shopping place" for Christmas shopping, and be entertained by the Big Band Society of Arizona. TFG will sponsor the event, and a portion of the proceeds will go to Junior Achievement for the development of young entrepreneurs.

XL Enterprises, Inc.—TFG has contracted with this San Diego, California, company to market NFL, limited edition, pewter beltbuckles. This will be a local, national, and international campaign, involving direct response, television, and mail-order advertising. Since the inception of this company, no one has marketed the beltbuckles quite like TFG. For this reason we expect to sell all 10,000 buckles for the Phoenix Cardinals in a 3-week time frame.

ABC Chiropractic—This local Chiropractic Clinic has reduced turnover and increased billing procedures as a direct result of the Paul Jones engineering and eight-week time management course offered to eight staff members of the clinic. We are presently developing a comprehensive marketing campaign for ABC Chiropractic.

Happy Vanilla—Brad Stevenson has been instrumental in taking this company offshore to have its product packaged and funded. A project that has been in development for three years will become an instant success, once developed marketing channels are totally open.

Seventy Seven Systems—A Tempe-based company that approached TFG about our "Triple-Tiered Corporate Engineering System." We are presently developing the organizational marketing and sales force divisions to be able to take this company public through stock purchases.

J & B Construction (JBC)—Recently contacted by JBC, The Fidelity Group was asked to apply its "Triple-Tiered Corporate Engineering System" for the further development of this construction firm.

Introduction

The Fidelity Group, Inc., is one of the first companies to combine years of research on marketing, financing, and leadership development. TFG is proud to announce the dynamic "Triple Tiered Corporate Development System" and the formation of a corporation dedicated to the development, improvement, and overall success of entrepreneurial-minded companies.

"Fidelity," according *The Synonym Finder,* is explained as "strict observance or faithfulness to promises and duties; obedience, devotedness, accuracy, the degree of exactness, constancy, loyalty, allegiance." We are building TFG step by step to ensure that we render creative and professional attention to our client's varying needs.

The founders of TFG, Brian Smith, Paul Jones, and Brad Stevenson, have created an unequaled system of corporate development that is fast becoming recognized as the "system" to use for developing a million-dollar business. Their combined talents in management, marketing, sales, and entrepreneurialism form the corporate nucleus and are supported with additional talent and resources. The vision of a new, dynamic, and innovative consulting company will establish a stronghold in the marketplace.

As we move forward to establish our consulting firm in a competitive marketplace, it is important that we stress integrity and commitment. We feel integrity is the main ingredient in running a company. When you do what's right, everyone benefits. That's the difference in long-term thinking and short-term thinking. TFG is in business for the long haul. When we work with clients, we are doing more than building a business, we are building our reputation.

We trust you will join us in our vision for the future, and the growth of our dynamic company.

Table of Contents

Business Overview

Company

The Fidelity Group, Inc.

Business Concept

The intention is for The Fidelity Group to be one of the leading corporate consulting companies in the world. TFG is developing and marketing services and products that increase overall profitability and efficiency in the complex world of business.

Market

TFG services and products are marketed for self-development, management and organizational improvement, and maximizing corporate businesses with emphasis on companies in existence 3 years or less. TFG is expanding to market products nationally and internationally.

Capital Required

The Fidelity Group requires $150,000 to meet expansion costs for additional office space, equipment, inventory, and personnel. The investment will be used to equip and staff offices, and for six months' operation capital. The six-month investment schedule is as follows:

Months 1-2	$ 75,000
Months 3-4	40,000
Months 5-6	35,000
Total	$150,000

The information contained in this report is confidential and is intended only for the persons to whom it is transmitted by TFG. Any reproduction of this business plan in whole or in part or the sharing of any of its content without the prior written consent of TFG is prohibited.

Capitalization and Risk Considerations

Purpose of Business Plan

The major purpose of this Business Plan is to:

Explain and define in detail the uses of One Hundred Fifty Thousand Dollars ($150,000) or more of capital funds for a startup corporation. The name of the corporation is The Fidelity Group, Inc., which hereinafter will be referred to as TFG.

Capitalization

It is the primary intent of TFG to capitalize the company in the amount of One Hundred Fifty Thousand Dollars ($150,000) or more, which may be in the form of debt, equity, or a combination of debt and equity financing. TFG is willing to pursue a stock offering of preferred and common stock or debenture offering.

The Business Plan, however, does not constitute an offer to sell or a solicitation of an offer to buy securities, nor does it constitute an offer to sell or a solicitation of an offer to buy from any person in any state or other jurisdiction in which such offer would be unlawful. Offers for the purchase of securities must be made by prospectus, which, if not exempt, has been duly registered with the Securities and Exchange Commission, Section 4 (2) of the Securities Act of 1933, as amended. The offer, purchase, and sale of any security is expressly conditioned on compliance with the appropriate federal and state security laws.

Resale of the securities discussed in this Business Plan may not be made unless the securities are registered under the Securities Act of 1933, as amended, or unless the resale is exempt from the registration requirements of the Securities Act of 1933, as amended.

Neither the delivery of this Business Plan, at any time, nor any sale hereunder shall in any way or through any circumstances create implication that the information contained herein is correct as of any time subsequent to its date.

Offers and sales will only be made to persons who have the knowledge and experience to evaluate the risks and merits of the investment and who have the economic means to afford the potential value of the securities offered hereby.

The information set forth herein is believed by the incorporators to be reliable. However, it must be recognized that the predictions and projections as to the Corporation's future and no warranty of such projections are expressed or implied hereby. All corporate documents relating to this investment will be made available to an offeree and/or offeree representative upon request to TFG.

TFG shall be under no obligation whatsoever to sell or issue any securities purchase agreement between TFG and the purchaser thereof.

Executive Summary

Four Essentials of TFG

TFG is a consulting firm dedicated to showing individuals and businesses how to achieve their financial goals. Our motto explains our objective: "The Fidelity Group—Arizona's Consulting Firm for Developing Million-Dollar Businesses." With this in mind, our concept is based on four key principles:

1. Low Risk

Too many businesses "bet the farm" on a business venture that, in many cases, fails. Others never get around to taking advantage of million-dollar opportunities because they feel they don't have the personal and financial resources to do it effectively.

The philosophy of TFG is that most good ideas never come to fruition because of fear of failure. We teach businesses the secrets of how to take a good idea, start small, and earn highly-leveraged returns. We specialize in showing businesses how to make money without taking major risks. There are a number of ways to create a profitable enterprise by teaching correct principles of leadership development, marketing, product or service development, financing, and time management.

2. Effective Marketing Strategies

Companies that learn how to strategically market their products and services become profitable in virtually every endeavor they enter. This is no accident. It is the result of applying some basic step-by-step principles of leverage that we teach our clients. TFG teaches companies to employ the strategies of successful marketers around the world. Our resource center is a consortium of consultants and business owners highly skilled in the areas of marketing, management, sales, and finance.

3. Financing

There is an ever-present need for qualified professionals who can serve both business and individuals in securing financing. This need is constantly growing as funds become more difficult to arrange through conventional sources and as interest rates fluctuate widely from quarter to quarter. There are two related needs in this regard: First, the need to help prospective borrowers approach conventional lending institutions in the correct way. Second, the need to help them approach nontraditional lending sources such as venture capitalists or other lenders in a way that can vastly improve their chances of obtaining the money they seek.

Conditions in the money market mean the financial broker must have an uncommon understanding of modes of financing, both conventional and innovative. We are prepared to offer these important services to our clients and supply them with forms, letters, applications, formats of proposals, and, most important, contacts.

4. Mentoring

The final secret that will make all of this work so effectively is a principle that has been the subject of a feature article in the *Harvard Review* under the headline, "Everyone Who Makes It Has a Mentor." Intense research has disclosed that highly successful people hardly ever make it on their own. They succeed because they enlist the help of experienced people who can lead them and guide them every step of the way—people to whom they can turn for counsel, for motivation, for key techniques and strategies that minimize risk and maximize success.

TFG is succeeding in assisting companies to build their "Million Dollar Businesses." Our goal is to help thousands of small, medium, and large companies become more profitable by offering concrete *solutions* to everyday business challenges.

Overview of Separate Divisions

The unique edge TFG has over its competition is that it is capable of helping a company in so many different areas. These areas include:

1. Marketing—Campaign Development

2. Personal and Management Self-Improvement Systems

3. Financial Planning

4. Investment and Venture Capital Sources

5. Sales Force Training Programs

6. Computerized Profile Reports for Hiring and Promoting Employees

Our objective when working with clients is to lead them through our four-part system, using a systematic approach for developing a million-dollar business. The first step is to assist our clients with *marketing,* beginning with their business plans. We have developed a comprehensive, step-by-step synopsis of how to write a business plan that gets funded. We want our clients to do the research and write the plan so that they will understand the intricate design of their businesses. They then can move into step two—*financing.*

Step two involves contacting investors about the particular business venture. TFG will contact investment groups and assist our clients to negotiate the best possible terms and repayment of the loan.

Step three consists of *leadership development*, management improvement, and sales force training. This step is included in our system to inspire individuals of the company to seek out and achieve personal as well as corporate goals.

Step four is making certain that our clients are turning a *profit*. Our consultants will monitor the progress of a company and teach it how it can become self-sufficient by using the proprietary strategies and techniques developed by TFG.

In addition to the expertise of the principals and associates of TFG, we have also invested capital to have the Consulting Divisions of the McKinley Institute on retainer. The McKinley Institute is directed by a National Council of Mentors comprising six millionaire achievers and 21 expert consultants who have agreed to make their success stories and strategies available to TFG.

Sales and Profit Projections

To date (July 1994) we are working with 16 companies in the four areas previously mentioned. We are experiencing tremendous success, and our clients are referring new prospects daily.

We are focusing 80 percent of our efforts on three specific projects. These projects and profit projections are as follows:

1. *Leaders Dynamic Group*—A division of TFG, focusing on leadership development, management, improvement, and sales force training. Paul Jones will be in charge of its operation.

	Sales	**Gross Profits**
1st Quarter	$ 87,000	$ 37,080
2nd Quarter	91,350	38,934
3rd Quarter	95,700	40,788
4th Quarter	100,050	42,642
1st Year (subtotal)	$ 374,100	$ 159,444
2nd Year	435,000	185,400
3rd Year	522,000	222,480
4th Year	609,000	259,560
5th Year	783,000	333,720
TOTAL	$2,723,100	$1,160,604

2. *Light and Hearing Co., Inc.*—A client of TFG that has developed a portable light and sound unit, which provides a portable means for reduced anxiety and improved concentration, memory, and creativity. The unit provides whole-brain synchronization. TFG will be part of the management team of L&R, and will be in charge of marketing and sales force training. In return, TFG will receive a percentage of sales.

   The financial forecast of management fees paid to the Fidelity Group over a five-year period will be as follows (These figures represent gross fees based on projections of Light and Hearing Co. See Light and Hearing Co., Inc., business plan.):

Fiscal Year One		Year Two	Year Three	Year Four	Year Five
First Quarter	$46,563				
Second Quarter	46,563				
Third Quarter	50,144				
Fourth Quarter	50,144				
TOTAL	$193,414	$281,042	$385,333	$414,528	$496,395
TFG Fees	$5,802	$8,431	$11,560	$12,435	$14,892
Five-Year Total					$1,770,712

3. *Direct Response Advertising Projects*—The Fidelity Marketing Group (FMG) offers several business opportunities for entrepreneurs who are seeking financial vehicles or programs that will enable them to reach their financial goals. FMG will be marketing such opportunities, giving a step-by-step structured plan for the novice and the professional. These programs will range in price from $15 to $500 and will be marketed through direct mail and direct response advertising.

Brad Stevenson will lead the project team that has developed the complete marketing program. The projected financial forecast over the next five years is as follows:

The figures listed are conservative and are based on the sale of a $15 program with one half of 1 percent response. These figures are also based on the placement of one local ad and one national ad. To see quarterly projections, these figures must be multiplied by 3, because we will be starting our campaign with 3 local and 3 national ads.

The first quarter figures are projected test results. Should our test results be favorable, we will increase the number of ads we place on a local and national basis. The second-, third-, and fourth-quarter figures are based on favorable results. The gross sales of local and national ads placed should be multiplied by 3 to reflect gross sales for the first quarter. Second-, third-, and fourth-quarter profits are based on a 30% increase per quarter.

Type	Circulation	Response	Revenue
Classified two-step ad	50,000/mo.	1/2%	2500 x 3 ads = 7,500 x 3 mo. = 22,500/qtr.
Classified two-step ad	250,000/mo.		6,250 x 3 Ads = 18,750 x 3 Mo. = 56,250

Fiscal Year	1	2	3	4	5
First Quarter	78,550				
Second Quarter	102,150				
Third Quarter	132,749				
Fourth Quarter	172,988				
	486,437	726,250	1,200,850	1,769,850	2,252,770
Total—Five Years (Gross Sales)					$6,436,157

Future of the Consulting Industry

The world is full of persons referring to themselves as "consultants." There are consultants in virtually all types of industries, and the competition is always growing. At TFG, we understand that there are companies and individuals who already have a "head start" on us. However, our market analysis shows that only two other companies offer competent advice and counseling in most of the areas of our focused markets. Currently, in Phoenix Metropolitan East areas of business, there are two other consulting firms that offer similar services to TFG.

Business Group and Management Resources International conduct seminars and offer one-on-one consultation in the areas of tax planning, business and personal finance, marketing, and sales training. These two companies have a very good system of consulting practice. A few other services they provide include discounts on business- and consumer-related products and public-speaking skills training. These consulting firms will be our main competitors in the East Valley of Metro-Phoenix.

We feel our management and marketing skills and our products are superior to those of our competitors. These three strengths will be outlined further throughout the plan.

Trends

Valley National Bank published the *Valley Statistical Review*, which indicated a census of selected service industries. According to their statistics, there are 3175 business-related service firms in Arizona with established payrolls. This number can be further broken down into six separate kinds of services: Advertising and marketing, 149; property managers, 561; computer services, 245; management, consulting, and public relations, 649; equipment rental and leasing services, 276; other, 1295.

Our analysis was focused on management, consulting, and public relations. There are currently 228 business consulting firms in the Metropolitan Phoenix area. Of these, eight are general business consultants, four are educational consultants, three are financing consultants, and 106 are considered marketing consultants.

Western Savings and Loan's "Forecast '87" points out that "it has often been suggested that the United States may lose its leading role in manufacturing, but it can maintain its world leadership in services industries. United States employment in services has been growing at a much more rapid rate than manufacturing employment." However, it is also quick to point out that "there is no safe haven in a competitive world economy, either in manufacturing or in services." We understand this principle. In Phoenix alone we will be faced with extensive competition, but our carefully tested companies will be able to offer professional services to virtually any type of business. The remainder are computer-related consulting services.

Let's refer again to the *Valley Statistical Review*, which points out that receipts paid in the consulting industry are very high. In 1984 receipts in Arizona totaled more than $161 million. Current figures are not available.

Also, according to *Entrepreneur Magazine's* catalog of new opportunities, the consulting business is "booming," and it is "time to cash in on the exploding consulting industry." It further states that it is very common "to make $900 a day giving advice to corporate presidents. Since the average consultant bills an average of 14 days a month to clients, this can put nearly $13,000 gross fees in your pocket every month."

Therefore, we are confident that TFG will turn a handsome profit in the months and years ahead. Our confidence comes from expertise. Our consultants and board of directors have many years of experience in management, marketing, sales force training, product development, and financial consulting. The most important area is people. We are in the "people business," just like every other company. However, the big difference between us and our competition is that we recognize that our business is *people*.

Profile of the TFG

Brief History

TFG is a newly formed Arizona corporation. However, two of our companies have been in operation since 1984 on a part-time basis. In January 1987, Leadership Development Group (LDG) began operating as a licensed, full-time entity in Mesa, Arizona. Due to the success of LDG, its management, and its dynamic products, TFG recently purchased LDG. Following is a description of the individual entities that make up TFG.

Individual Companies

Fidelity Marketing Group (FMG) has counseled businesses on marketing techniques and strategies for two years in Phoenix.

TFG offers professional marketing strategies to businesses through FMG. TFG will sponsor business seminars and workshops, which will be marketed by FMG. Other services provided will include:

- Writing business and marketing plans.
- Strategies for expanding a product or service.
- Developing a marketing campaign for startups and expansions.
- Developing effective advertising mediums.

FMG will be publishing and marketing a comprehensive "Entrepreneur's Survival Kit." The kit encapsulates the most aggressive concepts, philosophies, doctrines, and psychologies of modern business. The kit is a dynamic plan of action that gives a step-by-step analysis of management, product, and financing.

Leaders Development Group (LDG) has a philosophy based on the premise that men and women have an unlimited potential to make themselves whatever they choose—their only real limitations are self-imposed. It will be our task to prepare individuals and businesses to meet the challenge of becoming more successful. Our approach will be geared toward attitude change. LDG programs inform, motivate, and inspire participants and encourage them to seek out and achieve their personal goals, as well as experience growth in areas important to them.

Fidelity Investment Group (FIG) was formed to provide investment and venture capital to our clients. Currently, FIG relies on outside sources to find business and nonprofit ventures. However, it is our intention to establish a strong reputation and profitable enterprise to form our own venture capital group.

Principals of TFG

Brian Smith is president of TFG. At the age of nine, he began working for his father in their family-owned real estate and construction company. He became manager of maintenance and managed six employees at the age of 17. Brian started a landscaping company, and soon landed sizable contracts with two of the largest construction companies in Utah. During the four-year history of his company, "B. L. Smith Landscaping," Brian built up a very successful and profitable enterprise. Before moving to Arizona, he sold his landscaping business for a profit.

Mr. Smith received a bachelor's degree in Business Finance from Arizona State University, and a Masters of Business Administration degree from The University of Phoenix.

TFG was given its name for specific reasons. Brian could see that there were very few companies that offered "strict observance to promises and duties," as the word "fidelity" implies.

Paul Jones, cofounder of TFG, serves as executive vice president of Leaders Development Group. Paul developed his work ethic and independent spirit while growing up on the family farm in Idaho. During high school, Paul excelled in both athletics and academics. He was a member of the National Honor Society. He served on the student council and was elected Associated Men's Student Body President in his Sophomore year.

After graduating from Ball State College, Paul served three hears in the military, including combat duty as an Infantry Officer in Vietnam, where he received the Combat Infantryman's Badge and Purple Heart as well as other decorations. At Fort OK, Washington, Paul competed with 1000 soldiers for the American Spirit Honor Medal, which he was awarded by the commanding general.

From 1971 to 1972, Paul worked with a successful construction company headquartered in Ohio. He was vice-president and general manager responsible for construction projects and supervision of subcontractors, as well as the regular duties of managing a company of more than 70 employees. In 1976 Paul began a real estate business and purchased a Century 21 franchise to gain experience in the management and marketing of a franchise operation.

In 1984 Paul purchased a Leadership Inc. distributorship to expand his personal and management development skills. That decision led to a change of direction in his professional life. Because of his desire to help others develop their talents and abilities, Paul has put his full-time efforts into building the Leaders Development Group.

Brad Stevenson serves as executive vice-president of FMG.

As a young man growing up in New Mexico, Brad become very involved in student government, academics, and athletics. He was elected student body president his senior year, was a member of the National Honor Society, and received two scholarships from Brigham Young University: an academic leadership scholarship and a basketball scholarship.

Brad's educational background includes four years of college, where he studied Marketing and Business Administration. In 1980 Brad received a Certificate of Business Administration from the Center of Entrepreneurial Management. In 1984 he was awarded the Certificate of Entrepreneurial Management from New Mexico Technical College.

At the age of 19, Brad opened a chain of Discount Dry Cleaning Centers. The discount price of 99 cents per garment cleaned and pressed and the concept of "high volume, low prices" quickly became very popular. Within a two-year period, Brad had opened 5 stores. His stores were featured in *Entrepreneur Magazine,* and today there are hundreds like his in operation across the country. After operating this business for four years, Brad sold his company.

In early 1987, Brad and his family moved to Mesa, Arizona. To gain further experience in marketing, he went to work for the Chilton Corporation as the marketing director for a 45-store chain of convenience markets. Under Chilton employ, he developed successful marketing strategies that increased retail sales by 20 percent in a 6-month period.

Operational Details

We have anticipated that our company will grow quickly and we would like to be in an environment conducive to our growth. The executive suite we are presently leasing simply has become too small and is not suitable for expansion. Our 90-day projections include the remainder of our current lease agreement. We have already begun negotiation for a larger and more efficient office facility within a corporate center that has more space for expansion.

Our office is currently located at 1990 South Tree House Road, Suite 205, in Mesa, Arizona. Since this is a very good location for our targeted markets, we plan to stay in the general area.

We need the services of a secretary/receptionist immediately. With a sales staff of three, three principals of TFG, and an outside consultant, a secretary/receptionist is necessary to help organize the office.

Marketing Plan

Strategies

For the first 90 days, TFG will focus mainly on Leaders Development Group (LDG). LDG will become an immediate profit center. The products, training, financial planning systems, and established client base make LDG our obvious choice to market most heavily initially. We feel it is our quickest moneymaker to establish cash flow. However, as we are building LDG, there are opportunities to provide service to clients in the areas of marketing and investment capital.

Because of our drive to properly position LDG in the marketplace, we have written a condensed marketing plan about its purpose and overall operation. We feel that the concept of TFG as an operation of separate consulting service companies will allow each company to complement the others.

Paul Jones originally purchased the franchise in 1984. (Due to the enormous success of Leadership Inc., the franchise fee today is $20,000.) In what we feel is a tremendous opportunity to become a "total service" consulting firm, TFG purchased Leaders Development Group in July.

Profile of Leaders Development Group (LDG)

LDG's ability to provide a vehicle to help individuals and businesses realize more of their potential will tremendously enhance the present and future growth of TFG.

Every LDG program is designed to promote development of an expanding, positive self-image. The programs promote more meaningful goals. Clients discover that they have a great deal of control over their own destinies.

The goal of LDG is to assist clients to achieve their greatest potential in every area of life. Our methods are practical and have been demonstrated to be workable and successful.

Program Marketed by LDG

LDG offers a wide range of programs for children, teenagers, adults, and businesses. Our plans are to market these programs through a trained sales force. Before we outline how our sales force will operate, here is a brief overview of the dynamic programs we offer our clients.

Personal Leadership

Personal leadership is our basic motivation program. It provides personal motivation for every individual in any walk of life. The program recognizes that leadership is essentially an internal disposition, and through a comprehensive goals program, the dynamics of personal leadership help the individual develop the attitudes and confidence that provide that internal disposition.

Motivational Management

Motivational management is a motivational training program designed specifically for the manager. Its purpose is to develop the manager's ability to achieve results through other people by improving expertise in communication, human relations, and the application of effective management principles.

Supervision

The Supervision program is designed for those who, whether they are called managers, supervisors, or foremen, directly supervise the activities of other people. It not only teaches management and supervisory skills but encourages personal growth and development.

Organizational Goal Setting

Organizational Goal Setting guides the members of a management team in developing and implementing a complete system of organizational goals. When used first with the executive management team and then with departmental managers and supervisors, it gives all key personnel in the organization the skills and the information necessary to maximize personal and organizational productivity.

Growth in Children

Growth in Children builds a child's success and happiness in the critical years from six through twelve by teaching personal responsibility. It aids in setting goals and forming values and attitudes for success.

Champions Are Made

Champions Are Made is designed for young athletes from junior high through college age. It promotes development of the attitudes and habits necessary for reaching the desired level of achievement in athletics. The program is suitable for participants in team or individual sports and for those who want a career in athletics or who merely want to enjoy a sport for the contribution it makes to the total quality of life.

Executive Time Management

Executive Time Management offers executives, managers, and supervisors practical procedures for increasing their productivity and that of their people by improved management of time resources.

Selling Strategies

Selling Strategies is designed to build on, and to bring out, all of those natural positive qualities that lay comparatively dormant in every individual. It provides a vehicle to make use of one's inner strengths at a much faster rate than one is likely to achieve on one's own initiative. The unique plan of action activates internal motivation to develop the attitudes and habits necessary to achieve one's sales goals.

Personal Profiles Extraordinaire

Profiles is a program designed to help business owners and managers properly match individual talents with specific job classifications. Many companies literally spend thousands of dollars and enormous amounts of time selecting and training key employees—only to lose the individual months later due to inadequate screening of their skills and characteristics. The purpose of Profiles is to test the company's top personnel and establish a criterion for success. This pattern of success then serves as a basis when hiring other individuals, and clearly defines which person is best qualified to help the company reach its organizational goals.

Profiles is a personnel evaluation tool that meets all U.S. Government regulations. It measures six mental aptitudes, ten personality dimensions, and has two validity checks.

Comprehensive computer-generated reports include up to 28 pages of fully-graphic, job-related management information for any candidate for any job. Each user may choose the type of report, the amount of detail required, or the type of position in question. All reports are confidential and totally customized to the customer's requirements. The Profiles reports include:

> Hiring Reports
> (Whom to hire and why?)
>
> Succession Planning/Training Analysis Reports
> (Whom to promote and when?)
>
> Coaching Counseling/Training Analysis Reports
> (How can I/we increase productivity?)
>
> Personal Feedback
> (What does my Profile look like?)
>
> Career Planning Reports
> (What jobs am I suited for?)

This new product can be an additional tool to get associates into production and will help develop new clients. It will also generate add-on business. It can help our clients with hiring, training, and coaching decisions. Profiles can also assist us in hiring, training, and coaching our own associates.

When clients enroll in the Profiles program, they will receive a *Marketing Manual*, a *Reliability & Validity Manual,* and a complete price list of product and support materials.

We plan on targeting business schools, companies with sales staffs, misplaced executives, and housewives who suddenly have been shoved into the workforce due to divorce or death of a spouse. Our targeted markets will be contacted in the order listed.

This program will enable individuals to select a career best suited for their talents and characteristics. In addition, business owners will save thousands of dollars and eliminate the hours that might be spent training the wrong person for the job.

Sales Staff

Developing a Million-Dollar Distributorship

We have developed a system to identify the reasons why salespeople do not reach individual and company goals.

Generally, persons in sales do not succeed for two specific reasons:

1. Lack of skills

2. Poor attitude

With our "Sales Problem Identifier" we will train our staff to overcome obstacles that sometimes lead to inferior results.

Financial Projections

Capital Needs

Office Space

Included in the marketing plan are projections for our current lease agreement. We have anticipated that the lease will be increased to $550 a month for one office of 150 square feet. Since this facility is too small to meet our needs, we feel a much larger area is necessary. Therefore, we felt it necessary to negotiate for a larger space.

The office space we have targeted is the only space left in our complex that is left unbuilt. Fancy Properties is offering an allowance for build-out of $4440. The square footage available is 1260 feet. We plan on building our offices beginning September 1, 1995. Obviously this allowance will help out, but our capital needs will also include additional office furniture, telephone system, a fax machine, copy machine, a more comprehensive inventory of programs for Leaders Development Group, and a computer system.

Operating Projections

We have separated our operating projections into three separate areas, namely: 90 days, 12 months, and 15 months. The reason for this is because our move to a larger office space will increase our overhead after 90 days.

Inventory Expense and Savings

The average cost of an LDG program is $175 (wholesale) plus 8.5 percent added for sales tax and shipping expense, for a total of $189.88. Purchasing 20 programs at a time qualifies for a discount of 21 percent off the price of $189.88 or approximately $40 savings per program. Our savings per order would be about $800 for each 20-program order. Having inventory in stock that has been purchased in large volume will allow rapid service for our clients, as well as substantial savings for our company.

Twelve-Month Operating Projections

Authors' Note:

As suggested earlier, the financial presentation portion of the business plan needs to be well prepared. If assistance is needed, contact a reputable accounting or other business firm that will be able to provide accurate, reasonable, and meaningful information.

Appendix

Authors' Note:

List all supporting documentation in the appendix section as noted and referenced throughout your business plan.

Remember, this information should be clearly and neatly presented so the reader of your business plan can easily reference and understand the data being provided.

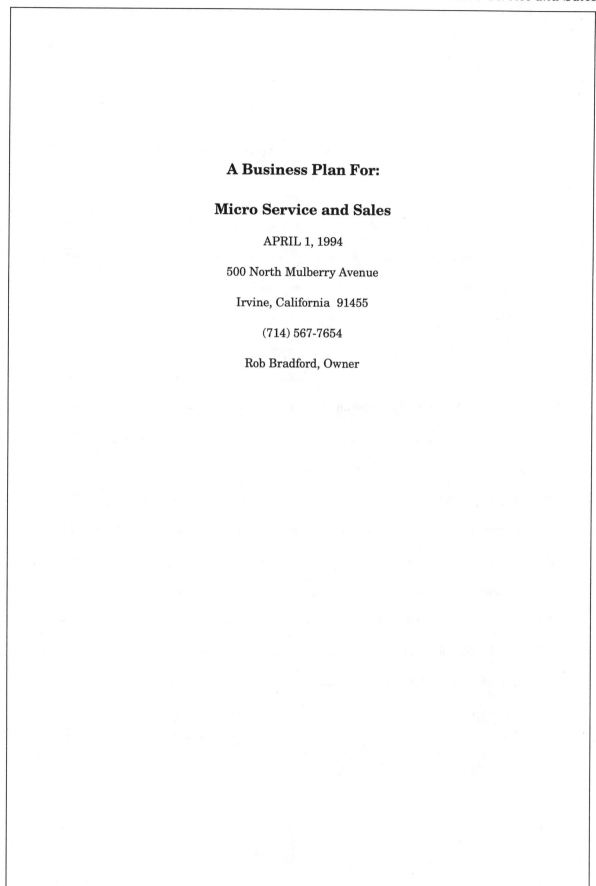

A Business Plan For:

Micro Service and Sales

APRIL 1, 1994

500 North Mulberry Avenue

Irvine, California 91455

(714) 567-7654

Rob Bradford, Owner

Table of Contents

Statement of Purpose

Micro Service and Sales, a computer sales and service firm, is a successful business that seeks financial aid to expand and continue building its profitable clientele base. The expansion would include a new location, additional inventory, and additional advertising.

The owner, Rob Bradford, desires to sell a portion of his interest in the business for the sum of $50,000. This figure includes all the money that the principal has put into Micro Service and Sales for the service equipment, spare parts, office furniture, service contracts, customer list, dealerships, and reputation.

Mr. Bradford, as well as Mrs. Bradford, would be willing to continue working for the business, building its clientele base and its reputation. Mr. Bradford seeks a salary of $2,500 per month to oversee the service and sales departments as well as the overall operation of the business, Mrs. Bradford seeks $1,000 per month to continue doing the bookkeeping, billing, and overseeing the advertising and marketing of the business on a part-time basis.

Micro Service and Sales is a successful business that needs a new location and more inventory in order to grow as it is capable of growing. The principal has put much time and effort into building the business and maintaining the highest possible reputation for honesty and hard work. An initial investment, in addition to buying out the equity of Mr. Bradford, of $56,500 for startup costs in a new location would put Micro Service and Sales on the road to becoming "the" computer store in Orange County for sales and service.

Description of the Business

Micro Service and Sales officially began operations January 1, 1991, at 500 North Mulberry Ave. It is a sole proprietorship, owned by Rob Bradford. It is a computer sales and service operation that is open Monday through Friday, 9:00 a.m. to 5:00 p.m. However, with a relocation, Micro Service and Sales (called MSS hereafter) would be open for business Monday through Friday from 10:00 a.m. to 7:00 p.m. and Saturday from 10:00 a.m. to 5:00 p.m.

MSS is a retail business that also specializes in providing the best computer repair for the best price. Along with computer repair, MSS also provides programming, consulting, and systems analysis services.

At present, the location of the business and lack of advertising funds is its only drawback. The environment is not conducive to sales and does not accommodate large numbers of people. When the business was first put into operation, the location was adequate because originally, MSS was devoted to computer repair only. However, as business increased, MSS became more and more involved in sales, programming, and consulting. MSS has also become involved in more and more service and presently has service contracts with Irvine School District and California Technical College Drafting Department. MSS has grown into a successful and thriving business, and to continue its growth it must be relocated.

A large part of the business comes from repeat customers for sales and service, which include Bills Lock and Safe, Patzi's of California, Lopger Paint and Glass, PLM Systems, WK Imaging, Sunstate Equipment, Harding and Associates, GTE Phone Directories, Irvine School District, California Regional Adolescent Center, and the Orange County School District, to name just a few. California Credit Service Corporation has also been a customer for the past year and has served as a sales outlet for MSS since July 1991.

MSS continues to build its customer list every day, and to date MSS has customers in Arizona, New Mexico, Colorado, Texas, Oregon, Washington, and California.

The reason why MSS has been so profitable (in its first full year of operation it grossed $226,735 in sales) is the dedication and hard work of its owner. The philosophy of MSS has been and continues to be that the customer deserves the very best service, whether it is in repairing computers, selling computers, or providing customer support after the sale. Repeat business is what keeps all businesses operational, and MSS has capitalized on its ability to bring back repeat customers because the customers have received such good service. With the expansion, MSS will better serve even more of the public.

May 1, 1994, is the date by which MSS would like to be relocated and open for business. With a new location, more inventory, and a sales staff MSS will be one of the fastest-growing businesses in Orange County. MSS will capture a large percentage of the market share for computer sales and service because it is well organized, efficiently run, and has state-of- the-art hardware and software.

The location chosen for relocation is slated to be the best location yet in Orange County, and it offers customer-oriented service. MSS wants to be a place where people can come in for free advice and where they can feel comfortable about asking questions. MSS wants to be the place where people come to learn what is going on in the computer industry with regard to both hardware and software.

In the past Mr. Bradford has spent a great deal of time on the phone answering questions and giving advice. He does not receive monetary compensation for this type of service, but he is paving the way for future business. When those he has helped decide to buy a computer, or have problems with one they already own, they will remember the willingness to help and the positive attitude Mr. Bradford displayed.

We believe that a good majority of these people will come to MSS because of the free advice given and time spent with them by Mr. Bradford. Hopefully they will also send in their friends. "Word of mouth" is by far the very best way to advertise, and that is something that cannot be forced. A business must earn trust and respect and that is what MSS will continue to do.

The previously mentioned investment capital of $55,000 will help MSS relocate to an ideal location that will produce foot traffic and generate more sales. The money will also help to buy inventory and set up MSS as a strong competitor with stores such as I-CON Computer Mart, Computers USA, and Computers of America. MSS plans to set up inventory in a showroom and make it accessible for people to use.

Many times people have in mind certain software that will only run on certain machines, and they want to see for themselves whether they are making a good purchase. At present, MSS allows anyone interested in purchasing a machine to try any software they have to see if it will run. This policy has allowed MSS to sell quite a few more systems than it would have without this practice.

MSS wants to make all the systems it sells available to the public for a "test drive." A computer is a major purchase, and people want to make sure they are getting the exact model they need. With the ability to try out the systems and the helpful atmosphere created by the employees, MSS will be a unique computer outlet and will be highly successful.

When a customer decides which system he or she wants and what peripherals he or she wishes to purchase, an employee will take the order. At the time the order is taken, the customer is required to pay 50 percent of the purchase price as a down payment. This deposit is nonrefundable in most cases. It is the responsibility of the employees at MSS to explain fully what the customer is paying for before he or she makes a purchase.

MSS will take orders because this practice will allow MSS to keep costs down; the customer will not have to "pay" for the cost of keeping the extra inventory, which would be reflected in the price of each system. Also, ordering allows customers to get exactly what they want with all the specific options they desire. At present, MSS is able to fill orders within one week from order date and plans to continue offering this time frame. Payment in full is required on delivery. The current policy of MSS is to extend no credit, thus keeping costs down.

Computer Market Analysis

The computer industry continues to grow and change every day. One of the latest innovations to hit the market is the development of the 80486-based computers. The 80486 computers are almost 20 times faster than the AT computers and almost ten times as fast as the 386 computers now available. The 80486 computers are slated to become the hottest selling items and will quickly become the industry standard. A forecast by Dataquest of the demand for 80486 computers in *Info World* estimates that yearly shipments of 80486 machines will grow from 60,000 in 1991 to 800,000 in 1995 and will reach 1.1 million by 1996 (*Info World*, November 10, 1993). MSS plans to sell these machines to businesses and the general public. (Please see Appendix A-1.)

Although the 80486 is predicted to become the industry standard, the worldwide U.S.-business-office installed base of personal computer systems of all processor types (286 and 386) is also estimated to rise. The installed base of all PCs is expected to rise from 30 million in 1992 to 64.7 million by 1995 (*Info World*, November 10, 1993). (Please see Appendix A-2.)

In addition, the number of laptop units shipped worldwide is estimated to quadruple the number shipped in 1993. In 1985, 169,000 units were shipped worldwide. That number more than doubled, to 397,000 in 1986. The number of units shipped in 1987 was 680,000. In 1991, 5.78 million laptop computers were sold (*Info World*, January 19, 1994). (Please see Appendix A-3.)

Worldwide demand for software is also estimated to rise dramatically. *Info World* predicts, "A special report by International Data Corp. of Framingham, Massachusetts, shows the worldwide market for personal computer software from U.S. vendors growing at an average annual rate of 28% up to 1995 . . ." (*Info World*, December 15, 1993). Sales of software in 1991 in the U.S. reached $10.5 billion. By 1994, sales are expected to reach $25.5 billion. (Please see Appendix A-4.)

MSS has a contract to repair the hardware of local area networks supplied by a company called LanFix that services the Novell systems. The growth of local area networks (LANs) looks very promising as well. Before 1984, according to a study done by International Data Corp., only 15,000 LANs were installed nationwide, and they estimate that in 1993 that number increased to more than 915,000 (*Info World*, January 19, 1994). (Please see Appendix A-5.)

The November 1993 issue of *Info World* predicts the total number of personal computers shipped will almost double in the next three years. In 1994, 20.12 million are expected to be shipped. A slight increase in educational use is expected, while business and home use will stay relatively the same. "Although there may be twice as many personal computers in 1994 as there were in 1992, they will perform the same functions."

It is clear from these reports that computer use and computer sales are expected to continue rising. The United States is a technologically-oriented society, and more and more people and businesses are seeing a need to implement computer systems. The expected growth of the computer industry combined with the expected growth of Orange and surrounding counties, addressed below, make Irvine an ideal place to exploit the computer market. MSS is the business that can take advantage of this growth and profit by it.

Customer/Local Market Analysis

The market that MSS targets for sales is men and women 25 to 45 years old, with an annual income of $35,000 or more per year. MSS also targets the local student population at University of California at Irvine and California Technical College because more and more students are being required to use computers for their classes.

California Credit Service Corporation (CCSC) is MSS's link to the student population at the present time because CCSC lends money to students who wish to purchase a computer. Basically, the markets for MSS consist of (1) men and women who are able to purchase computer systems on their own and (2) students who borrow the money to buy the systems. These are two distinct markets that are reached through two different ways. To reach the students, MSS relies mainly on CCSC but occasionally advertises in the *Daily University Chronicle*. To reach the general public, MSS advertises in the Yellow Pages, on the radio, and through direct mailers.

Both of the markets continue to grow. National Decision Systems has estimated that the general population within a 6-mile radius of the proposed relocation of MSS will increase 74,551 by 1995. The number of households within the same radius is estimated to increase 34,924 by 1995. Currently, the student population at U.C. Irvine is approximately 28,264. New students make up 23 percent, integrating with the market. An additional 4 percent represents new students enrolled during the winter semester, according to U.C. Irvine.

The student market as well as the general public market is continuing to grow every year, and combined with the increase in computer sales, the possible market share to be captured also grows. With relocation, MSS plans to capture a larger market share by being the best-priced and most service-oriented computer store.

Concentrating on service, whether actually repairing a computer or selling a system, MSS will have a unique selling advantage. The market will accept MSS, as it already has, because of the friendly service available and the comfortable atmosphere for learning it will offer in its new location. To some people, computers seem unfriendly or hard to use, and MSS wants to bridge the gap between the public and the computers with a helpful learning environment.

MSS wants any person of any age to be able to come in and learn all they need to know about any computer and how to operate any system effectively. This policy will bring in the customers, and MSS will capture the largest market share of potential computer buyers and present computer owners and users.

MSS will also be price-conscious because Orange County tends to be very price-oriented. People want to feel that they are getting a good deal, and most people in Irvine shop around and compare prices. For this reason, MSS will also be competitively priced with the other computer stores in the area and will generally be $15 to $35 lower in price. The computer stores in the area mark up their products between 25 percent and 35 percent. MSS plans to mark up its products only 25 percent. This way, MSS will be competitively priced, thus promoting the fact that MSS's products are of comparable quality and, at the same time, have some of the lowest prices available in the valley.

MSS has, in the past, discounted for package buys. For example, a customer who buys the 386 compatible system, a printer, a modem, and a hard drive will pay less for the whole package than a customer who buys these goods at different times. MSS plans to continue this practice because it moves more inventory and makes more money for the business.

The market that MSS targets for service is mainly businesses and schools. The businesses targeted include accountants, lawyers, engineers, travel agencies, medical clinics, computer-aided design firms, and computer software firms. To reach these businesses, MSS sends out direct mailers. To reach the various schools in the area, MSS sends out letters to each principal. At present, MSS already handles the service contract for the Irvine School District and has done quite a bit of work for schools in the Costa Mesa School District.

With the markets that MSS targets for both sales and service, there is a potential to make a large amount of money. The potential of MSS, with the appropriate funds, is excellent. The principal, as well as other respected industry colleagues, believes MSS will rival any computer operation already in Orange County and any potential competition.

A greater market could be reached and maintained for sales and service with a new, more visible, more easily accessible location. Walk-in traffic, as well as advertisement response, needs a showroom area to promote sales and to "test drive" computer equipment and software. A new location would also give Micro Service and Sales the professional, competent image it seeks for growth.

Competition Analysis

In analyzing the four main competitors, one can see that MSS will definitely have an advantage over the competition, because it will be set apart from all of the above-mentioned businesses. It is not uncommon to walk into the local retail stores and find the salespeople talking to each other and more interested in each other than in the customers. Generally speaking, the employees also lack the knowledge to really help customers. Although some of the computer stores are priced right and the employees are helpful, they lack adequate knowledge to answer technical questions.

MSS has the right prices, the right atmosphere, and the right personnel to answer questions about hardware or software. MSS has the best combination and has learned from its competitors what is desirable and what is undesirable. The only thing that any of the competition has over MSS is location. MSS has everything these stores have and more, but its location is not easily accessible, nor is it highly visible, as are the locations of our competitors.

MSS will also carry a full line of the most popular products and not devote itself to merely one type, such as IBM. MSS will be a store where anyone, whether they want to purchase an IBM, an IBM Compatible, or a Macintosh Computer, can find the product they need.

Location Analysis

To bring in more revenue and build even more business, MSS should be relocated in the PlumTree Shopping Center. PlumTree is a new shopping center located at 1984 West University Drive in Irvine, California. Its target date for opening is May 1, 1994. PlumTree will have two anchor stores in the mall, one being Food-4-Less and the other being Shopko. Additional tenants are a video store, beauty shop, bakery, restaurant, and a 6-plex Cinema Theater. Extensive research has gone into this project, and the developers of PlumTree optimistically plan to make this shopping center "the hub of activity."

According to the 1993 Department of Transportation Report, 49,975 vehicles travel University Drive every day, and an additional 14,185 vehicles travel 1984 West and 7550 South. Therefore, an average of 64,160 vehicles pass by the location of this shopping center every day. University Drive is probably one of the most heavily-traveled streets in all of Irvine, and PlumTree is highly visible to this heavy traffic.

From 1985 to 1990, the population within a two-, three-, and five-mile radius of PlumTree has increased 43 percent. According to National Decision Systems' 1990 Census the population increase since 1970 is as follows:

	2-mile radius	3-mile radius	5-mile radius
1995 projection	370,187	310,792	353,599
1990 Census	365,345	302,810	339,861
1980 Census	160,406	194,648	225,870
1970 Census	144,153	167,386	130,822

Over the past six years, median household income has increased 30 percent. According to National Decision Systems' 1990 Census, the figures are as follows:

Median Household Income

	2-mile radius	3-mile radius	5-mile radius
1995 estimate	$42,473	$42,887	$43,441
1990 Census	37,571	37,779	38,106

PlumTree is designed to be an easily accessible shopping center, and MSS wants to be a part of it. A move to PlumTree could realistically double, if not triple, the business that MSS already handles because of increased customer flow. The anchor store, Food-4-Less, has already signed a sixty-year lease and is expected to bring in 5500 cars per day, according to studies done in other areas where Food-4-Less is located. According to the placement of MSS in relation to the position of Food-4-Less, most of the traffic will have to pass by MSS. MSS can also be seen by those traveling University Drive.

By virtue of the fact that the shopping center is new, many people will come to see what it offers and MSS can capitalize on this. There will also be a huge grand opening for the mall and MSS will benefit from the advertisements and publicity of the newest and best location in the valley. This location will be ideal for MSS because the mall will have a grocery store, a restaurant, a video store, a bakery, and a beauty salon. These businesses will draw customer traffic from which MSS will benefit. Once people know where MSS is located and have experienced the friendly, helpful attitude of its employees and compared the prices, MSS will have a substantial clientele and customer base.

The actual physical location will be on ground level with glass as its face. It will have 3700 square feet and will have heating, electricity, and air-conditioning, as well as a bathroom for employees. The carpet and walls will reflect relaxing and nonthreatening colors. Background music will also be relaxing, promoting the comfortable feeling MSS seeks for its atmosphere. The office furniture will all be new and state-of-the-art. There will also be plants in decorative pots and decorative pictures on the walls to make people feel welcome. Smoking will not be allowed.

There is ample parking at PlumTree and accessibility to MSS will be very easy. Parking stalls will afford approximate and convenient access to the store. (Please see Appendix D for the actual layout of MSS and its position in relation to Food-4-Less.)

The location will be acquired by lease. The lease can be for one year or up to sixty years. The price is $11.50 per square foot per year. The developers estimate an additional $2.30 per square foot per year will include the utilities, landscaping and maintenance of the parking lot, fire insurance, parking-lot lighting, and garbage removal.

The increased cost of this location will be reflected in a minor price increase. However, even with the price increase, MSS plans to be as low if not lower on most items than any of its competitors. (Please see price comparisons under Competition Analysis.)

The location is yet to be completed, so the developers will work with the intended occupants to make adjustments as needed. Partition walls are needed for office and service areas and will be provided by the developers. The service area will be for repairing computers and the office will be for the secretary to do the paperwork. The developers have a set budget on what they will spend on improvements, and additional improvements must be paid for by the occupant. MSS only needs the partitions put up, so there should not be too great a cost involved in the improvements.

Management Expertise

Rob Bradford, the owner, has been acting as chief technician, salesman, and office manager for MSS since it opened in 1991. Mr. Bradford has been involved with the computer industry since 1978. He has attended the University of California at Irvine where he studied electronic technology and also attended San Jose College where he again studied electronic technology. In 1982, Mr. Bradford went to work for IBM as a field technician. During the summer of 1984, Mr. Bradford was approached by Senior Management of IBM to become the Director of Field Operations for the Southern California Region. Mr. Bradford continued as the Director of Field Operations for IBM until he started MSS.

Mr. Bradford's expertise is mainly in IBM, IBM-compatible, Commodore, and Apple computers, as well as printer and terminal repair, although he is not limited to these by any means. Aside from computers, Mr. Bradford has repaired VCRs, video cameras, televisions, and stereos. He is a capable and competent technician and manager. He has successfully managed two different businesses, the most recent being MSS.

Support Personnel

Mrs. Bradford has served many functions at MSS. She has kept all of the books, handled the advertising and marketing, and taken care of the accounts receivable and accounts payable. She graduated from Stanford University in 1986 with a degree in advertising and sales. She has worked for various organizations including a boys' club, a theater, and Stanford University. She had no previous experience in bookkeeping but has become quite adept in maintaining orderly books. Her area of expertise is advertising, but a limited budget has not allowed her to use her talents as she would have liked. However, with an appropriate advertising budget she could increase business dramatically for MSS.

Appropriation of Funds for Relocation/Expansion

Initial Investment:

Equipment $18,390

> IBM system
> AT&T system
> Commodore 128
> AT clone
> Letter quality printer
> NEC monitor
> Cable system
> Toshiba printer
> Laptop system

Advertising $7,350

      Ads in *Daily Universe*
      Ads in *Daily Herald*
      Giveaway items for Grand Opening
      Radio remote and ads
      Mailers/coupons

Furniture 3,100

      Chairs
      Computer desks
      Magazine racks
      Manuals
      Plants

Signs 2,000

      Van
      Building

Accessories for sale 500

      Diskettes
      Cables
      Surge protectors

Paperwork 100

      Sales books
      Repair books
      Pens
      Stamps
      Postage stamps
      Staples

First month's rent (includes utilities) 2,000

Three months' wages 10,500

      Manager at 2,500

      Secretary at 1,000

Operating capital 8,000

Phone startup cost 575

Three-month shipping cost 3,000

First-month business insurance 200

First-month van insurance and gas 285

Miscellaneous (checking account) 500

Initial Total Cost 56,500

Monthly Costs

Rent (includes utilities) $2,000

Wages 5,000

Advertising 1,000

Phone (local, long distance, Yellow Pages ad) 415

Shipping 1,000

Business insurance 200

Paperwork 50

Van insurance and gas 285

Total Monthly Cost $9,950

Summary

Micro Service and Sales is a successful, thriving business that is suffering at the moment from its location. It has a good reputation for being honest and fair. MSS has strong customer backing, but to grow as it potentially could, it needs a new location. The reason PlumTree has been chosen as its first priority for its new location is because PlumTree is a new shopping center; it is going to open with a bang, and MSS wants to be a part of it.

The developers of PlumTree feel that this shopping center is going to be better than the Mall at Orange, and they expect more than 5500 cars per day to come through the center. MSS needs this kind of exposure. People who have brought their computers to MSS to be serviced and those who have bought their computer systems from MSS have been very pleased with the service they have received. Growth would be achieved by exposing more of the public to this kind of desirable service. Location in PlumTree shopping center would allow MSS to grow to its full potential and would pave the way for opening subsequent stores in other areas of the country.

Existing Inventory

	cost	make	model	serial #
10 printers	$5,500.00	Silent Scribe	DP-962OA	N012210
12 desks	2,200.00			
6 computer desks	1,000.00			
1 cash register	350.00	MAX	RE 1011	G84B38459
12 computers	18,000.00	Beltron	386	M101,M102
1 phone/answering	150.00	Panasonic	KX-T2415	5ECHF121768
Test equipment	10,000.00			
4 oscilloscopes		BK Precision	1479 B	12924
misc. tools				
5 meters				
Work benches	250.00			
Spare parts	12,000.00			
Chairs	425.00			
Total	**$49,895.00**			

Break-Even Analysis

New Location Only:

Total monthly fixed costs	$9,950.00
Approximate total monthly variable costs	250.00
Total	$10,200.00

To break even every month, MSS would have to sell:

64 — IBM Compatible 386 systems or	$ 158.18 profit
29 — 386 Laptops or	$ 348.00 profit
18 — IBM AT systems or	$ 557.00 profit
15 IBM systems, 15 printers,	$ 235.00 profit
11 XT compatibles, 1 IBM AT,	
2 AT compatibles	

This includes sales of hardware only. Of course there are numerous combinations of hardware, software, and service that will allow MSS to break even every month. The hardware mentioned above is merely an example of what could be sold to break even. However, MSS plans to do much more than simply break even every month.

Partial Customer List

California Technical College
California Credit Service Corporation
Irvine Lock and Safe
Patzi's of California
Lopger Paint and Glass
LanFix
PLM Systems
WK Imaging
Strate Western
McClean Clinic
Sunstate Industries
Planned Management
Rollins, Brown and Gunnell, Inc.
Robyn Reed, International
Harding and Associates
University of California at Irvine Personnel Department
Cubco
GTE Phone Directories
Irvine School District
Regional Adolescent Center
Travel Station
Ford Construction
Riverside School District
Peripheral Equipment
Telum, Inc.
Thornhill Corp.
Frameworks
Multipoint

This list includes businesses and schools only; individuals have not been included. (Please see Appendix B for letters of recommendation.)

Job Descriptions

On the Payroll

Service Manager The service manager oversees the operation of the service department, making sure all the repairs are done on a timely basis and that the cost of repairs is kept down for the customer. The service manager also functions as the chief technician, repairing the machines as well as overseeing the operation of the department. This is a full-time position.

Technician The technician handles the service work and the service calls that the chief technician is unable to attend to. The technician also handles customer support where necessary. This can be a full-time or part-time position.

Secretary The secretary takes care of all the bookkeeping, billing, bank deposits, and keeping the office inventory of staples, postage stamps, etc., up to date. This is a part-time position.

Independent Contractors

Advertising Director The advertising director makes the media buys as well as implements an advertising campaign. The advertising director is also responsible for the marketing of MSS. This position has been combined with the position of secretary in the past. This is a part-time position, and if a separate advertising director is hired, payment would be by the job.

Sales Manager The sales manager oversees the sales department, making sure customers are treated well and that sales prices are competitive. This is a full-time position.

Salespeople The salespeople sell the computer systems and software. These are part-time positions.

To begin, MSS would need a service manager, who would also act as chief technician; a secretary, who would also act as the advertising director; and a salesperson, who may be promoted to sales manager at a future date. The service manager and secretary would be paid salaries, while the salesperson would work strictly for commission. Additional salespeople hired in the future would also work strictly for commission. The reason the salespeople are not paid salaries is because commission-based pay tends to make people work harder and more efficiently, and top salespeople can make money for MSS as well as making a nice sum for themselves.

Salaries

Service manager	$2,500 per month
Secretary/advertising director	$1,000 per month
Future technician	$700 per month

Commissions

Sales manager	12 percent retail
Salespeople	10 percent retail
Advertising director	By the job

Memberships

MSS is a member of the United States Chamber of Commerce, the Better Business Bureau, the National Federation of Independent Businesses, and the Orange County Chamber of Commerce. These memberships allow MSS certain privileges and also give customers confidence that MSS is a dependable and reputable business.

Future Plans for Micro Service and Sales

In the future, MSS would like to add four to six 80386-compatible systems to its inventory for instructional use and for renting to students or the general public. A rental fee of $10 per hour for the computer is a competitive price with U.C. Irvine; although it is not much, it would bring in additional potential customers. These units may also be used for instructional purposes, and classes could be held nightly, weekly, or monthly to teach anyone who is interested in how to use a computer. An additional use for these units would be to let people come in and try out software they have already purchased or may purchase in the future. MSS would be a learning environment as much as anything else, and the customer would be the center of attention and importance.

Future plans would also include opening additional locations throughout the country. A possible second location in Orange County would be in Costa Mesa. In California other possible locations would be San Bernardino, Riverside, Santa Barbara, San Diego, and San Francisco. A possible location in Arizona would be Phoenix. Eventually, MSS would like to be located in all of the western states. The first chain location could be opened within two years of the relocation of MSS.

Profit and Loss Sheet for 1993

January	Loss	$2,673.11
February	Profit	710.63
March	Loss	3,282.30
April	Profit	1,842.30
May	Profit	2,721.34
June	Profit	2,069.71
July	Profit	3,351.57
August	Profit	2,988.40
September	Profit	4,324.12
October	Profit	5,528.06
November	Loss	225.98
December	Profit	9,466.62
Total credits for 1993		$226,735.90
Total debits for 1993		$193,733.15
Total profit for 1993		$26,821.36
Average profit each month in 1993		$2,750.23 (including salaries)

Sales Forecast for Remainder of 1994*

New Location

month	gross sales	gross cost	gross profit	fixed costs	net profit
May	$60,000	$43,000	$17,000	$10,200	$ 6,800
June	60,000	43,000	17,000	10,200	6,800
July	50,000	35,000	15,000	10,200	4,800
August	50,000	35,000	15,000	10,200	4,800
September	61,000	43,825	17,175	10,200	6,975
October	61,000	43,825	17,175	10,200	6,975
November	62,000	44,650	17,350	10,200	7,150
December	72,000	51,650	20,350	10,200	10,150
Total	$476,000	$339,950	$136,050	$81,600	$54,450

To arrive at the figures above, the gross sales achieved at MSS's present location were doubled. MSS began sales in January 1991. From January 1991 to December 1991, average gross sales per month were $30,000. This figure was simply doubled, giving the base figure of $60,000. The markup used for these calculations was 25 percent. The commission of the salesperson has also been figured into these estimates. The net profit forecasted for 1994 is $54,450.

Sales Forecast for 1995*

New Location

quarter	gross sales	gross cost	gross profit	fixed costs	net profit
First	$202,025	$146,170	$55,855	$40,800	$15,055
Second	202,025	146,170	55,855	40,800	15,055
Third	202,025	146,170	55,855	40,800	15,055
Fourth	202,025	146,170	55,855	40,800	15,055
Total	$808,100	$584,680	$223,420	$163,200	$60,220

These numbers reflect a 41 percent increase in sales from 1994, which is the estimated increase of sales according to Dataquest (*Info World*, November 10, 1991). The salesperson's commission has been figured into these estimates. The net profit forecasted for 1995 is $60,220.

Sales Forecast for 1996*

New Location

quarter	gross sales	gross cost	gross profit	fixed costs	net profit
First	$292,401	$210,528	$81,472	$48,500	$32,972
Second	292,401	210,528	81,472	48,500	32,972
Third	292,401	210,528	81,472	48,500	32,972
Fourth	292,401	210,528	81,472	48,500	32,972
Total	$1,169,604	$842,112	$325,888	$194,000	$131,888

These figures reflect a 30 percent increase in sales from 1995, which is the estimated growth in sales according to Dataquest. The salesperson's commission has been figured into these estimates. The net profit forecasted for 1996 is $131,888.

Numbers have been rounded to nearest whole number

Return on Investment

New Location

year	net profit
1994	$ 54,450
1995	60,220
1996	131,888
Total net profit at end of 1994	$246,558

Initial investment (equity buyout of Rob Bradford)	$ 50,000
New equipment and relocation costs	$ 56,500
Total	$106,500

Net profit minus initial investment: $246,558 - $105,000 = $140,058

The actual net profit for the investor at the end of 1994 is $140,058 which is 31.5 percent interest on the initial investment of $106,500. The investor would have to wait almost three years to make money on this investment, but at the end of this time the investor could make 31.5 percent interest on his investment.

Tentative Advertising Plan, May 1994-April 1995

June
   Daily Universe, 3 days/week, 2 x 3, 4 weeks, $351.36
   Daily Herald, 7 days, 2 x 3, $388.08
   120D Printer giveaway, $190.00

July
   Daily Universe, 3 days/week, 2 x 3, 4 weeks, $351.36
   WordPerfect giveaway, $180.00
   Coupons/mailers

August
   Daily Universe, 3 days/week, 2 x 3, 4 weeks, $351.36
   Daily Herald, 7 days, 2 x 3, $388.08
   Dac Easy Accounting giveaway, $80.00

September
   Daily Universe, 5 days/week, 2 x 4, 4 weeks, $958.40
   PC Paint/Mouse giveaway, $130.00
   Coupons/mailers

October
   Radio
   Modem giveaway, $95.00

November
   Daily Herald, 7 days, $388.08
   Dac Easy Accounting giveaway, $80.00
   Coupons/mailers

December

    Coupons/mailers

    Print Shop giveaway, $30.00

    Daily Universe, 3 days/week, 2 x 3, 4 weeks, $458.64

January

    Daily Universe, 5 days/week, 2 x 4, 4 weeks, $958.40

    Modem giveaway, $95.00

    Daily Herald, 7 days, $388.08

February

    Radio

    Modem giveaway, $95.00

March

    Daily Universe, 3 days/week, 2 x 3, 4 weeks, $458.64

    Daily Herald, 7 days, $388.08

    Diskette holder giveaway, $8.00

April

    Daily Universe, 3 days/week, 2 x 3, 4 weeks, $458.64

    Coupons/mailers

    Head cleaner kit giveaway, $12.00

This is merely a tentative plan for advertising. It is dependent on how these particular media perform and whether or not they bring in customers. The budget for all months except September and January is $1,000. The budget for September and January is $1,500 to reflect additional advertising to the returning students at U.C. Irvine. All the advertising listed above is within the advertising budget for the month. Some figures have not been included because exact costs cannot be determined at this time; however, the total cost for the month will not exceed the budget. Advertising is a variable cost and MSS would go with what does best. In the past, MSS has found that the ads placed in the *Daily Universe* have drawn in students and MSS would expect the same thing to happen with additional advertising in the *Daily Universe.* The radio station to be used is not specified; it would be up to the discretion of the advertiser, because radio stations frequently change their formats and research of the station at the time of advertising is required to make sure the proper buy is made.

The giveaways will bring in additional customers who want to win the item to be given away. These giveaway items will not cost MSS too much, and at the same time they have the potential of bringing in numerous potential customers. The rules of the drawings will be: "No purchase necessary, 18 and older, must be present at the drawing, participants may enter as often as they wish, winners cannot be any employees or relatives of employees of MSS, the drawing will be held the last Friday of every month at 6 p.m., winners' names will be posted following the drawing to verify there was a drawing and a winner."

There will be a special display set up with the item to be given away as well as a box for entry slips. A free drawing for these items is a gimmick that should bring in many people who may be potential customers.

Plan Summary

Micro Service and Sales is a profitable and successful business. Although MSS has done well in its present location, a move to the new PlumTree Shopping Center would enable MSS to grow as it should and would allow sales to increase dramatically. This is an ideal opportunity for someone who wants to own a successful business, see it grow, and make money on his investment.

MSS started under very humble circumstances with only a desk, a chair, and a phone. Under the direction of its present owner, Rob Bradford, MSS has grown into a successful and highly respected business in Orange County. Starting with absolutely nothing, not even a computer, MSS has acquired loyal clientele in the public community as well as service agreements with local businesses and schools. MSS could become bigger and better than any computer retail outlet in Orange County and has the potential of growing into a chain that would certainly rival the larger computer stores.

MSS is set apart from the rest of the competition because it offers real service. From repairing the actual machines to giving customer support after the sale, MSS is dedicated to giving the customer the very best service. Mr. Bradford at the present time spends many hours every week just talking to potential customers and giving support to those who have bought equipment or those who have used MSS to service their system. MSS will also be different from its competition because with the proper backing, MSS will have all the popular brands of computer hardware and software and individuals will be given the opportunity to "test" the equipment and the software before purchase.

There are numerous possibilities available to MSS, from sales and service to programming, but it needs a new location and money to make it into a better-recognized computer store of Orange County.

Micro Service and Sales has all the ingredients for a successful business except location and appropriate funds. MSS already has the reputation, the contacts, the dealerships, and the clientele. All MSS needs is a more-visible, more-easily accessible location, and appropriate funds.

Appendixes

Appendix A: Graphs

Appendix B: Letters of Recommendation

Appendix C: Newspaper Articles

Appendix D: PlumTree Information

Author's Note:

List all supporting documentation in the appendix section as noted and referenced throughout your business plan.

Remember, this information should be clearly and neatly presented so the reader of your business plan can easily reference and understand the data being provided.

A Business Plan For:

Rancho Sporting Goods Company

by Daven Porter

May 1, 1994

Table of Contents

Summary Statement

Rancho Sporting Goods Company is slated to begin operations in April 1995 under a business-wise team of three executives in response to an unfilled need in the Durango area for quality outdoor sports equipment. The business venture was conceived to be viable from the following conditions:

1. The market for sports equipment has demonstrated substantial growth in the past decade (5 percent, to $989.9 million).

2. The existing competitors in the area do not carry the goods and services most consumers need and want.

3. Rancho Sporting Goods can supply normal sporting goods in an array that competitors cannot match.

As a result of these conditions, Rancho Sporting Goods believes it can capture 20 percent of the market share in the first three years of operation. This market share would produce forecasted sales of $234,000 and an after-tax profit of $32,346 by the third year.

By providing goods and services that are not readily available from competitors and continually catering to the wishes of the consumer, Rancho Sporting Goods will be able to hold its customers and finance its operations after an initial investment of $800,000.

Company Analysis

Company Name: Rancho Sporting Goods Company

Type of Business: Retail/Service

Location: 4225 W. PineTop Road

Durango, CO 85555

Owner: Daven Porter

Company History

The proposed date of opening for Rancho Sporting Goods Company (Rancho Sports) is April 1995. Rancho Sports has a very narrowly defined purpose, which is to provide quality outdoor recreation equipment and service to the consumer at an affordable price.

Currently, there are no sporting goods stores in the Durango area that carry the quality or quantity of goods and services Rancho Sports will be carrying. Although Wal-Mart and K-mart have outlets in the same geographic area, neither has the quality of products or the service Rancho Sports will provide. The nearest purchasing outlet with any similarity to Rancho Sports is in the Denver area.

At Rancho Sports, the main focus will be the personal attention we can provide for the customer. Since ultimately the customer is the one who decides whether Rancho Sports will prosper, customer service will be a top priority.

The Durango area was chosen as the location for Rancho Sports for several reasons:

1. The community is close to major areas of outdoor recreation.

2. Durango and the surrounding communities house a large, untapped client base, with a population of 148,400 people between the ages of 15 and 65.

3. The geographic area is expanding tremendously, with an average change of +73.5 percent from 1980 to 1990.

4. The economic stability and average income of Durango and surrounding areas will support this type of operation. With an average annual income of approximately $20,000 and retail sales of $235,899,000 in 1993, the area looks promising.

5. The influence of outdoor recreation on the people of the area is outstanding. Having grown up in the area, I know that the people of this area respond favorably to sporting goods stores.

Principals

Currently, Daven Porter is the only principal working on the venture in the capacity of creating a business plan. However, a proposed management team consisting of Daven Porter, John Porter, and Kathy Porter is currently under consideration.

As president and CEO of the venture, Daven Porter would be responsible for the overall development and strategic movement of the company. He will also maintain a position as a floor manager and deal with selling, purchasing, and stocking goods.

John Porter would be mainly involved in selling, purchasing, stocking, and promoting Rancho Sports goods and services. He would occupy a position in the organizational structure as vice-president of operations.

Finally, Kathy Porter would be responsible for the accounting and financing portion of Rancho Sports operations. Her position in the organizational structure would be vice-president in charge of financing/accounting (Appendix A-1).

Organizational Structure

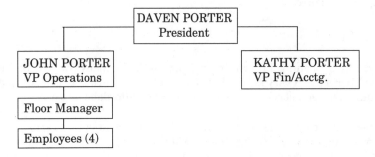

Products

Being involved in the retail sale of outdoor recreation goods and services, everything from Frisbees to baseballs to camping equipment could be included in this category. However, Rancho Sports has chosen to create a niche in the market by concentrating its efforts in the areas of hunting, fishing, and camping equipment and the subsequent servicing of this equipment.

The following list comprises the goods and services that will be offered at Rancho Sports.

Fishing Equipment (specializing in trout)

A. Spinning rods and reels

B. Fly-fishing rods and reels: Orvis, Fenwick, Eagle Claw, Garcia

C. Custom-built rods and fishing combinations

D. Accessories: waders, nets, float tubes, flies, line, hooks, tackle boxes, stringers, bobbers, lures, live bait, weights, containers, scales, scalers, fly-tying equipment and supplies, fishing vests, fish finders, electric motors, and rod/reel cases

Archery Equipment

A. Compound bows: PSE, Browning, Hoyt-Easton, Pro-line, Oneida

B. Recurved bows

C. Crossbows

D. Aluminum/Graphite/Fiberglass/Wooden Arrows: Easton

E. Crossbow bolts

F. Accessories: strings, cams, limbs, sights, silencers, paints, tape, blunts, field point, broadheads, bow cases, targets, arrow straighteners, arrow fletchers, scents, face paint, wax, sharpeners, tools, scales, stabilizers

Firearms

A. Rifles: Weatherby, Sako, Winchester, Remington, Colt

B. Pistols: S&W, Ruger, Colt, Baretta, Taurus, Browning

C. Accessories: scopes, mounts, bore sights, targets, slings, recoil pads, ammunition, cleaning equipment, holsters, grips, sights, rests, vises, clay pigeons, trap machines, premade stocks, muzzle brakes, stock finishing equipment, blueing equipment, calls, pack saws, ultraviolet reducer, game bags

Camping

A. Backpacks/Daypacks: Jansport, North Face, Mountain Sports

B. Tents

C. Sleeping bags

D. Accessories: lanterns, mantles, generators, stoves, white gas, pumps, stakes, waterproof spray, tarps, utensils, cook gear, dry food, pads, space blankets, first-aid kits, small axes/ shovels, ropes, heaters, boots, rain gear, canteens, water purifier

Knives

A Hunting/Fishing Knives: Buck, Schrade, Gerber, Boker

B. Sharpening equipment

Clothing

A. Camouflage shirts, pants, jackets, gloves, socks, hats

B. Thermal underwear

C. Fashion outdoor wear—wool, flannel: shirts, pants, hats, socks, shorts, gloves, coats, jackets

Optical

A. Binoculars/Monoculars: Redfield, Bausch & Lomb, Steiner, Bushnell

B. Spotting scopes

C. Tripods

D. Defogger

Reloading

A. Powder

B. Primers

C. Cases

D. Bullets

E. Dies

F. Presses

G. Manuals

H. Classes

I. Accessories

Services

A. Gun repair

B. Stock building/checkering

C. Custom gun building

D. Blueing

E. Gun accessorizing: grips, sights, mounts, etc.

F. Classes: gun safety, checkering, stock building

G. Custom bows/arrows

H. Bow repair/accessorizing

I. Shooting tips, lanes, range

J. Archery classes

K. Custom rods/reels

L. Custom hand-tied flies

M. Fly fishing classes (private pond)

N. Information on surrounding areas (Appendix A-2)

Other

Guided tours of area by horse, maps, videos, muzzle loader kits and accessories, airguns, hearing protection, decoys

Equipment

The very nature of a retail organization requires a substantial investment in different types of fixtures and equipment for the venture. Because of the expensive nature of some of the goods Rancho Sports will be offering, locking display cases will be used. Knives, optical equipment, ammunition, and guns will remain locked up until a customer wishes to view a particular item. Shelving, racks, and islands will be needed to display the inventory, along with display cases. The total costs for these fixtures will run in the range of $4,000.

For purposes of recording sales and accepting payment from customers, electronic cash registers will initially be rented at a rate of $200 per month with thought being given to purchasing the registers at a later date.

Complementing the electronic registers will be a personalized computer system for Rancho Sports. The computer will track sales, forecast profits/expenses, control inventory, and maintain a current list of customers. Initial estimates for the hardware and software tally around $6,000. Exact figures have not been computed at this time because of the extremely fast-changing technology in the computer information field.

Other equipment for fly-tying, arrow construction, and gun customizing, along with supplies such as stationery and business cards, will cost approximately $1,250.

To protect Rancho Sports from vandalism and theft, a security system consisting of alarms, cameras, and retractable bars for the windows will be installed at a cost of $4,500. Although this is a rather high cost for a security system, the adage "An ounce of prevention is worth a pound of cure" holds true. Spending a little money now can prevent big losses later.

As indicated in Appendix A-3, insuring a sporting goods operation is rather costly, due to the type of goods (guns/ammo) that are carried. However, if a quality security system is installed, USF&G insurance offers a 15 percent discount for the overall policy.

Markets

Major Market: Small towns within the county.

Combined Population (total): 151,900 as of July 1, 1993.

Primary Market: Males, ages 20 to 49, with strong interest in outdoor activities (hunting, fishing, camping).

Secondary Market: Females, age 20 and up, interest in outdoor activities or buying for significant other.

Other Markets: Specialty groups, persons in immediate geographic area, tourists, 15 to 19 year age group.

Technology Position

Rancho Sporting Goods Company must keep abreast of new trends, ideas, and goods in the outdoor recreation field to provide the best goods and services for the consumer.

Bases of Competition

The main reason that consumers buy from Rancho Sports over other competitors is the quality of its goods and services. Along with this, customers buy from Rancho Sports because of the personal attention to the customer and the intangible goodwill created in the store (Appendix A-4).

Key Success Factors

The main factors contributing to the success of Rancho Sports are quality goods in a sizable quantity, dependable and fast service, and competitive pricing. Our service is a main point that will separate us from the rest of the pack.

Industry Analysis

Industry Definition

The sporting goods industry as a whole occupies two different but overlapping economic sectors, one being retail and the other the service sector. Although many sporting goods stores tend to concentrate more on the retail distribution of their products, the service sector plays an integral part in maintaining profitability. A store that is unable or unwilling to provide service on its goods (or get the service from another business for its customers) will invariably end up in a very unprofitable position.

Although the sporting goods industry has been in existence for well over 150 years, the range of products and services has remained fairly consistent over the years. Currently, the product lines of most sporting goods stores consist of the following goods:

1. Hunting equipment

2. Firearms and accessories

3. Fishing equipment

4. Archery equipment

5. Camping equipment

6. Reloading supplies and equipment

7. Outdoor clothing

The number of retail sporting goods outlets that offer many services is quite limited. Most of the large stores, such as Wal-Mart, K-Mart, Oshmans, and others, have based their service operations on two main points: (1) helping the customer at the point of sale and (2) returning defective or broken goods to the manufacturer for repair or replacement. The smaller stores, however, are more likely to provide service in the form of instruction and replacement rather than repairing the damaged goods themselves.

The surrounding areas, consisting of rural counties, would be the local market for Rancho Sports. In this geographic area there are two major suppliers of outdoor recreation equipment, Wal-Mart and K-mart. At the present time, there are four other small (profits under $2,500 per year) retail outlets competing for a share of the market (Appendix B-1).

Geographically, the retail sporting goods industry is mainly confined to a national market. Although many large companies do sell sporting goods equipment internationally, people in the United States are, by far, the largest purchasers of outdoor sporting equipment. Private ownership of guns, ammunition, reloading equipment, and miscellaneous survival equipment in the United States outnumbers that of many countries' militaries.

Industry Size and Growth Rate

More than 105 million Americans participate in outdoor recreation activities and support the industries while doing so. More than one third of the population are regular participants in nonmotorized outdoor activities—hiking, camping, rock-climbing, canoeing, hunting, and fishing—in many cases, year around.

Well-located sporting goods stores have the ability to gross over $500,000 per year. Most shops, however, have annual sales between $90,000 and $250,000.

The industry is looking forward to a 7 to 10 percent real annual growth rate for the coming decade. In the past 25 years, participation in wilderness activities increased by 300 percent.

Well-run wilderness shops turn over inventory completely three or more times a year. Net pretax profits for sporting goods outlets are typically in the 17 to 22 percent range, with costs of sales around 51 percent and overhead maintained at 27 to 30 percent. A store grossing $150,000 to $250,000 annually will carry $20,000 to $50,000 to the bottom line (Appendix B-2).

Key Growth Factors

There are many significant growth factors for the outdoor sporting equipment industry. These factors, being beyond the control of the retailer, can have both positive and negative repercussions on the business. Although many of the growth factors that follow have a direct influence on the industry, it must be noted that in the years to follow many new and previously unknown growth factors will arise.

New legislation regarding the banning of weapons, limiting or completely banning hunting animals for sport, and restrictions on areas where an individual may participate in such activities plays a key role in influencing the success or failure of the business. Should legislation pass limiting the hunting of animals or the sale of weapons, the industry would show significant losses.

Another factor related to the growth of the industry is societal attitudes toward activities such as hunting and fishing. Groups such as Greenpeace and People for the Ethical Treatment of Animals (PETA) have considerable influence over the prosperity of the industry.

Factors that are more immediate are financial factors facing the people of the area. The amount of discretionary income they have to spend, the economic stability of the area, the population growth, and the unemployment rate could all create a "boom or bust" situation for anyone in the outdoor recreation market.

The current trend of people "getting back to nature" and rediscovering themselves in the outdoors is giving the sporting goods industry a tremendous boost. The shift of people away from the metropolitan areas to the more rural communities where they can enjoy the outdoors is a promising factor relating to the growth and stability of the industry (Appendix B-2).

Finally, the pollution and destruction of popular outdoor recreation areas will eventually limit the sporting goods industry. The cutting of the National Forests to supply wood products for the world, the expansion of modern civilization, and the inevitable pollution created by man and industry will eventually force the retail owner of a sporting goods outlet to either go out of business or seek new types of products to keep up with the changing times.

Cyclical Influences

The sporting goods industry, especially in the Durango area, is affected very little by cyclical influences. Granted, there are times when the aspects of outdoor recreation may seem trendy, but for the most part there is a stable base of consumers that supports this type of operation.

Seasonality

Being involved in the sporting goods industry, especially with hunting and fishing equipment, Rancho Sports would be influenced by the seasonality of its goods.

During the months of July through December, there would be a upward trend of sales of hunting equipment. This type of product would account for approximately 60 percent of the sales during the specified time period (Appendix B-3).

The months of April through July would be most profitable for sales of fishing equipment. During these months, the weather is warmer and the number of people out fishing is far greater than during the other months. Fishing equipment would, therefore, account for approximately 65 percent of the net sales for that period (Appendix B-3).

Looking at the year-round picture, the months of January through March would be the slow months, accounting for 40 percent of net sales, due to the low outdoor activity during these months. The time frame of April through December would account for 60 percent of the net sales for the year, due to the seasonality of the activities and products needed for these activities (Appendix B-3).

Industry Life Cycle

The following table indicates the life cycle of the sporting goods industry as a whole. In each of the following criteria, the industry exhibits the characteristics of the mature life cycle:

1. Growth rate = Stable

2. Market share = High

3. Product line = No change

4. Financial = Cash rich, low debt

5. Market share stability = Entrenched

6. Ease of entry = Difficult

7. Typical volume growth rate = Peak and decline

8. Managerial style = Critical administrator (Appendix B-4)

Market Analysis

Market Scope

Rancho Sports will occupy a local market base covering the Durango area and surrounding communities. We will cater to those individuals with interest in outdoor activities such as hunting, fishing, camping, and hiking. Although the outdoor recreation market consists of many areas of interest, ranging from skiing to off-road racing, Rancho Sports will focus its efforts on those activities relating to the pursuit of wild game and fish.

Market Segmentation

Geography

> *Region:* Southwestern United States
>
> *County Size:* Land Area—9,955 square miles
>
> *Climate:* Mainly Ponderosa pine forest, with temperatures ranging from below 0 degrees Fahrenheit in the winter to 90 degrees Fahrenheit in the hottest summer months
>
> *Elevation:* 7,000 feet above sea level

Major Customers and Concentration

Typical Customers

Typical patrons of Rancho Sports will mainly be male, between the ages of 20 and 49, with strong interests in outdoor activities such as hunting, fishing, and camping. They will usually be involved in all areas of outdoor sports, as they will participate in rifle and bow hunting, fishing and camping. Typical customers will spend approximately 25 to 30 minutes in the store just looking around if they aren't buying anything. Those customers that do buy the products offered will spend an average of approximately one hour in the store. These customers will constitute 60 percent of sales.

Rancho Sports will appeal to many different customers. These customers will include, but are not limited to, the following:

Females, age 20 and up: interested in outdoor activities; introduced to outdoor recreation by husband or boyfriend; buying for self or significant others.

Males, ages 16 to 20: interest in outdoor activities; introduced to sports at young ages by family; shop where the "neat" products are.

Specialty groups: persons looking for specific items, such as hand-tied flies, or checkering equipment; will include persons in immediate area as well as those from surrounding communities and tourists.

Sales Tactics

Rancho Sports will use a sales force located inside a retail outlet to sell the products and services available. The store size will be approximately 5,000 square feet, thus requiring a minimum of three people on the selling floor at any given time. The sales procedure will not be an obnoxious hard sell, but rather a helpful, informative sell in which the customer isn't pressured into buying something that is not needed. All sales will be on the basis that satisfied customers are return customers.

Any and all discounts or special prices will be approved through Daven Porter or John Porter. Normal sales terms will be cash, check, and a lay-away program. Credit sales will be approved for certain long-time, dependable customers, with the following terms: for small items, balance due in 30 days, larger expensive items on an individual basis. Other credit terms will be approved through management for certain individuals such as doctors, family members, and other special customers.

Pricing Trends

Average gun prices have risen steadily over the past five years, a symptom that the market has matured and is not attracting very many new buyers. Prices range anywhere from $150 for the small, low-quality pistols to $900 for the more expensive items in the firearms field.

Camping and fishing equipment, on the other hand, have maintained a relatively low, stable price throughout the market. The only exception in this area is the state-of-the-art graphite and custom-made fishing equipment, which tends to occupy the upper end of the price scale.

Rancho Sports will maintain its competitiveness by keeping within a ± 2 percent pricing structure compared with the major competitors in the area.

Promotion and Advertising

The advertising strategy Rancho Sports will employ will consist of advertising in the following media:

1. Yellow Pages

2. Magazines—*Colorado Hunter and Angler*

3. Newspapers—*Durango News* and the *Denver Times*

4. Radio—KDJI, KVWM, KFRM

5. Direct Mail—Mailing list

The initial media blitz will be allocated as 40 percent radio, 20 percent Yellow Pages, 20 percent newspaper, 5 percent magazine, and 15 percent direct mail. These expenditures will be based on 3 percent of total sales for the first year, then reduced to 2 percent of total sales thereafter.

Promotional advertising will be done through workshops, archery tournaments, special contests during specific seasons, sponsorship of local activities, and occasional promotional giveaways. The costs of completing this type of advertising/ promotional blitz as suggested above is broken down as follows:

	Yr. 1	Yr. 2	Yr. 3
Yellow Pages	$ 2,100	$ 2,800	$ 5,040
Colorado Hunter/Angler	525	700	1,260
KDJI, KVWM, KFRM	4,200	5,600	10,080
Durango News/Denver Times	2,100	2,800	5,040
Direct Mail	1,575	2,100	3,780
Total Expenditure	$10,500	$14,000	$25,200

Competitor Profile

Appendix C-1 indicates Rancho Sports' major competitors, their sales volume, growth rate, degree of integration, strengths, and weaknesses.

Management Team

The management team of Rancho Sports will consist of Daven Porter, owner and CEO; John Porter, vice-president of operations; and Kathy Porter, vice-president of finance/accounting. The following breakdown shows the responsibilities each principal will be either directly (D) or indirectly (I) associated with:

Daven Porter:

Objective Setting (D), Communicating (D), Coordinating (D), Controlling (D), Organizing (D), Staffing (D), Planning (D), Leading (D), Public Relations (I), General Administration (D), Risk Management (D), Advertising (I), Purchasing (D), Operations (D), Personnel (I), Marketing (I), Finance (I), Sales (D), Legal (D) Taxes (I)

John Porter:

Objective Setting (D), Communicating (D), Coordinating (D), Controlling (D), Organizing (D), Staffing (D), Planning (D), Leading (D), Public Relations (D), General Administrative (D), Risk Management (I), Advertising (D), Purchasing (D), Operations (D), Personnel (I), Marketing (I), Finance (I), Sales (D), Taxes (I)

Kathy Porter:

Objective Setting (D), Communicating (D), Coordinating (D), Controlling (D), Organizing (D), Staffing (D), Planning (D), Leading (I), Public Relations (D), General Administrative (D), Risk Management (I), Advertising (D), Purchasing (I), Operations (D), Personnel (D), Marketing (D), Finance (D), Sales (I), Taxes (D)

Rancho Sports will involve participatory management. Certain principals will have talents in areas that others do not; therefore, they will hold primary responsibility in the area. However, the management team will be expected to have a broad overview of all aspects of Rancho Sports, even if it is through indirect involvement.

Functions of Key Personnel

To determine any and all special functions performed by the principals of Rancho Sports, Appendix C-4 delineates which functions will be the primary responsibility of each individual.

Manpower Milestones

In determining the number of employees needed for the first three years of operation, the chart entitled *Manpower Milestones* (Appendix C-5) gives the number of employees that will be needed to successfully operate Rancho Sports in the following areas: General and Administrative, Marketing, Finance/Accounting, and Sales.

Strategic Planning

The upper management of Rancho Sports will not be complacent with a venture restricted to the Durango area. The long-term goal of Rancho Sports is to become a leader in the sporting goods industry through expansion, increased sales, increased product lines, and quality of service. The first five to ten years of operation will be dedicated to growth, financial stability, and goodwill. In this time frame, Rancho Sports will be the first name in quality sporting goods *and service*. Management and employees will strive to achieve total market domination. Because of the large inventory, competitive pricing, and quality service, Rancho Sports will be working toward more than $350,000 in sales after the fifth year of operation.

After the initial stabilizing period (long enough for Rancho Sports to become financially independent), one of two courses will be pursued. Rancho Sports will either (1) expand into other geographic areas, or (2) begin a mail-order business, such as Cabela's, Gander Mountain, or the past king of mail-order sporting goods, Herter's.

If Rancho Sports decides to expand into other geographic areas, such as the metropolitan Denver or Colorado Springs areas, store ownership will be held by the original principals, Daven Porter, John Porter, and Kathy Porter. Management for the different regions will be decided on by the original principals, and in-depth background and qualification checks will be performed. This direction will not be one of franchising, but rather of expansion and maintenance of ownership.

Should Rancho Sports decide to follow the alternate path of the mail-order catalog business, Cabela's, Gander Mountain, and Herter's will serve as the model for Rancho Sports. The catalog will be distributed on a nationwide basis and will contain all products currently available to the sporting goods consumer.

Each alternative will be evaluated by using a simple weighted payoff matrix considering probability and criteria as follows: cost, profitability, efficacy, and feasibility.

The alternatives follow both a generic and a master strategy.

Generic Strategy

This strategy is used as a approach to outperform competitors.

FOCUS (Niche): Focusing on product development and marketing efforts to a particular market segment in which the firm has a cost or differentiation advantage (Appendix D-1).

For Rancho Sports this means focusing on the present location where there are no other sporting goods stores that provide the quality goods or services that we will.

Master Strategy

This strategy involves internal growth at a steady rate each year through innovation and development.

Market Development: Developing new markets, meaning Rancho Sports would pursue other market areas such as Denver or Colorado Springs.

Concentric Diversification: Meaning acquiring new-but-related forms of business for new customers, such as going into the mail-order business.

The criteria used to evaluate the alternatives are:

1. Efficacy: Will the alternative solve the problem?

2. Cost: Will the cost of implementing compare favorably with the returns?

3. Acceptability: Will management accept the alternative?

The alternatives will be evaluated on a 1 to 5 scale, where 1 = No, 2 = Probable No, 3 = Neither Yes nor No, 4 = Probable Yes, 5 = Yes.

Consequences are indicated by the probabilities shown in parentheses under each alternative (Appendix D-2). They are determined by calculating (1 minus P), where P is the subjective probability that negative consequences will be associated with the alternative.

Milestone Schedule

Rancho Sports will use the following activities as critical milestones to plan and time the operations of the venture:

1. Business plan completion = April 30, 1994

2. Business plan update = January 1995

3. Financing = February 1993 through May 1995

4. Incorporation = February 1995

5. Construction = March 1995 through April 1995

6. Supplier/dealer agreement = March 1995

7. Order placement = April 1995

8. Order receipt = May 1995

9. Grand opening = May 1995

Appendix D-3 shows the time schedule for each of the above-listed activities in a time-line form. Note that each of the activities has a contingent plan for unforeseen problems that may arise.

Plan Assumption

Economic Conditions

Durango Country	Percent Change
Population	+31.0%
Wage/salary employment	+ 2.2%
Retail sales	+96.2%
Bank deposits	+44.6%
Vehicle registration	+29.3%

The above assumptions of the economic conditions are based upon projections from the *Colorado Statistical Review,* published by Valley National Bank.

Industry Trends

New technologies such as lightweight space-age polymers for the construction of clothing and camping equipment, new types of firearm design and calibers, and new methods in hunting and fishing techniques will all affect Rancho Sports' competitive position. To maintain a competitive advantage over other sporting goods dealers, Rancho Sports must continually strive to keep abreast of new advances in the sporting goods field.

Market Trends

The sporting goods market will be experiencing an increased demand for outdoor products such as camping equipment and fly-fishing supplies because of the recent trend of more people "getting back to nature." Visitors to the National Parks have increased from 263.4 million people per year to 269.4 million people per year. Sales of backpacks, tents, sleeping bags, and other camping equipment are up 5 percent, to $989.9 million. All of this translates into an increased demand for outdoor recreation equipment (Appendix B-2).

Outside Influences

Other influences that will directly or indirectly affect the sporting goods industry, including Rancho Sports, are government regulations of gun sales and hunting regulations. Along with the government, pressures from special interest groups such as GreenPeace, PETA, and other radical environmentalist groups will have a profound effect on the industry.

Red Flags

In the process of completing this business plan, several red flags that cannot be resolved at the present time must be noted for further investigation. Government regulations, new laws concerning hunting and gun control, and pressure from environmental and animal rights activists will all play a significant role in Rancho Sports' success. Although Rancho Sports has no direct control over these influential factors, they still must be kept in mind as red flags to serve as warnings, not only for Rancho Sports, but for the industry as well.

Company Strengths to Exploit

Rancho Sports' strengths are its quality goods and the service provided with the sale. Management will promote the service to the fullest extent possible, because this is where the two main competitors of Rancho Sports, Wal-Mart and K-mart, cannot compete. To exploit the company's strengths, only friendly, knowledgeable salespeople will be employed. These employees must know the ins and outs of all the goods carried at Rancho Sports and will offer their knowledge to customers in every way possible. Services such as reloading, custom gun finishing, and instructional courses will also be completed by only the most competent individuals who demonstrate a genuine concern for the needs of the customer. Any sporting goods store can provide quality goods, but how the store takes care of its customers is what sets it apart from the rest of the competition (Appendix E-1 and E-2).

Company Weaknesses to Overcome

In creating this business plan, all possible attempts have been made to eliminate any weaknesses that Rancho Sports may have. At this time, the only visible weakness of Rancho Sports is the seasonal nature of the industry. To overcome this shortcoming, a wide variety of goods will be offered to keep up with the different seasons involved in the sporting goods arena. All in all, only the months of January and February are predicted as "slow" months. The amount of projected sales for the other 10 months of the year will allow Rancho Sports to operate during the slower months without experiencing difficulties in financial stability.

Market Opportunities to Exploit

Rancho Sporting Goods Company will focus its activities on the previously untapped market surrounding Durango.

Risk Analysis

Every company in existence experiences risk in one way or another, and Rancho Sports is no exception. Several elements are delineated as important risk factors that Rancho Sporting Goods Company should be concerned with. They are:

    Industry
    Market
    Competitive position
    Strategy
    Assumption
    Financial performance
    Management performance
    Level of future performance

These risks are tallied and an overall rating of high, medium, or low risk for Rancho Sports is computed (Appendix E-4).

Business Strategies

Rancho Sports is presently in several strategic positions. Not only is management working for the short-term goals, but it also will be looking to the future for ways to make the business grow by using market strategies to concentrate on the immediate geographic area surrounding Durango and capture market share, product line strategies to keep the lines of products that the customer wants, technology strategies to keep abreast of new and rapidly changing technological advances in the outdoor products market, operations strategies to focus on performance related to sales and services, and financial strategies to help provide capital for ongoing operations and growth (Appendix E-5).

Company Thrusts and Business Strategies

In the Durango geographic areas, Rancho Sports' competitive position will definitely be considered strong because of the lack of competition. From this competitive position, different thrusts over the life cycle of the business have been determined. During the embryonic stage, the company thrust will be focused on startup, differentiation, and fast growth. Startup thrust is designed to introduce Rancho Sports to the area, with its main objective being to satisfy the demand for quality sporting goods and services where there previously had been none. This requires a risk-taking attitude on the part of management, along with capital expenditures and expenses. Results that can be expected are negative cash flow, low to negative returns, and a leadership position in the market. Risks are high but worth taking (Appendix E-6).

After the initial startup period, a fast-growth strategy will be employed to aggressively pursue a larger market share and a better competitive position. During this time, volume and market share will increase faster than the immediate competition and industry. Results expected are a greater market share, above-average returns in the long run, and competitive retaliation. By taking advantage of an untapped market and doing well, Rancho Sports risks that someone else will enter the market and try to play smarter and harder (Appendix E-7).

During the differentiation stage, customer perceptions of the best goods and service in the market with acceptable costs will be associated with Rancho Sports. The objective will be to insulate the company from switching, substitution, price competition, and loss of loyal customers and suppliers. From this position, high margins, above-average earnings, and a highly-defensible position will be attained (Appendix E-8).

The chart entitled *Guide to Company Thrusts* (Appendix E-9) gives a detailed guide to the thrusts Rancho Sports will be pursuing over the business life-cycle while occupying a strong competitive position.

Strategy Plan

Rancho Sports' main thrust will be to focus and develop a niche. The Durango area chosen for operation will allow Rancho Sports to select this niche and protect its strategic target area efficiently, fully, and profitably from such broad-line competitors as Wal-Mart and K-mart. This strategy will require a disciplined management, persistent pursuit of a well-defined scope and mission, premium pricing, and careful selection of targets. Rancho Sporting Goods Company expects to be the low-cost producer in the area while attaining high differentiation and above-average earnings.

Tactics

To pursue the above strategic plan, the following tactics will be implemented:

1. Continually redefining the scope and mission of the business;

2. Careful selection of targets;

3. Determining the products and services that are consistent with consumer wants and needs;

4. Continual steps to maintain loyal customers;

5. Perpetual reviews of objectives, financial position, and ways of improving performance.

Timing

The time frame involved in implementing the above tactics will begin immediately on opening and continue throughout the years of operation.

Responsibility

The main responsibility for seeing that the tactics are implemented and continually reviewed will fall on the shoulders of the main principals: Daven Porter, John Porter, and Kathy Porter. As the management team, each principal will be involved in a weekly meeting to determine short- and long-term needs of the company and ways of obtaining its goals.

Estimated Costs

The costs involved in implementing the strategies will mainly be manpower costs and the time it takes to run the weekly meetings to come up with solutions to problems.

Licenses and Taxes

Licenses

Durango does not require a city business license, only that the business file a joint tax return with the state (Appendix F-1).

The Durango Building Commission requires that operation in specific areas conform to the established zoning laws. Therefore, Rancho Sports has selected a location that meets the current zoning restrictions.

Since Rancho Sports will be selling such items as gunpowder and ammunition, a permit from the local fire department will also be obtained.

Regulations

Aside from the local licenses and permits, other state and federal regulations apply to Rancho Sporting Goods Company. Laws designed to encourage competition prohibit practices such as contracts, combinations, and conspiracies in restraint of trade; they prohibit discrimination in price between different purchases of commodities similar in grade and quality that may injure competition; they make unlawful "unfair methods of competition" and "unfair or deceptive practices."

The term *deceptive* refers to any false advertisements, misrepresentation, simulation of competitive products, and bad-mouthing competitors. Even in the case of violations by a manufacturer or distributor, a retailer who knowingly accepts an illegal concession offered by the vendor may be considered equally guilty.

A fairly common statute forbids the sale of any article at less than the seller's cost if the intent is to injure competitors. Other laws deal with "bait and switch selling," withholding appropriate refunds on deposits made by customers, misrepresenting warranties and guarantees, and quality requirements for certain products.

Due to the complex nature of these regulations and the penalties for violations, Daven Porter will be responsible for seeing that all laws and regulations are met.

Taxes

As a business owner and employer, we understand that various state and federal taxes will need to be collected and remitted to the proper agencies.

Although research has been conducted on current tax information, it must be noted that by the time Rancho Sporting Goods Company opens, certain laws may have changed. Therefore, current tax laws will be investigated before opening to ensure that our tax structure complies with the latest regulations.

As an employer, withholding tax and Social Security tax must be withheld from each employee's paycheck and transferred to the proper tax-collecting agencies.

An employer tax number will be obtained from the federal government using the IRS form SS-4. The federal agency will send Rancho Sports the tax number as well as charts to determine payroll tax deductions, quarterly and annual forms, W-4 forms, tax deposit forms, and instructions for each form.

The Federal Insurance Contribution Act, or FICA, requires Rancho Sports to pay an amount equal to the employee's contributions to the Social Security tax. Currently the rate is 7.65 percent.

Four different reports must be filed with the IRS district director in connection with payroll taxes:

1. Quarterly return of taxes withheld on wages (form 941)

2. Annual statement of taxes withheld on wages (form W-2)

3. Reconciliation of quarterly returns of taxes withheld with annual statement of taxes withheld (form W-3)

4. Annual Federal Unemployment Tax Return (form 940)

Colorado has a payroll tax that must be collected and remitted to the proper agency. The tax is calculated as a percentage of total payroll and remitted at the end of the year.

Financial Analysis

In acquiring the capital needed to get the venture started, the main sources will be the principals and their friends and relatives. These sources, having deep pockets, will be furnished with monthly income statements for the first year of operation and on a yearly basis for the following four years. The pro forma income statements will show monthly and yearly revenues and expenses for the first five years, thus giving investors a good indication of the profitability, sales, and expenses for the first few critical years of operation (Appendix G-1).

Along with the income statements, a balance sheet also will be issued to possible investors. The breakdown includes cash, accounts receivable, and other assets, as well as the liabilities to be incurred (Appendix G-2).

Finally, the break-even analysis shows at what point Rancho Sports will be able to handle its fixed and variable costs and start making a profit (Appendix G-3). This chart is based on sales over a twelve-month period, and indicates the amount of fixed and variable expenses needed to be covered before making a profit is possible.

Pro Forma Income Statement

The pro forma income statement covering the first five years of operations will be broken down on a monthly basis for the first year to indicate the seasonality and expected fluctuations in revenues and expenses that could be overlooked if represented by only simple yearly figures. The sales dollars show fluctuations from January ($8,000) to December ($15,000). The increases are related to the major hunting and fishing seasons that extend from April to October, plus the Christmas shopping season. At the end of the first year of operation Rancho Sports expects a total net profit after taxes of $9,790. Profits for the next four years of operation increase to $23,096, $32,346, and $64,039 respectively (Appendix G-1).

Break-Even Analysis

Rancho Sporting Goods Company has general fixed costs of $57,300 and variable costs of $74,700. With these expenses of $132,000, Rancho Sports will be able to start turning a profit in mid-July. At this point, all expenses will be covered and additional revenues will be considered profit for the business. By the end of the first year of operation, Rancho Sports will be looking at a profit for the year of $9,790 (Appendix G-3).

Financial Ratios

Liquidity ratios for Rancho Sports have been calculated and are as follows:

1. Quick ratio

2. Current debt to inventory

3. Total debts to total assets

4. Current debts to total assets

5. Current debts to tangible net worth

6. Total asset turnover

7. Net sales to tangible net worth (Appendix G-4)

Along with the calculations, descriptions of the ratios are presented in Appendix G-5.

Store Layout

Appendixes H-1 and H-2 show the projected store layout for Rancho Sporting Goods Company.

Appendixes

Authors' Note

Note: The Pro forma Financial Statements may be included in the Appendix as is the case with sections G-1 to G-5 in this business plan. However, we suggest that you include your financial statements in the main body of the business plan in a sole and separate section entitled "Financial Projections."

Business Plan for:

Residential Realty, Inc.

2222 West DiamondBack Road

SUITE B-1200

Memphis, TN 88998

(555) 555-0204

January 1994

Business Plan Copy Number _____

Table of Contents

Executive Summary

Residential Realty, Inc., was formed to provide a professional real estate service to buyers and sellers of residential real estate in the Greater Metropolitan Memphis area. Tom and Randy Jones are the founders of the company.

Residential Realty, Inc., opened its doors for operation January 1, 1993. The office is located in the DiamondBack Corridor, to provide services to the higher income sections of Metropolitan Memphis.

Residential Realty, Inc., is part of the Worldwide International System of independently-owned offices. The company is proud of its association with Worldwide International.

In two recent surveys of homeowners, buyers and sellers of residential real estate and potential sales associates preferred to do business with a Worldwide office. Worldwide continuously ranked higher than any other real estate organization.

The Joneses chose to become a part of this organization because of the high success ratio of the Worldwide System.

Statement of Purpose

For many years Tom and Randy Jones have been involved in the real estate market as investors. The primary reason for establishing Residential Realty, Inc., was to develop a profitable business enterprise from which other investments may be developed.

Each of the business investments is planned to have a future acquisition value at the end of three years. The Joneses plan to review the investments at the end of three years, and evaluate whether to continue to nurture the investment or to offer it for acquisition.

While so doing, the company will always continue to strengthen its position in the target market area by providing superior customer service to clients and to sales associates.

The objective of our extensive recruiting process is to hire at least 25 sales associates by January 1995. At present, we have hired 13 sales associates, and we expect to reach our intended goal ahead of schedule.

Management

Our management team consists of experienced managers whose backgrounds consist of more than 50 years of combined marketing, real estate, and sales experience.

Tom Jones has several years' experience as a successful entrepreneur in the real estate industry. Prior to operating his own business, he developed a solid background in the same field with other well-known agencies in Tennessee.

Randy Jones has extensive experience as a corporate vice-president in the cellular phone industry for Southern Bell Telephone Co.

Our sales manager and designated broker is Bill Thomas. He brings to our team 25 years of successful real estate experience in sales and as an investor.

Marketing

The fundamental thrust of our marketing strategy consists of recruiting the very best personnel available, many of whom live within our targeted market area. We intend to reach six primary market segments in the affluent areas of Memphis.

Our company can be characterized as an aggressive marketing company that is very serious about the quality of service we provide to our clientele. We intend to continue our advances in the marketplace by following this plan of action.

Finance

In two years we will have achieved our initial goals, and our investment will be generating profits from which other opportunities will arise for further investment in the real estate market.

Gross revenue projected for the first 12 months of operation (January 1, 1994, through January 1, 1995), without external funding, is expected to be $234,000. Gross margin (company dollars) for the same period of time is projected to be $124,500. Annual growth is projected to be 10 percent per year through 1996.

Present Situation

Market Environment

The real estate marketplace is undergoing rapid changes in the Memphis metropolitan area. Due to the strengthening of the economy in the Memphis area, more homebuyers today are looking to purchase homes. These changes in attitudes of homebuyers are a tremendous boost to real estate firms.

We are poised to take advantage of these changes, and expect to become a recognized name and profitable entity in the Memphis real estate market.

Current prices of residential homes in Metropolitan Memphis are increasing, and revenue to real estate companies is also increasing. With the average home price up 6 percent during the past two years, prices have increased from an average of $76,500 to $80,851. We are seeing the marketplace turn around, as the value of homes begins to increase.

We chose to locate our office in the area of most revenue potential. Our targeted market area, the DiamondBack corridor, shows stability and growth. The average selling price for homes in our area for the past 15 months is $187,400. The average price is considerably higher than the rest of the Metropolitan Memphis area. (Please refer to the Market Analysis Section for a more comprehensive analysis.)

The present situation of our organization is very exciting. We have a beautiful 4500-square-foot office, centered in the DiamondBack corridor of Memphis. This location will enable our sales associates to work in an area that will allow them to make more money in a shorter period of time.

Management

Our management is in place and each manager has his or her specific responsibilities outlined. (Please refer to the Management Section.)

Objectives

The primary objectives of our organization are to:

1. Become a profitable enterprise to allow us the freedom of taking advantage of other real estate investment opportunities as they become available.

2. Recruit and hire self-motivated, success-oriented, and hardworking sales agents.

3. Maintain an office of at least 25 sales agents who meet the previous requirements.

4. Develop a solid, corporate identity in our specified targeted market area.

5. Become one of the Top Ten Regional Worldwide offices by our fourth year of operation, or before.

6. Realize a positive return on investment within the first 12 months of operation.

Rationale

We believe the above-mentioned objectives are obtainable because of the professionalism of our managers and sales associates. Our management team is highly skilled in the critical areas that are required to develop a successful real estate office. Each comes from an environment where he or she experienced managing large organizations, rapid growth, development of quality control, and building a strong, client-centered team of sales professionals.

Financial Objectives

Item	(1/1/95) Year One	Year Five
Gross revenue	$234,000	$356,000
Gross margin (company dollars)	124,500	189,000

Broker Objectives

We have set the following objectives for our broker to accomplish. The broker will be responsible for:

1. Recruiting and maintaining a level of at least 25 sales associates.

2. Retaining successful sales professionals.

3. Motivating the sales associates to produce quality listings.

4. Developing checks and balances to evaluate the productivity of the sales associates.

5. Ensuring the highest possible level of penetration into our targeted market by number of listings and closings.

6. Maintaining the highest possible profile within appropriate real estate organizations and associations.

7. Ensuring the highest possible quality of service to our clients.

Management

How We Started

Residential Realty, Inc., was founded in early 1993 by Tom and Randy Jones. The Joneses invested a great deal of time and energy looking for a business development opportunity in Tennessee. Since they came from service industries, they concentrated their investigations in this sector. They came to believe that a niche existed for a real estate company with an extraordinarily high commitment to customer service.

The legal form of Residential Realty, Inc., is a Subchapter S Corporation, incorporated in the State of Tennessee.

The founders have been issued 100 percent of the original stock issue. Tom Jones holds 50 percent of the stock and Randy holds 50 percent.

Management Team

Three people make up the development staff:

> Tom Jones, President
> Randy Jones, Vice-President and Marketing Director
> Bill Thomas, Vice-President of Sales and Designated Broker

The founders and key managers of Residential Realty, Inc., have combined experiences exceeding 15 years in the real estate industry, and combined experiences exceeding 50 years in general business management.

The strength of the Residential Realty management team stems from the combined expertise in management, real estate, and sales areas. Those years of experience and successful operations in other companies will produce outstanding results.

The leadership qualities and characteristics of our management team have resulted in broad and flexible goal setting to meet the ever-changing demands of the quickly moving marketplace requiring our services. This is evident when the team responds to situations requiring new and innovative capabilities.

Responsibilities

Tom Jones, President

Management of working capital, including receivables, inventory, cash and marketable securities; financial forecasting, including capital budget, cash budget, pro forma financial statements, external financing requirements, financial condition requirements, and facilitating staff services.

Randy Jones, Vice-President, and Marketing Director

Manage market planning, advertising, public relations, sales promotions, identify new markets, develop marketing strategies, and direct market research and analysis.

Bill Thomas—Vice-President of Sales and Designated Broker

Manage field sales organization, territories and quotas; manage sales activities, including customer support service; develop and maintain a high industry profile, and be signatory to all company contracts.

Outside Support

An outside team of highly qualified business and industry professionals will assist our management team to make productive decisions and take the most effective actions to generate the greatest possible profits for our enterprise. However, they will not be responsible for final management decisions.

> Legal—Jack Anderson, Attorney
> Accounting—Emily Smith, Certified Public Accountant
> Management Consulting—Trico Business Solutions, Inc.
> Quality Control—Worldwide Real Estate Corp.

Management Team

Following their participation in the Tennessee real estate market, the Joneses turned their attention to the Memphis market. They have purchased three dozen separate real estate properties in Tennessee for investment purposes, and they plan to pursue other real estate investments in the Tennessee market.

Tom Jones

After several years of learning the real estate business, Tom opened his own agency in Chattanooga, Tenn. He developed the company into a successful enterprise, and in 1989 sold the agency to Banner and Banner, Ltd.

Tom's successful sales and promotion experience covers the spectrum of all types of real estate properties, including residential, commercial, and industrial. He has also participated in the promotion of the oil and gas industry.

Randy Jones

Randy's career path has been a distinguished one in sales and communication as a corporate vice-president and executive. He was the vice-president of the Fortune 100 Company, Southern Bell Telephone Co. Prior to Southern Bell he was with ATT&R, one of the world's best known International Telecommunications companies.

Randy has developed successful sales and marketing campaigns for these companies that have produced outstanding results. He was awarded the prestigious Malcolm Smith sales award while at ATT&R.

Bill Thomas

Bill has been successfully involved in the Tennessee real estate industry for 25 years. He is the designated broker to Residential Realty, Inc., and oversees the development of the entire sales force.

Bill is a graduate of the Realty Institute, and has received the GRI designation for his real estate educational training. He is also a member of several industry associations and committees.

Outside Support

Finance and Accounting—Emily Smith, CPA

Emily holds professional designations as Certified Public Accountant in both Tennessee and Kentucky. She is a member of the American Institute of Certified Public Accountants and the Tennessee Society of Certified Public Accountants.

Her original contribution to Residential Realty, Inc., was in the incorporation and original setup of the company and its accounting procedures. Her ongoing contribution is in the role of accounting services and as a tax and financial consultant.

Legal—Jack Anderson, Attorney

Mr. Anderson is a graduate of the Harvard School of Finance & Commerce, The University of Tennessee School of Law, and Stanford University School of Law.

Jack was admitted to the Tennessee State Bar in 1978. His areas of preferred practice are estate planning, real estate, and business law. He has extensive experience as an instructor and lecturer at the college and university level, as well as for a variety of businesses, industry organizations, and community groups.

Jack is a member of the American, Tennessee, Jackson County, and Memphis Bar Associations.

His original contribution to Residential Realty, Inc., was in the incorporation of the company. His ongoing role is in all matters of business law, as they arise, concerning the company.

Management Consulting—Trico Business Solutions, Inc.

Trico Business Solutions, Inc., is a professional management consulting firm located in Memphis, Tenn. Its diverse client base includes businesses in manufacturing, wholesale, retail, and service industries. The senior management team of Trico consists of executives with more than 40 years of combined management, marketing, and sales experience.

Joseph A. Thomas, MBA (Finance), is a graduate of Fairleigh Dickinson University. He has 15 years' experience in accounting and upper management. He has been vice-president of finance and general manager in large manufacturing and distribution corporations. Joe is also an instructor for business and human relations courses at Memphis College.

Brian J. Hanson, BA (Marketing), is a graduate of Western International University. Brian has been a top sales representative and regional sales manager in large service and distribution companies. He is also a licensed REALTOR® in Tennessee.

Brian has appeared as a guest on several radio and television talk shows regarding business plan development and marketing strategies.

Quality Control—Worldwide Regional Headquarters

A team of professional managers with direct, hands-on experience within the real estate industry is always available to assist Residential Realty, Inc. These professionals are constantly in touch with our senior managers to assist and make suggestions for the overall benefit of our business in the areas of sales and marketing support and training.

Functional Organization Chart of
Residential Realty, Inc., as of January 1, 1994

President
Tom Jones
Financial, Administrative,
Long Range Planning

Vice-President/Marketing Director
Randy Jones
Marketing, Advertising,
Public Relations

Designated Broker/Sales Manager
Bill Thomas
Sales Associate Training

Outside Support
Finance/Accounting
Emily Smith, CPA

Sales Associates
M. Wicks
G. Steppon
C. Stevens
R. Rich
H. Pachoe
D. Rutan
L. Walker
L. Benson
L. Holtman
G. Wright
P. Sharrock
M. Ashby
K. Krieger
C. Morrison
C. Watson
S. Roach
M. Cook

Legal
Jack Anderson, Attorney

Management Consultants
Trico Business Solutions

Secretarial
S. Haymond

Quality Control / Operations
Worldwide Regional Headqtrs.

Service Description

At Residential Realty, Inc., our principal service consists of selling residential real estate in a targeted market area. Our target market is located in the DiamondBack corridor of Memphis. This particular area covers from 10th Street to Amazon Road, and from Washington Drive to Stenson Road. (Please refer to the Market Analysis Section.)

Residential Realty, Inc., is a full service residential sales agency. The development of three other services is already in progress. These additional services will allow us to satisfy several different needs of our clients. These services are:

1. Property Management,

2. Commercial Real Estate Sales, and

3. Business Brokerage Services.

Useful Purpose and Benefits

Our services provide our clients with an international network of buyers and sellers through the Worldwide International System, as well as the local multiple listing service (MLS). Because of our capabilities to network with other brokers, we will sell homes faster than our clients could if they tried to market their home without the assistance of a licensed real estate agent.

In addition, our customers will list their homes with our agency because of our aggressive and highly-skilled professionals. We will continuously have an above-average sales force to generate and close residential listings.

The owners and management team of Residential Realty, Inc., are committed to success in the real estate market. Our high level of commitment will enable the company to attract top professionals as sales associates and clients looking to buy and sell residential real estate.

Benefits of Belonging to the Worldwide System

As part of the Worldwide System, Residential Realty, Inc., is able to offer detailed services that help make the sales and purchases of residential homes much easier for our clients. Residential Realty, Inc., is a full-service real estate office. The following categories of services help make up this dynamic format of customer service.

Residential Real Estate Sales

Residential real estate is the foundation of the Worldwide and Residential Realty, Inc., systems. While continuing to strengthen its position in the residential real estate market, Worldwide Real Estate Corp. has also renewed its commitment to additional services, which allows Residential Realty, Inc., to become more influential with our clients.

Broker-to-Broker Referrals

Broker-to-broker referrals continue to be one of the hallmarks of the Worldwide System. In an increasingly mobile society, the referral opportunities available to Residential Realty, Inc., and other Worldwide brokers are a lucrative income source. And with approximately 12,000 offices worldwide, referral capabilities are a valuable benefit to our buyers and sellers.

Worldwide Military Program

The Worldwide Military Program has been in operation since 1982. This system was developed in cooperation with U.S. Military officials. The military program features substantial savings to military transferees on fees required to purchase a home, plus a variety of other specialized services. The Worldwide System is officially endorsed by the military to provide this service.

Corporate Real Estate Services Department

The corporate Real Estate Services Department at Worldwide conducts a national corporate calling program and administers real estate services to corporate clients. Through this program, corporate clients have access to services such as:

1. Home purchase assistance,

2. Home search assistance,

3. Early sales program assistance,

4. Mortgage and insurance assistance, and

5. Household goods transportation assistance.

Residential Realty, Inc., will utilize the vast library of knowledge provided to us as a Worldwide franchise owner. As our sales associates use the successful tools also provided by Worldwide, our firm will generate more revenues in a relatively short period of time.

Sales Support Materials

The sales materials used by our sales associates are developed by the Worldwide organization. Our sales materials reflect the enormous success of the Worldwide network. These materials are easy to understand and follow. Their purpose is to assist our sales associates when giving presentations to clients. We feel that our sales materials will help our agents list and sell more properties.

Key Benefits of all Services

The combination of all services provided by Worldwide enabled the Joneses to make an intelligent decision of which franchise to purchase. To illustrate this point even further, a national survey and a local Metropolitan Memphis survey was performed by The Thomlinson Group, a leading survey research organization. The results of the surveys clearly indicate why Worldwide enjoys the rating of "Number One" in the world. (Please refer to the Market Analysis Section.)

Market Analysis

Market Definition

Key points in defining the market segment for our service are our geographical location and the life-style of our targeted customers. Currently, the market distribution is shared by several participants due to overlapping segments of the targeted market.

We will show where our targeted markets are in the Memphis area and provide figures for the number of homes presently listed, as well as the number of homes that have sold during the past 15 months.

For our market analysis, we will provide facts and figures from the following areas listed in the Multiple Listing Service (MLS) for the Memphis area:

1. MURRAY (Area 105 on the map);

2. DIAMONDBACK MOUNTAIN (Area 104);

3. LAMBSON VALLEY (Below the Memphis Mountain Preserve) (Area 106);

4. WASHINGTON DRIVE TO SOUTHERN AVENUE (Area 103);

5. AMAZON ROAD TO 10TH STREET, AND STENSON ROAD TO 20TH STREET (Area 406);

6. DIAMONDBACK ROAD TO THOMASSON DRIVE (Area 410).

Market research (as of December 15, 1992) indicates that there are currently 987 to 1,003 active listings in these areas. This is our targeted market area, and gives our office a tremendous boost, because all the homes listed are in medium- to upper-income areas.

Like most of the southern region of the United States, this market segment has been unstable in the past few years. However, the trend is swinging upward for the number of listings and number of sold homes, particularly in our target area.

During the past 15 months, our area has produced approximately 1,009 sales of middle- to upper-income homes. The approximate average selling price for these homes in all the combined areas of our target market is $187,400. The average selling price in the Metropolitan Memphis area is $80,851.

Based on the real estate market performance over the past 24 months, the average selling price in the Memphis area has increased almost 6 percent. The trend is expected to continue for the next five years as our market begins to rebound from a slow period from 1987 to 1990.

Figures from the Tennessee Regional Multiple Listing Service show that 1,908 buyers and sellers connected in December 1992. That is the highest figure recorded in the five years the organization has kept monthly statistics.

In November 1990, the average home sale price increased $2,500 more than posted increases in October 1990. Homes are moving quickly in Memphis. The Tennessee Regional MLS figures show that nearly half of all homes sold in December 1992 had been on the market for 60 days or less *(The Memphis Business Journal,* December 29, 1992).

The following list illustrates what the average selling prices are for our specific areas during the past 15 months.

Area	Average Selling Price
106	$ 87,000
105	215,000
103	120,000
410	108,000
104	407,000

The overall target market for the DiamondBack Corridor is presently generating about $217 million. It is projected to be $266 million by the end of 1996. (This is based on a 4 percent increase of sales over the next five years.) (Tennessee Regional Multiple Listing Service.)

The major competitors in our market are:
Red Canyon
Jack Holmes and Associates
Realty People
Connors
Other Worldwide offices

Strengths

In terms of our service strengths, we will recruit sales associates who live within our target market to gain even greater influence. It is very important for sales associates to live in the area where they will generate most of their leads and, consequently, their sales.

The physical location of our office is a definite strength. We are located in the heart of our target market at 10th Street and DiamondBack in Memphis. This is only a few minutes from four of the most influential and high-income residential areas of the immediate area.

In the corporate arena, Residential Realty, Inc., is supported by Worldwide System. Our market strengths are the recognized symbols of quality, success, and professionalism. These several advantages have already been outlined in the Service Description Section.

Opportunities

The upside potential for a real estate agency like Residential Realty, Inc., backed by the Number One real estate organization in the world is tremendous.

Based on existing conditions, we are poised to take full advantage of the current market in Memphis. As we follow the detailed educational process provided by Worldwide Real Estate Corp., there really is no way for our firm to fail.

We will succeed in becoming one of the major competitors in the Memphis real estate market, because of our management team, the superior service that we provide, the powerful training provided by Worldwide, and our focused market segment, located a few miles from our office.

National and Local Survey Results

The following surveys, conducted by The Thomlinson Group (referred to in the Service Description Section), offer further positive references for our decision of owning and operating a Worldwide franchise.

The national survey included 1,500 telephone interviews with a random sample of homeowners from across the United States, and was conducted during August 5-9, 1993. No coaching or preferences were provided by the survey company to persuade the homeowners to state any specific answers.

The local survey included 300 telephone interviews, and was conducted during August 15-19, 1993.

National Survey

QUESTION: Which company would you say is the company you would want to join if you were going to work in real estate?

WORLDWIDE	33 %
Connors	6
E.S.S.A.	3
Bigger Homes	2
Maximum	2
Presidential	2

QUESTION: Supposing you were going to sell your home, which one of the following types of agencies would you most likely select to list your home?

An agency associated with a national organization	58%
An agency not associated with a national organization	16
An agency owned and operated by a national organization	14
Does not matter/Would not use a real estate agency	12

QUESTION: Which real estate company would you say can do the most to help someone like you sell a home?

WORLDWIDE	22 %
Connors	4
E.S.S.A.	2
Maximum	2
Bigger Homes	1
Presidential	1

Metropolitan Memphis Survey

QUESTION: Which real estate sales organization would you most likely use to sell your home?

WORLDWIDE	13 %
Realty People	7
Red Canyon	3
Connors	3
E.S.S.A.	2
Realty Professionals	2
Jack Holmes	1
South USA	1
Southern Bell	1

QUESTION: Which company would you want to join if you were going to work in real estate?

WORLDWIDE	15 %
Realty People	7
Connors	4
Red Canyon	3
E.S.S.A.	2
Bigger Homes	1
Help Us Sell	1
Jack Holmes	1

QUESTION: Which one of the following types of agencies would you most likely select to list your home?

An agency associated with a national organization, but which is independently owned and operated by local business people	55%
An agency owned and operated by a national organization	21
An agency not associated with a national organization	11
The type of agency doesn't matter/Would not use a real estate agency/ Don't know	14

Customers

Our customer service philosophy is unique. In a philosophic sense, Residential Realty, Inc., has three distinct customer groups: *sellers, buyers,* and *agents.*

Sellers of real property are our *first* customers. Listers of properties (sellers) pay commissions from the sale of their property and are the direct clients of the real estate brokers. We will never lose our focus that clients who have retained Residential Realty, Inc., to list and sell their properties are our first obligation.

Our second real customer is the buyer of residential real estate. We will provide superior personal service to buyers.

Our *third* real customer is the licensed real estate sales *agent.* It is the agent's job to provide a professional service to both sellers and buyers, specifically in this order. Therefore, it is the direct responsibility of Residential Realty, Inc., to provide service to our sales agents.

Typical Customer

We have identified the most typical buyer for our office. The purpose of the following information is to illustrate the age, income level, and emotional biases of our targeted clientele base. This information is also intended to assist our sales associates in understanding who our typical clients are:

Corporate Executive

Title:	President, VP Finance, VP Manufacturing, Office Manager, Advertising Manager, etc.
Power:	Permitter, decision-maker, influencer, initiator
Viewpoint:	Big picture, financial, personal
Emotional Influences:	Status, power, nice neighborhood, low crime area
Practical Influences:	Saving money, efficiency
Education:	Ph.D., MBA, college graduate
Limitations:	Geographical, purchasing approval from spouse

Housewife

Age:	35-55
Household Income:	$50,000 +
Sex:	Female
Family:	Full nest
Geographic:	Suburban
Occupation:	White-collar family
Emotional Influences:	Comfort, safe surroundings, close to schools, church, and shopping

Young Professionals

Age:	25-45
Income:	Medium to high
Sex:	Male or female
Family:	Bachelor or married
Geographic:	Suburban
Occupation:	White-collar
Emotional Influences:	Status, power, close to work

Young Married Couples

Age:	35-45
Income:	Medium to high
Sex:	Male or female
Family:	Married, with or without children
Geographic:	Suburban
Occupation:	White-collar
Emotional Influences:	Comfort; safe surroundings; close to schools, church, and shopping

Wealthy Rural Families

Age:	35-55
Income:	High
Sex:	Male or female
Family:	Full nest
Geographic:	Rural
Occupation:	White-collar
Emotional Influences:	Status; power; close to work; comfort; safe surroundings; close to schools, church, and shopping

Older Couple

Age:	55-70
Income:	High or fixed
Sex:	Male or female
Family:	Empty nest
Geographic:	Suburban
Occupation:	White-collar or retired
Emotional Influences:	Comfort, safe surroundings, close to church and shopping

Selling Agent

Recruiting Guidelines

The typical selling agent that we will constantly recruit will fall under the following categories:

- Middle Management personnel, earning approximately $60,000 a year.
- Retired persons in search of a second career.
- Persons who have a burning desire to earn a good living.
- Spouses who can contribute an above-average income to a family unit as a second income.

During the recruiting process and once the sales associate is hired, we will emphasize three key areas that are important attributes for all of our sales associates to maintain. They are

- Commitment to individual success and to the success of Residential Realty, Inc.
- Attitude and direction
- Knowledge and skills

Recruiting Goals

As part of our ongoing recruiting process, we have established recruiting goals to project our profit potential. These goals are based on the following important parameters:

1. What our monthly expenses are to keep the doors open.

2. The number of sales each month needed to meet the budget.

3. The amount of profit we should be earning each month on our investment in the company.

4. Minimum number of salespeople needed.

5. The average number of sales per sales associate per month.

Marketing and Advertising Strategies

Residential Realty, Inc., is committed to an extensive promotional campaign. This must be done aggressively and on a wide scale. To accomplish our initial sales goals, we require an extremely effective promotional campaign to accomplish two primary objectives:

1. Attract quality sales personnel that have a burning desire to be successful, and

2. Attract sellers and buyers that we will represent as their broker.

Residential Realty, Inc., plans to advertise in trade magazines and newspapers in the Memphis area. *Memphis Executive* is one publication that our ads have been placed in for recruiting quality female sales associates.

The Memphis Times has a wide distribution network that allows us to advertise for sales associates as well as to list properties.

The Memphis Guide is one of the more influential magazines for newcomers to the Memphis area. This publication gives us some very good exposure to potential home buyers.

Unique Homes is distributed nationally. We will be advertising homes that list for $500,000 and above in this publication.

Due to the high Jewish population in our target area, we will be advertising for sales associates and listing homes in two prominent Jewish publications: *Jewish News* and *Jewish Living in Memphis.*

Old Times is a tabloid newspaper, which covers a diverse psychographic audience. We will use this publication for recruiting.

On the DiamondBack Corridor is a business tabloid read by persons who work in the area, and may wish to move or relocate to the area. We will advertise in this publication for home sales.

We will also take advantage of the promotional opportunities provided by our memberships in both the Memphis and the Chattanooga Chambers of Commerce.

Advertising will be done independently and cooperatively with Worldwide of The Southern Region, Inc. A fixed amount of sales revenues will go toward the national Worldwide advertising campaign. The amount will be a minimum of $230 and a maximum of $690 per sale. These figures are a part of the agreement between Residential Realty, Inc., and Worldwide Inc.

Media Strategy

It is the practice of Residential Realty, Inc., to position the company in a compatible editorial environment consistent with communication objectives. We have selected primary publications with specific and tactical market penetration.

Promotion

In addition to standard local advertising practices, we will gain considerable recognition through the national advertising campaign from Worldwide Real Estate Corp. Worldwide ranks in the top 100 advertisers and enjoys an awareness factor of 90 percent with the American public. It is the only real estate organization to do so.

This is very important to our recruiting process, as well as to the buyers and sellers who may consider working with Residential Realty, Inc. People naturally want to be associated with successful organizations.

As a benefit of membership in the Worldwide System, we have available to us the services of the professional public relations firm, Jorgan & Haas, which has undertaken a promotional campaign on our behalf. Jorgan & Haas is located in Manhattan, N.Y.

Incentives

As an extra incentive for customers and recruits to remember Residential Realty's name, we plan to distribute coffee mugs, t-shirts, and other advertising specialties with the company logo. This will be an ongoing program to promote the company, when appropriate and where it is identified as beneficial.

Corporate Capabilities Brochure

Objective: To portray Residential Realty, Inc., as a leader in the Memphis real estate market. *Recommended Contents:* Utilize the powerful messages already created by Worldwide that have been proven successful. We will develop three separate brochures initially: one to use for recruiting, one to be used to promote sales, and another to promote referrals within the Worldwide Network.

Investment in Advertising and Promotion

For the first 12 months of operations, advertising and promotion is budgeted at approximately $12,000. On an ongoing basis, we feel that we can budget our advertising investment as 10 percent of revenues to Residential Realty, Inc.

Financial Projections

Assumptions, Definitions, and Notes

Revenues

1. Gross Revenues—Three percent has been used to determine the amount per side (a side may either be a listing or sale of a home) to be applied against the selling price of homes. The following has been used in the time periods indicated:

	Avg. Sale Price per Home	Gross Revenue per Side
January 1993-December 1993	$100,000	$3,000
January 1994-December 1994	120,000	3,600
January 1995-December 1995	140,000	4,200
January 1996-December 1996	150,000	4,500

The increase in the average sale price per home is a result of having a greater number of experienced and knowledgeable sales associates on staff.

Annual gross revenue is projected to increase by 25 percent for year three and 10 percent for years four and five.

Cost of Services

1. *Agent Commission*—Sales associates are paid on a commission only basis. The average commission rates used were as follows:

	Avg. Comm. Rate
January 1993-December 1993	50%
January 1994-March 1994	55
April 1994-December 1995	60

The average commission rate was applied against the net of gross revenues less Worldwide service fees and cooperative advertising costs.

2. *Worldwide Service Fee*—Six percent of monthly gross revenue is paid to Worldwide of The Southern Region, Inc., as a service fee per the franchise agreement.

3. *Cooperative Advertising*—Two percent of monthly gross revenue is also paid to Worldwide of The Southern Region, Inc., for advertising media per the franchise agreement, with the following limitation:

On an aggregate monthly basis, the amount to Worldwide of The Southern Region, Inc., must be at least $230 but must not exceed $690.

General and Administrative Expenses

1. *Advertising*—For year one advertising expenditures are estimated to be 15 percent of company dollars. This amount will be needed to gain immediate market recognition. Advertising amounts for years two through five have been reduced to approximately 11 percent of company dollars.

2. *Rent*—Has been recorded per the actual signed lease, including rental sales tax. The lease is a gross lease.

3. *Wages, Clerical*—One clerical support staff member has been hired for 1994. Another support staff member will be added at the beginning of 1995. No additional support staff will be needed through 1996.

4. *Wages, Broker, and Brokers Commission*—Base wages to be paid to one broker as a monthly fixed salary. The Broker will also receive as commission 5 percent of all company dollars.

5. *Wages, Officers*—Officers will not receive wages until loan to officers has been fully repaid. Wages are anticipated to begin January 1995.

6. *All Other Expenses*—Have been recorded on estimated usage for each category for all years. Anticipated inflation of 6 percent has been included.

Assets

1. *Cash*—Reflects limited amount of cash on hand at any balance sheet date. Positive generation of cash is to be applied against loan payable officer until fully repaid and then distributed to stockholders.

2. *Fixed Assets*—Projected purchase of all furniture and fixtures and office equipment for years 1993 through 1996 is recorded in January of each year. Depreciation will be calculated per Modified Accelerated Cost Recovery System (MACRS).

3. *Franchise Fee*—The actual cost to purchase a Worldwide franchise has been recorded. Straight-line amortization will be used systematically over a ten-year period.

4. *Rent Deposit*—Actual rent deposit required by landlord upon execution of the rental lease has been recorded.

Liabilities

1. *Accounts Payable*—Represents balances due vendors for items such as supplies, telephone, legal and accounting, travel, and entertainment.

2. *Accrued Liabilities*—Include unpaid Federal, State, FICA, FUTA, and SUI, withholding taxes payable, as well as other miscellaneous items not recorded through accounts payable.

The Financials

Authors' Note

As suggested earlier, the financial presentation portion of the business plan needs to be well prepared. If assistance is needed, contact a reputable accounting or other business firm that will be able to provide accurate, reasonable and meaningful information.

As a general guide, the financial section may include the following data:

- *Notes, definitions, and assumptions used in preparing the financial data*
- *Profit and loss forecasts: years one and two by month, years three through five by year*
- *Balance sheet forecasts: years one and two by quarter, years three through five by year*
- *Cash Flow forecasts: years one and two by quarter, years three through five by year*

Appendix

Authors' Note:

List all supporting documentation in the Appendix section as noted and referenced throughout your business plan. Remember, this information should be clearly and neatly presented so the reader of your business plan can easily reference and understand the data provided.